MAN'S CONQUEST

of his environment is a recent achievement; his past history has been dictated almost entirely by the conditions of his surroundings. He has had to survive ice ages and encroaching deserts; earthquake, volcano, wild beast, and hostile terrain. This absorbing book examines man's environment from the dawn of the race and shows how the ancient human communities developed their various cultures depending upon the environment in which they lived.

I. W. Cornwall reconstructs the primitive world with its radically different land forms, river systems, forestation, and climate. He emphasizes the importance of land bridges; relates the discovery of irrigation and fertilization, traces the patterns of prehistoric trade and the birth of industry with the use of gold, copper, silver, and iron. He details the detection methods employed by archaeologists: how pollen-analysis has helped reveal the environment of Mesolithic man; how tree rings can document the climatic patterns of thousands of years ago. His provocative survey of an ancient world and the men who lived in it is beautifully illuminated by unusual diagrams, drawings, and maps.

MENTOR and SIGNET SCIENCE
Books of Related Interest

The World of
ANCIENT MAN

by I. W. CORNWALL

With Illustrations by
M. MAITLAND HOWARD

and Maps and Diagrams
BY THE AUTHOR

A MENTOR BOOK

Published by The New American Library, New York and Toronto
The New English Library Limited, London

*Published as a MENTOR BOOK
by arrangement with The John Day Company, Inc.,
who have authorized this softcover edition.
A hardcover edition is available from The John Day Company,
Inc.*

FIRST PRINTING, MARCH, 1966

MENTOR BOOKS are published *in the United States* by
The New American Library, Inc.,
1301 Avenue of the Americas, New York, New York 10019,
in Canada by The New American Library of Canada Limited,
295 King Street East, Toronto 2, Ontario,
in the United Kingdom by The New English Library Limited,
Barnard's Inn, Holborn, London, E.C. 1, England

In grateful memory of
the late
Professors S. W. Wooldridge and F. E. Zeuner,
my teachers in many things.

Foreword
and Acknowledgments

THE FULLEST study of man's past requires the examination of evidences from very many fields of knowledge, so that it is clear that, nowadays, no one man can write about even such a part of it as the natural environments of ancient cultures and societies from first-hand knowledge alone. More than ever before in history, to be a Jack-of-all-trades is to remain master of none. The day of the polymath has gone for ever.

The putting together of this book, therefore, has required much reading and digestion of the work of others, with a view not so much to summarizing what is known of different environments of the past as to showing why and how they should and may be studied, using selected cases to exemplify the sort of results which may be hoped for.

The writer is a prehistorian, resident near London, so that the majority of the examples is naturally taken from the areas and periods with which he is most familiar, though occasional travel in the European continent, and even, briefly, to Jordan, Mexico and California, has enabled him to see at first hand something of other lands, where man's conditions today are very different from those which obtain in western Europe. The overseas reader is therefore invited to supply his own, more familiar, illustrations from nearer home.

For the rest, reliance has been placed on the atlas and on books and scientific papers from a wide field.

In a work of such scope, written primarily for non-specialist readers, it seems unnecessary to give references to authorities for statements and examples. Fully to do so would call for a Bibliography nearly as bulky as the text. To select would be invidious. For those interested, some titles for further general reading are suggested at the end of the book and these will afford access to the vast specialist literature. Again, European sources must necessarily preponderate.

To my friends and colleagues in many fields, whose brains I have picked, whose works I have consulted, whose experience has been willingly shared and some of whom have been kind enough to read and criticize parts of this book in manuscript, my best thanks.

If I have inevitably committed some errors or have misunderstood, let it be attributed to ignorance, not intention.

Miss Howard, my skilled illustrator, needs no recommendation from me—her drawings speak for themselves. My gratitude, on this as on former occasions, has been expressed directly.

I. W. C.

Contents

List of Illustrations

Maps and Diagrams

xi

Drawings

The World of
ANCIENT MAN

Introduction

TIME WAS when the archaeologist had first to be a classical and oriental scholar, when his subject began with the Assyrians, Egyptians, Greeks and Romans and the study of their languages, histories and literatures, extracted from ancient manuscripts, papyri, and inscriptions on clay tablets and cut on stone. Having learned as much as was known about the history, myth and legend of his place and period from written sources, he would take spade in hand and travel to the land of his choice to see whether he might discover, by collecting and digging on sites of ancient cities, temples and cemeteries, something tangible about the kings and priests, the heroes and warriors named in the books. Very occasionally this was successful and the fantastic wealth of art-objects and treasures of antiquity from Troy, Mycenae, Ur of the Chaldees, the Palace of Minos in Crete or the royal tombs in the Valley of the Kings at Thebes brought lasting fame to their discoverers, brief wonder and speculation to the man in the street and a vast heritage of artistry and learning to the great museums of the world and private collections.

Such collectors' pieces, however, were not for all. On the whole, the rich tombs and buried palaces associated with the mighty names of the past were, as are all outstanding discoveries, rather rare and elusive. Robbers and looters in antiquity and later treasure-hunters, man's forgetfulness of the very sites of many recorded civilizations, vandalism through the centuries and natural decay had done their work too well. The excavator's trenches laid bare, as often as not, only the footings of the palace buildings; his questing lamp revealed tombs gutted and sarcophagi empty, so that only the indestructible sherds of pottery in the midden and other unconsidered and intrinsically valueless rubbish were left to tell of lost and all but forgotten glories.

All was not lost, nevertheless. In time, even the rubbish was shown to have a fascinating story to tell in the hands of the skilful and systematic inquirer. Careful, slow excavation, with due regard to the telltale streaks of stratified de-

17

posits, the exact plotting of the positions of finds and the separate study of the yield from different layers enabled the painstaking building up of sequences in time of pottery and building-styles, in their due order of appearance, development, degeneration and decay. This was not the history of the rise and fall of kings and empires so much as of the development of some obscure, undated settlement from hamlet to village to town, and then, overrun by the hordes of some unnamed invader, of its return in ashes to the dust, to rise again on its trampled ruins under some new occupants—a process often many times repeated on some favoured sites such as Jericho.

The archaeologist, from being only a historian and collector of antiquarian show-pieces, turned detective and reconstructor of the buried past. Where history was deficient or non-existent, archaeology was able to fill in some gaps, or even, as prehistory, to set up a scaffolding of fact on which a sort of history could be sustained.

Equipped with this outlook and some new techniques, more archaeologists in western Europe began to look, nearer home, at the less impressive monuments of their own unrecorded past. Only a generation ago in Britain, for example, history really began with the Roman invasion of 55 B.C., preceded by some slightly garbled accounts taken directly from classical authors of the 'Ancient Britons' who were already living in the Islands. Prehistory, by then already firmly based on evidence from field-surveys and excavation, had not yet found a secure place in education.

Beyond the immediately pre-Roman Britons, Gauls, Germans and Helvetians of Julius Caesar's time, we, today, know a good deal about *their* predecessors, the Early Iron Age, Bronze Age and even the Neolithic, the New Stone Age, inhabitants of Europe. Whereas the historian deals with kings and conquests, the relations between States, the growth of law and order and the thoughts and doings of prominent known *personalities*—human studies, in fact—the prehistorian is chiefly and most directly concerned with *things*—sherds of primitive pottery, flint tools, bronze axes and swords or the post-hole plan of a hill-fort entrance or of a herdsman's hut. We have no names and only the most approximate dates, changing as knowledge and theory advance from year to year, for the people who made and used these things. Chiefs and kings and priests and policies they doubtless had, but of these we know next to nothing. On the other hand, we *do* know a fair amount about how the common man lived and died and was buried, what sort of axes, knives and pots he used, the ornaments he and his wife wore. From these, something of connections between peoples and of migrations from place to place of users of particular weapons and household equipment may be made out. Thus in Britain we speak of the Beaker Folk or the Long-Barrow People or the Corded-Ware Makers, these names being convenient labels for the assemblages of implements, ways of life and burial customs which the archaeologist calls 'cultures'. Amid all this impersonal and dry-as-dust detail, it is too easy, sometimes, to forget that it is once-living *people* that we are really studying!

Now, while the frontiers of knowledge were being pushed by the humanists back into the past, beyond written documents and inscriptions and even beyond classical travellers' tales into the realm of prehistoric potsherds, bronzes and beads, they were being advanced, too, by the scientists.

Geology and palaeontology are, respectively, concerned with the nature, structure and revolutions of our earth and with the earlier history of its living inhabitants as these are to be read in the rocks of the accessible crust. They deal with periods of many millions of years, during which the leading forms of animal life developed from unicellular organisms, through marine worms and shellfish, fishes, amphibians, reptiles and mammals, until at length came man.

Most geologists were interested in Eras and Periods, dating between hundreds of millions of years up to some few millions of years ago, in which the differences from the world we know are very great. In deposits of some of these can be found almost the same marine fossils, whether in South Wales or New South Wales, in England or New England.

The accessible geological deposits of the Pliocene and Pleistocene, however, the latest Periods, are another matter. They are largely terrestrial rather than marine and so are much more diverse, both in their character as rocks and in their contained fossils. Seldom are they widely extensive or easily correlatable in time over considerable distances by their stratigraphic positions. A generation ago, therefore, many textbooks of geology grew thin at the upper end of the story of the rocks, partly through lack of interest, where the science presented so many larger problems for solution, and partly because, only where there had been intensive geological fieldwork and mapping was much known of deposits so relatively thin, various in character and scattered.

History and prehistory, similarly, tended to lose themselves in the mists of antiquity and legend at the lower limit of their fields of interest, so that, for most parts of the world, there lay a gap, only here and there bridgeable, of perhaps a million or two years between the end of the Era of the Mammals, the Tertiary of the geologists, and the beginnings of the Neolithic, a mere three thousand or so years before Christ, at the earliest, in the West; perhaps a few thousand years earlier in the Near East.

Archaeologists, for their part, had long known of early Old Stone Age (Lower Palaeolithic) hand-axes and flakes, of flint and other hard stones, coming from old river gravels, and of the more skilfully-worked 'points', blades, scrapers and so on found in caves with some bone tools, called Upper Palaeolithic—all associated securely with the remains of extinct animals, which proved their great antiquity as compared with the traces of Neolithic man, maker of 'polished' stone axes, well-designed arrowheads and pottery.

Still the 'hiatus' between geological deposits containing traces of Old Stone Age man and the habitation-sites of the New Stone Age remained unbridged—a gap now only of a few thousands of years, yet a period longer than all that has elapsed between the Neolithic and our own times. That bridge has been firmly constructed, chiefly within the last forty years, by the discovery and dating to this interval of numerous varieties of Middle Stone Age (Mesolithic) remains in peat-bogs, on beaches and open sandy tracts, on desert margins and in the upper strata of caves, over the greater part of the Old World.

Since the evidences of earliest man, in the Palaeolithic and Mesolithic stages of tool-making technique, occur chiefly in natural deposits, archaeologists interested in those remoter periods have, from the first, been accustomed to employ the geological approach and methods of study. They have thus always been at least in part scientists, because without science, or scientists of one sort or another at call, they were practically helpless to interpret their finds or to assign dates to them. Prehistorians concerned with the Neolithic and later stages of culture have, on the other hand, tended to be mainly humanist in outlook, since they work on the whole with purely archaeological, i.e. largely artificial, deposits—the mounds of occupation-debris, ruined structures, earthworks and so on—associated with more or less static settlements. They are, none the less, using the scientific method of destructive analysis as they excavate, and their records, to be of value, must be as conscientiously complete and their deductions therefrom as rigorously logical and as firmly based on hard facts as those of chemical analysis. Whereas some of the deposits which contain and cover their finds are clearly natural in origin and include natural, as well as artificial, evidence, archaeologists should be (and generally nowadays, are) as much aware of what the natural sciences can do to help them as are students of the earlier periods, if less exclusively dependent than the latter on the purely scientific evidence.

Thus we find that, over the whole of Prehistory at least, science and the arts may march hand in hand, to the profit of both; and, indeed, there are practitioners in both camps who may be formally attached by training to the one or the other, but, in fact, have a foot firmly planted in both, which is as it should be.

Archaeology may be defined as the study of the material equipment—buildings, household goods, ornaments, clothing, tools, weapons, vehicles, grave-furniture, etc.—of early men and communities of the past. Any archaeological investigation is undertaken with the purpose of learning through these objects as much as may be discovered by inference about the people concerned, their way of life and even something of their origins and history, where these are not recorded in writing or where the record is incomplete. The methods of archaeology are applicable to such materials, dating from the earliest human times right up into the immediate historical past. In the former case, the archaeological material is all we have; in the latter, though written history may record in great detail public events and the important personalities of the time, only their outworn and outdated material equipment tells us anything of the daily lives of the common people—peasants, farmers, artisans or townsmen. Even the discarded implements of only a generation ago are now, in this age of automation and space travel, becoming museum exhibits for our children, who have never seen them in use. Unless they are preserved and recorded, a time will come when the special purposes for which they were made may have been forgotten. Archaeology is as close to our own lives as the wooden yoke with which the dairyman carried two full buckets of milk in our childhood and which is unknown, save as a curious 'bygone', even to twenty-year-olds today.

While we, and even the middle-class parents of a generation

ago, who were well on in the industrial revolution, are and were but little conscious of the natural setting of our civilization, the producers of primary natural raw materials and foodstuffs—minerals, timber, fibres, hides, meat, vegetables, fish and dairy-produce—are still relatively close to the land, the seas, the soil from which their living, and ours, ultimately comes. In the days, not so long ago, when every man was his own gardener, wool-farmer and builder, the shape of the hills, the weather, the seasons of the year, the raw materials, food-plants and food-animals which Nature permitted him to win or to grow for personal use or for sale were very much in the forefront of his interests. Even more was this the case before man had learned to produce any of these things for himself, but was a hunter and collector of what Nature might provide for taking.

The archaeologist, we have seen, may bring his study to bear on any period of man's past that is beyond living memory or is without exact record. The further back into that past that his interest takes him, the more important to the people whose works he is studying becomes the nature of the surroundings in which they lived—and, through them, to him.

Within the last half century it has become apparent that archaeology is only one part, if an important one, of the study of man's past.

The study of early human societies cannot be confined to the cultural equipment of the people concerned. They lived in a world which provided them, as ours provides us, with food, clothing, shelter and common materials only in exchange for intelligent appreciation of natural resources and much hard work in exploiting them. Since their knowledge of natural laws and materials and their degree of social organization were less than ours, they were more dependent than we are on what nature afforded for their use in their immediate surroundings. Thus, if we seek to reconstruct their ways of life we have to take into account, in detail, the sort of natural setting in which they had their being, which was often very different from that which exists at the same place today. The whole complex of conditions which influence the natural habitats of living things, including human dwelling-places, is known as the environment.

The further back in time that we take our study, the greater are the probable differences in environment that we shall find, for nothing on this earth is static or eternal, and even conditions outside the earth itself, such as the quality and amount of solar radiation which reaches us, are subject to fluctuations in time, sometimes of a cyclic nature. Our environment as we know it is the product of extremely slow development under the changing forces of nature, but when we turn back thousands, or even tens and hundreds of thousands, of years, the differences to be noted may prove to be extreme. Thus we know that, at several different times within the last million years, the climates of what are today the temperate zones have been much colder, even arctic in character—the so-called Ice Ages—during which in Europe some Old Stone Age cultures flourished under conditions quite different from those we experience. If we are to understand them as living human groups we need to visualize our Palaeolithic forbears in their true natural environments.

The environments of civilized societies at the present day are much changed by thousands of years of man's own interference with, and increasing command of, nature, yet the larger forces which govern our ways are still beyond our full control—geography, climate, the seasonal produce of the earth. As we go back beyond the last few centuries of the historic period the natural settings of peoples are seen more and more to determine their ways of life. Geography made the inhabitants of Britain a seafaring and trading people, while the Hungarian *puszta* and the plains of south Russia gave rise to horse-owning nomadic pastoralists. Still further back, the culture possible to man was strictly conditioned by the character of the particular environment which existed where he happened to be. No sensible modification of the environment itself was within his powers so long as his technological achievements remained at the primitive level. Thus, a change of climate to arctic conditions would forbid the survival of a culture which knew neither the use of fire nor the means to catch and kill large mammals, which alone make a hunting economy possible in such surroundings. A change involving notably drier seasons than before might force primitive agricultural folk to migrate elsewhere, where regular harvests were less problematical.

It is clear, therefore, that environmental knowledge is essential to the best understanding of the activities of any human community. For the earliest times it is scarcely possible to know anything at all about them without the study of the environment. Even when dealing with later, settled, urban and historic peoples, information about their environ-

ment greatly enhances the picture of civilization which the
archaeologist compiles from the artifacts. We need, in addition, to understand the relation of the town to its immediately
surrounding country and to other near-by peoples, the sources
of its day-to-day sustenance, materials, exchange and ex-
ternal influences. Ecology, the study of the natural relations
of wild living creatures with their environments, merges with
civilized man into economics.

1

Factors of Natural Environment

NATURAL ENVIRONMENT may be defined as the sum of all the natural circumstances of the place or region in which any organism, including man, lives. It comprises earth, air, water, radiation and the other living creatures, both vegetable and animal, which share it. In the case of man, some of the circumstances will be favourable to his living and culture, some unfavourable. He may seek, if it be possible, to improve the former and to modify the latter by artificial means. In this he is different from all other animals. The possibility of improvement or modification depends, in large part, on man's own technological status and the degree of social organization which he has attained, for much may be achieved by co-operative effort that one man or family are powerless to effect. Some circumstances of his environment are, save in the most modern times, unalterable directly—such as the distribution of land and water, outdoor climate and the availability or otherwise of particularly desirable materials which occur naturally. Not being rooted in one situation, like in a tree, man can either move his dwelling permanently to another place with more favourable environment or undertake occasional or periodic (perhaps seasonal) journeys elsewhere, in order to make the most of resources or conditions not so readily obtainable at home.

Even the unalterable circumstances, if unfavourable, may be made tolerable artificially, as, for instance, a severe climate by adequate warm clothing and housing, or one naturally too dry for agriculture, by irrigation. These call, however, for a certain degree of development of technical ways and means not available to man in the more primitive stages of culture. Such environments are, for him, uninhabitable, except perhaps temporarily.

Existing environments all over the globe, from the Poles to the Equator, from oceanic islands to the hearts of great continents, from sea-level up into the high mountains, have been extensively studied by geographers, biologists and others interested in the relations of living things to the various conditions existing in different parts of the world. Just as many wild organisms, both plants and animals, display astonishing special adaptations to the particular circumstances in which they live, so does man, the most adaptable of all animals, though little specialized physically, develop cultural traits of the greatest ingenuity to enable him to survive in reasonable comfort, even in the most difficult environments. One need only consider the Eskimo, among surviving peoples at the hunter-fisher level, to see how admirably housing, heating, clothing, transport and hunting equipment can be adapted to difficult conditions.

Human environment, as a whole, is clearly a matter of great complexity, governed by a number of natural factors. Though it is possible to isolate on paper some of the chief of these and to examine their influences on the environment separately, this cannot easily be done in a particular actual case, for the factors, themselves in most cases not simple, interact with each other, so that it is not often easy to point to one in particular and say with confidence that it is *the* controlling factor for the environmental phenomenon being examined.

In order of importance, the main factors determining the characters of natural environments are (see Fig. 1):

1. Place

This is the exact situation of the area being studied, in relation to its surroundings. Place includes more than the geographical position which an area occupies in terms of latitude and longitude, though this is obviously fundamental, because of the influence of mere latitude on climate and the seasons. The position of a site as part of a land-mass, in relation to coasts and seas, the existence of near-by rivers, lakes or mountains and other natural barriers or routes of communication are very important. The whole geography of the place, physical and economic, must be taken into consideration as part of the environment which it affords for human occupation—its height above sea-level, its exposure or otherwise to prevailing winds and the sun in its yearly courses, and to such possibilities as flooding.

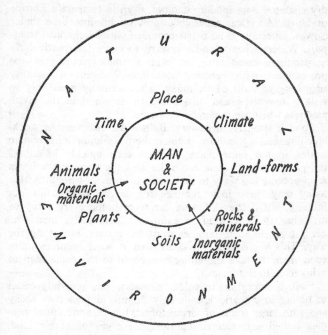

Fig. 1. Man in his natural environment and the various factors which contribute to it.

1. Place
2. Climate
3. Land-forms
4. Rocks and minerals
5. Soils
6. Plants
7. Animals, including man himself
8. Time

The list, thus barely stated, is not very informative without some elaboration. The remainder of this chapter will be devoted to defining and enlarging on their scope and interactions.

The places where men choose to live have regard, naturally, to privacy and concealment as well as to accessibility and communications. Where primitive people are scattered in small groups over wide areas of country, defensibility of the dwelling-site (against wild animals, as much as against possibly hostile neighbours or invaders) is a prime consideration. Nearness to water-supply is especially important in hot, dry climates. Any modern camper, even in temperate Europe or North America, experiences this on his first time under canvas, especially if he is not provided with mechanical transport. Water is heavy and awkward to carry far, particularly in primitive containers, but even a small group (not too preoccupied with personal cleanliness!) needs a quantity surprising to most of us today, who normally need only to walk a few steps and turn a tap to obtain it in the lavish amounts which we use and even waste.

Food is similarly necessary. Before the discovery of stock-breeding and agriculture, hunters could seldom long remain settled in the same place, because they quickly killed off the game close to their camp-site and the surviving animals soon became too wary to approach. Bushmen of South Africa today may leave their families for several days while out hunting, but if they kill very far from home every scrap of meat has to be carried to camp. Unfortunately, men who carry meat to their families must have nourishment on the way. This so reduces 'pay-load' that it soon becomes more economical to take the entire household to the game than to bring meat back to camp.

Fuel, if important in colder climates, was generally easier to obtain in a world less densely populated than ours today and with large tracts of virgin forest, but as agricultural peoples settled and cleared considerable areas of arable land, wood still had to be gathered, cut and carried, perhaps for some distance. The woodcutter is a prominent character in story and legend in northwest Europe. In the Near East today, firewood for cooking presents a serious problem, largely owing to a flora that often is naturally scanty and has been greatly depleted by man himself and his browsing animals over many centuries. Coal and oil as fuels scarcely enter the picture until the Western industrial revolution, though mineral coal was used by Palaeolithic man in Czechoslovakia and locally in Britain also, perhaps as early as the Bronze Age. The early metallurgy of Asia Minor may well have been largely based on the use of mineral coal.

Minerals, in the restricted sense of metal ores, were virtually unknown until the coming of the metal ages, but mineral materials such as hard stones for making implements, clays suitable for pottery, and mineral pigments for colouring were of great importance in earlier times. Their availability at any particular place is a matter of geology, and, if not present in the immediate environment, it was necessary for man either to use what he could find, however inferior to the best materials, or to travel elsewhere to secure better, perhaps by exchange with a neighbour. With knowledge of metals, locally occurring ores became of great economic importance. Areas favoured with accessible deposits of copper- and tin-bearing minerals, though not common, were specially desirable to early bronze-metallurgists.

Though men in the hunting and collecting stage of culture were necessarily fairly mobile, because they soon exhausted the local natural resources of food, they probably did not, as individuals or groups, undertake very long journeys, at least while their neighbourhood afforded a living. Doubtless the slow changes of Pleistocene climate, due to advance and retreat of ice-sheets or of rainfall-belts, caused some on the whole uni-directional migrations over great distances in the course of generations, but place, in the sense of general area of activity, as a factor in environment remained an important one for a given group of individuals. Farmers and miners are not so easily displaced from their fields or mineral-veins, save by invasion or main force. Once a more or less sedentary culture had been developed, place must have meant, for most groups, their own settlements and their neighbourhoods within half a day's march in any direction. Even today some country people do not often travel far. Indeed, even modern townsfolk may be stay-at-homes by preference. A middle-aged Londoner, living south of the Thames, was recently heard to say that she had not crossed the river for fifteen years. Cases like this could certainly be multiplied.

2. Climate

The very important climatic factor is obviously directly involved in determining, or in any case modifying, at least three of the others—soils, plants and animals. Among the last, it is a great controller of the ways of man also.

Climate itself consists of two main sub-factors, temperature and precipitation (mainly rainfall), but others come into it also, for places having equal annual means of temperature and rainfall can have very different climates, according to their seasonal ranges of temperature and distributions of rainfall, or different exposure to wind.

Place is also a potent determinant of climate. To some extent this is only a matter of latitude—higher temperatures nearer the Equator, lower near the Poles—but position in relation to land and sea areas and to prevailing winds and ocean currents is all-important for access of moisture. In the sub-tropical zones the world-pattern of prevailing winds is easterly, so that in these latitudes the eastern coasts of continents receive plenty of rain off the oceans, while the western coasts are very dry, with off-shore winds. For contrast, one need only instance the climates, in similar latitudes, of Labrador and Great Britain, the one with shores washed by an icy current from the Arctic, the other enjoying sea-warmth from the tropics, brought thousands of miles across the ocean by the Gulf Stream and the North Atlantic Drift.

Height above sea-level and coastal or inland position further modify temperature and precipitation, so that the third factor, land-forms, here comes into the picture. Vera Cruz, at sea-level on the Gulf coast of Mexico, is tropical and moist; Mexico City, very little farther north, but far inland and on a plateau over 2,200 metres (7,000 feet) higher, is cool and rather dry. Rain-bearing easterly winds expend their moisture on the coastal plain and the seaward slopes of the mountains, while, once over the crest, they have little left to give. Western Europe and northwestern North America have a mild, 'oceanic' type of climate, since the oceans act as thermostats and the moist westerlies prevent temperatures from falling very low in winter or rising very high in summer. In central and eastern Europe and in the American Middle West, however, the moderating influence of the oceans is scarcely felt and wide seasonal extremes of temperature are experienced—the hot summers and very cold winters of a 'continental' type of climate. This is accentuated in North America by the westerly position of the Cascade-Sierra mountain systems and the Rockies, which sharply cut off the ocean influence from the interior of the continent.

A type of climate with hot, dry summers and moderate rainfall only in the mild winter, is known as 'Mediterranean', and, in the Old World, is typical of the lands surrounding that sea. It is shared by relatively small areas, such as the more southerly of the Pacific coastal areas of the United States, in the Northern Hemisphere, and the Cape of Good Hope, south-western and south-eastern Australia and a narrow strip of the Andean foothills in northern Chile, in the Southern. It is the wine-growing climate *par excellence*.

Equatorial lands have both heat and moisture at all seasons. At the other extreme, the arctic snowfields and tundras and the great coniferous forest regions of the northern continental areas demand specialized cultures in human beings, with the emphasis on maintaining body-temperature by heavy clothing, heated dwellings and a diet of high calorific value, especially in winter. The Eskimo, Lapps and inhabitants of northern Siberia are modern examples of such peoples. The Middle and Upper Palaeolithic occupants of Europe, during the Last Glaciation,* must have had to withstand similar conditions, with the difference, in their case, of a much lower latitude and hence an improvement in the relative length of the summer season and of winter daylight, both of which would have been in their favour.

Hot deserts form an environment as forbidding in its own way as the arctic wastes. They may be hilly, rolling or flat, carved into mesas and canyons, gravelly, sandy or salt-encrusted. The limiting factors, in every case, are enormous diurnal temperature-range and lack of water. Such life as can exist, plant or animal, is highly specialized to withstand desiccation. Primitive man, by nature ill-fitted to survive in such conditions, can do so only by continuous effort, the exercise of special skills, such as water-finding, dictated by the generations of experience, and by due caution not to overreach his physiological capacity to endure water-privation.

The culture and equipment of man, therefore, are very closely connected with climate. It is evident that the original homeland of the human species, whether in Africa or Asia, enjoyed a tropical climate, in which clothing was not required for warmth. Outside this zone, clothing, shelter, and the use of fire for warmth become necessary for comfort, if not for survival, at some seasons, especially in elevated or exposed situations. Only within the tropics does Nature provide vegetable foodstuffs and fruits for the gathering at all seasons, so that elsewhere primitive man has to be at least to some extent a hunter. Once man has learned husbandry and winter storage of cereals and roots, this habitable climatic range is greatly extended. Settlements become more or less permanent and we find solidly built houses, granaries and other structures. The poleward range of the farmer depends very much on the hardiness of his staple crops and the length of the growing season they may require. Wheat and barley are sub-tropical in origin and prehistoric and early

* See Table, p. 96.

historic strains did not flourish far north of Latitude 50°.
Oats and rye are quicker to mature and so permit a more
northern range in the shorter summers. Maize (Indian corn)
is not frost-tolerant. It can be grown, even in most English
summers, but is here not safe without protection until the
end of May.

As human knowledge advanced, so did technical adaptation to climate. The inward-looking courtyard-house is a
worldwide answer to the need for reasonably shady and cool
quarters under a hot sun. Wood fires, warm clothing and the
compact, snugly thatched timber or stone house made life
tolerable in cold, wet, or snowy conditions before the advent
of steam-heating. Since Neolithic times irrigation-water drawn
from a river has extended the possible range of agriculture
in lands with insufficient moisture.

3.   Land-forms or topography

The shape of a country, both in the horizontal and vertical
planes, has an important influence on environment. A large
flat area in the centre of a continent, for instance, will provide for man very different advantages and problems from
those presented by a much-indented and mountainous coast-
line. The one, if not thickly forested, will encourage travel
and rapid cultural and economic exchanges over long distances. The other tends to isolate even the inhabitants of
adjacent valleys and make them take to the sea for easier
communication. Islanders, unless self-sufficient, also necessarily become seafarers.

Mountain ranges have important climatic effects. Situated
near coasts where sea-winds bring moisture, they concentrate
the rainfall by diverting moist air-masses to higher altitudes,
where they are cooled and precipitate. Over depressions or
plains in their lee may be a correspondingly intense 'rain-
shadow'. The lofty Sierras and the semi-arid to arid Great
Basin afford the classic examples of this effect. Mountains
may thus delimit major regions of different environment. Even
in low latitudes, their upper slopes may be temperate, or even
glacial, climatically speaking.

Rivers, on the other hand, tend to unite peoples. Cultural
influences follow the valley-paths up and down stream,
climbing the hills only to cross a watershed into another
stream-valley. Mountaineers and plainsmen lead very different lives and are often politically at odds. River-peoples,

travelling and, indeed, living on the stream, are a race apart
from the sedentary farmers on the banks. Some rivers, such
as the Nile, Euphrates and Tigris, actually *make* the lands
through which they flow.

Extensive high plateaux (that of central Mexico has already been mentioned), sunken rift-valleys such as the Rhine
Rift between Mainz and Basle, and basins, may form islands
that differ from their surroundings in climate, environment
and human culture.

Low-lying marsh-lands and river deltas, intersected by
many streams and creeks and frequently overgrown with
forest, are cut off from higher, drier areas and tend to become cultural refuges, backward and self-sufficient. The Ever-
glades of Florida or the Usumacinta River region of Tabasco,
Mexico, and, on a much smaller scale, the English Fenland,
before modern drainage-works, are examples. The inhabitants
are boatmen perforce, fishers and fowlers by calling and predi-
lection and rugged individualists, resistant to interference,
political or cultural. Their environment may be dangerous
and malaria-ridden, but human adaptability is apparently almost unlimited and necessity may be rated by such people
as virtue.

Lakes, both large and small, may similarly divide and
isolate. They are most numerous in recently glaciated areas
such as Finland and the Canadian North. Open in summer
or frozen over in winter, they afford by boat or sledge the
easiest lines of communication and transport in heavily
wooded country. Aesthetically, lakesides are desirable sites
for occupation in warmer surroundings. They offer other
environmental advantages—fish and waterfowl for food, timber for buildings, reeds for thatch, permanent water for
stock, and the protection afforded by pile-dwellings built out
over the shallows.

Coasts and beaches afforded, in the past as today, a living
for many peoples. In tropical or sub-tropical surroundings
the beachcomber's life has many attractions—sea-food in
plenty, coastwise communication where the interior may be
wooded, swampy or otherwise impassable, and the advantage, on rocky coasts, of abandoned sea-caves as dwellings.
In the Far North, on the other hand, the sea's driftwood may
be almost the only available source of timber for house- or
boat-building and other essential purposes. The prehistoric
'shell-mound' peoples of the world, from Chiapas, Mexico, to

Denmark, via the Strandloopers of the Cape of Good Hope, and the Capsians of north Africa, are examples.

Peninsulas, especially if of great extent, form cultural culs-de-sac and the ultimate refuge before extinction of human groups under pressure from the invasion of technologically more advanced peoples. The Bushmen and Hottentots, with a pure Stone Age culture, occupied great areas of south and east Africa up to the Middle Ages of Europe. First the iron-using Bantuspeakers from the north and west, pressing south-wards, drove them ever farther towards the Cape, then the Portuguese settled on both east and west coasts, and finally the Dutch and British invaded from the Cape itself. The lingering remnants of the Bushmen still survive in the Kalahari Desert region, which has been of no economic value (hitherto!) to any later comers. Near Cape Horn, the extremely primitive Yahgans similarly retain a toe-hold in the unwanted wilderness of Tierra del Fuego. Their marginal environments are not chosen, but obligatory. Beyond their coast lies no land at all.

4. Rocks and minerals

Next to the shape of the landscape comes the geology which underlies it. We are not, here, so much concerned with the structural role of the sub-surface rocks, though this is an important factor in topography, since the harder beds, which are less quickly attacked by weather and de-nuding agencies, tend to stand up as hills and ridges while the softer are easily worn down into plains and valleys.

The physical and chemical nature of the bedrock is of great importance, controlling to a large extent the nature of the soil formed from it by weathering and, through the soil, that of the plants and animals which inhabit the region. Further, the harder limestones, and, to a lesser extent, basalts and other basic igneous rocks, provide caves and overhangs which serve as ready-made shelters for man.

Subsoil geology determines the availability or scarcity of the mineral materials useful to man. In the earlier Stone Ages, the most important rocks from man's point of view were hard, easily flaked stones, such as flint, for the manufacture of essential cutting tools. Where flint itself was unobtainable, the earliest human inhabitants had to use the best material at hand or go elsewhere in search of something better. Many kinds of workable stone, other than flint, were used at many periods and in many places, but the roughness of implements made from second- or third-rate materials shows how far the nature of the available stones restricted the worker in obtaining the desired sharp working edges. Only a very few rather uncommon rocks, such as obsidian, chalcedony and opal were as good as, or even superior to, flint. Most other rocks are far less easily worked and even the superior few are often obtainable only in rather small pieces which called for great skill and economy of material in the course of manufacture. In many places good stone for cutting tools was brought to the most favoured settlement-sites, often for considerable distances.

In Neolithic times stone still served for cutting tools and weapons, so that the same considerations as before applied to flaked work. Neolithic knappers were more particular about obtaining the better materials on which to exercise their skill and quite deep shafts were sunk in Chalk country to reach layers of high quality flint not otherwise obtainable.

In addition to flaked implements, Neolithic people had axes or 'celts', which, though roughed out by flaking, were finished to a smooth surface by grinding and polishing. For such axes the best materials had to be rather tougher, if less hard, than flint, generally a crystalline igneous rock. A regular industry for their manufacture and trade for their distribution grew up, so that the ground axes were often found far from the places where their parent rock occurs naturally.

The Neolithic, in Europe, also brings the beginning of pottery-making, so that suitable clays for this purpose were important mineral materials to be sought conveniently close to human settlements.

Still later came the knowledge of metals—first those, like gold and copper, which usually, or at least sometimes, occur 'native' (i.e. already in the metallic state), then bronze, an alloy of copper and tin, much superior to copper for tools and weapons, and latterly iron. Unlike gold and copper, tin and iron are seldom or never found 'native', but occur as their compounds with oxygen, sulphur or other elements. The metals are obtainable from these 'ores' by some fairly difficult industrial processes involving great heat and specially built furnaces. Moreover, though iron ores are common enough in nature, they are much harder to smelt than those of copper and tin, but copper and tin ores, especially the latter, are rather restricted in their occurrence, so that only in a few places favoured with suitable ores could bronze be made.

It was widely distributed by trade and exchange, but must always have been rather expensive.

Building materials (apart from wood and thatch) are nearly all mineral in nature: earth or turf, stone, bricks and tiles made from clay and sand, slates, lime-plaster, mortar, concrete and latterly cement and glass. Most involve at least some industrial processing of the raw materials. All are heavy to transport and are best found as close as possible to the site of the intended building. Only in fairly modern times are materials other than those quite locally available extensively used in building.

5. Soils

That the soil mantling the 'solid' geology is a very important factor in environment is known to all of us, but especially to farmers, gardeners and stock-breeders, who depend directly on the sorts of plants that will grow in it. Even to unscientific farmers, guided only by accepted practice and tradition, local differences in soil are apparent—they are known as 'rich' or 'poor', 'fat' or 'hungry', 'heavy' or 'light', and so on. Their working properties in different seasons and weathers very soon impress themselves on the man with the plough, spade, hoe or digging-stick.

Soil is a natural formation, whether or not eventually exploited by the farmer, market-gardener or grazier, and has great influence on the wild grasses, herbs, shrubs and trees, which Nature, unaided, enables to grow. It is formed from the minerals available in the bedrock by the action, physical and chemical, of 'weather'—sun and air, rain and drought, frost and thaw. To the mineral basis is added humus—organic matter chiefly derived from the decay of the natural cover of larger plants, but also including the remains and excretia of the myriads of its small and microscopic inhabitants, both vegetable and animal.

On and in the soil grows the natural flora, and whereas the climate of the place is a potent factor, through weathering, in determining the nature of the soil formed from a given bedrock, it is, clearly, together with the soil itself, also a major determinant of the species and luxuriance of the flora that naturally grows there. Given a constant climate, different sorts of bedrock will give rise to different types of soil and different floras, exactly those assemblages of plants which are best suited to the prevailing soil-conditions.

Thus, in the temperate zone of Europe a rich, heavy moist soil, such as forms on a valley clay, will tend to grow a close forest of broad-leaved deciduous trees. Soils which are poorer in mineral plant-nutrients, light, and perhaps liable to drought in summer, such as those on chalk or coarse sandy bedrock, may produce, under Nature, little more than scattered scrub of oak and thorn in the way of trees, but have plenty of open space for herbs and grasses to provide natural pasture for grazing animals. The same soil-materials under a somewhat warmer, drier climate might form a semi-desert, clothed only with some sparse grasses and herbs in the moister seasons, with cacti and drought-resistant shrubs as the only perennials.

Among the other factors of natural environment the soil is evidently an important one. While, in some archaeological contexts, animal and plant remains may be lacking to give us an idea of past conditions, an original soil of the time has sometimes been preserved by becoming buried, either by some natural agency or under some structure erected by man, and this may straightway suggest the sort of conditions of climate and flora under which it was formed.

Modern soils in the most varied existing environments, both natural and of human making, have been studied, so that when we happen on such a fossil soil we can often make a good guess as to its contemporary natural environment, and, hence, that of any human group whose cultural remains may be stratigraphically associated with it.

Agricultural operations or any other extensive human interference with the environment will be reflected in the character of the soil. Forest clearance for fields and pastures, for example, generally result in some impoverishment of it, except under careful modern management. Man's numerous domestic grazing animals also prevent the regeneration of trees, so that man himself, in later times, becomes a factor in soil-formation or degradation, of which the soil itself may betray the action.

Under a given climate and exposure, the natural soils, via the vegetation, determine man's environment as forest or heath, scrub or grassland, and his ways of life will clearly differ accordingly in those environments.

6. Plants

The natural plant-assemblage of an environment depends

in part on soil-conditions, but is greatly affected also by the other factors already discussed. Place does so for bio-geographical reasons: where the typical semi-desert shrub in the sub-tropical zone of the Old World is the camel-thorn, the corresponding plant in the new is the mesquite. Climate, exposure and the nature of the bedrock will also have their characteristic influences. Compared with these factors, the flora is much more varied and flexible. On the same general kind of soil and under the same major climatic régime, the plant-assemblage may vary greatly within a few feet, according to minor changes in environment. In southern England a river-bank may be overgrown with alder and willow (water-loving trees), while on ground only a little higher, near by, the woodland may consist almost exclusively of oak, haw-thorn and holly, which prefer drier conditions. Where sand or gravel overlies chalk, there may be patches of gorse, heather and bilberry, or even rhododendron (an imported lime-hater, now widely naturalized on acid soils in Britain), while all around is grass pasture, or beech, ash and hawthorn forest—all trees which prefer a calcareous soil. A plant may grow prolifically on one flank of a hill, while not a single individual of that species will be found on the opposite slope. This is likely to be due to special heat- or light-requirements, which are adequately met on south-facing slopes, but not on slopes that face northward.

Most wild species are less particular as to the exact conditions than those just mentioned. Oak-trees grow in very wet conditions on sheltered hillsides of schist in the western Highlands of Scotland, on shaly screes high up in Cumberland and on dry sands in the New Forest of Hampshire, but the largest and best oaks in Britain grow on heavy clay in the Weald of Surrey, Sussex and Kent, and this is clearly the environment which the tree prefers—warm, well-watered and rich in mineral nutrients. Near the edges of the Weald is an outcrop of coarse sands and sandstones—the Greensand. Here the predominant trees are pine and birch. The oak will grow there also, but the conditions are, on the whole, too dry and acid to give fine specimens such as are to be found a mile or two away, on the clay.

For the archaeologist trees and plants generally are valuable indicators of human environment. They are represented in archaeological deposits by their airborne pollen, which is well preserved in acid soil-conditions, especially where the ground is perennially damp, as in river-valleys and peat-bogs. Timber may be well preserved either in very dry conditions, as in Egyptian tombs and in caves in arid country (e.g. Mexico), or, in the opposite circumstances, where the soil is waterlogged and air is excluded (rivers, lakes and bogs). With both air and moisture, wood rots away completely in a few years. It is also permanently preserved if once charred by fire, so that charcoal from hearths is useful. Softer plant-remains (leaves, bark, fruits, fibres, etc.) require the most favourable conditions—those of waterlogging or complete dryness—if anything is to remain. As in the case of the oak, many species determinable from such remains do not give any very exact indications of environment, taken in isolation. When, however, a fairly complete spectrum of the local flora can be obtained, as by pollen-analysis, the presence or absence of some of the more sensitive species may lead to quite definite environmental conclusions.

The flora of a countryside provides man with innumerable valuable commodities; fruits, seeds, succulent stems, roots and foliage for food; wood for implements and weapons and hafts for his stone or metal tools; wood or charcoal for fires; fibres from stems, barks or leaves for lashings, cordage, netting, basketry, clothing and bedding; timbers for buildings, house-furniture, fencing, boats and other vehicles; roofing materials as varied, according to the part of the world, as heather, straw, reeds, bark, leaves, cleft shingles or weatherboards; osiers for baskets, cleft willow and birch-bark for containers, large and small, and even canoes; oak-bark for tanning leather; dyes, medicines and arrow-poisons from appropriate plants; herbs for flavouring, maple or cane-sugar for sweetening and fermented liquors (the last also obtained from grain, roots, tree saps and fruits); forage for animals.

Out of this list one thinks, naturally, first of the familiar home-produced materials and particular equipment of rural house, farm and workshop of a generation or two ago, but every country has its own products and the reader may choose any instances with which he may be most familiar. The list could be prolonged almost indefinitely. Clearly, wherever trees and plants grow, there ancient, as well as modern, man learned the values of their products and put them to good use. Where we can discover recognizable remains of some of these things in an archaeological context, we can use botanical identifications to reconstruct the natural environment from which they were taken.

Cultivation by man assures the supply of some of these

plant products. Selection of the finest and most high-yielding strains has given us, today, the very large number of highly specialized cultivated races of original wild species which are commonly exploited. Something of the history of cultivated plants is known from remains found in association with Neolithic and later settlements. Food-grains, especially, have been studied, but all the varieties of food and industrial plant products regularly cultivated today must at some time have passed through similar processes of improvement. The entire history of their adaptation to human needs is known only in the cases of some fairly modern introductions, such as rubber.

7. Animals

Both invertebrate and vertebrate animals live directly or indirectly on the vegetable kingdom. Man, as we have seen, eats and uses many vegetable products directly. At most times and in most places he has also taken a certain proportion of animal food and, in the special case of the Eskimo, the diet is almost exclusively animal, at least in winter, because his arctic environment includes hardly any useful plants and these only during the short summer. Some Palaeolithic peoples, during the Ice Ages, must have been in a very similar situation, living mainly on the meat of the large game which they hunted.

The fauna available to man depends, as does the flora, very much on the other factors contributing to the environment. Herbivores live directly on the plants and both flesh-eating animals and man prey on them. In the earliest times, indeed, man, as a hunter, must often have been in direct competition with the larger carnivores for his food supply. The bones of the animals which he hunted and ate he sometimes preserved in great profusion at his dwelling-sites, so that the archaeologist, seeking the stone tools of Palaeolithic and Mesolithic man, turns up, as he excavates, plentiful evidence of the contemporary animal environment, which is of the greatest service for viewing the human culture in its natural ecological context, and for dating.

Because early hunters largely lived on mammals and because, for the palaeontologist, the mammals evolved sufficiently quickly to show significant morphological changes in the comparatively short spans of late geological time during which man was also on the scene, in studying the earlier

Stone Age it is on this group of animals that the chief emphasis naturally falls. This is not to say, however, that early man concerned himself only with the mammals in his environment. We know, from the analogy of the living Australian aborigines, who are still in a Stone Age stage of culture, that almost all zoological groups available—even insect larvae—contribute to the food supply. When larger game is scarce, not only the smaller mammals, such as rodents and insectivores, but birds, lizards, snakes, amphibia, fishes, land and marine invertebrates such as worms, snails and shellfish, are welcome substitutes on the menu. No doubt this was the case with ancient Stone Age peoples also. With the change from glacial to temperate conditions after the retreat of the Last Glaciation in Europe, tundra or steppe gave way to forest, and the herds of large game, such as reindeer and wild horses, were no longer available. The Mesolithic inhabitants of northern lands became fowlers, fishermen, collectors and beachcombers, living very much on shellfish and other sea-food. *Any* animal remains, therefore, not only mammalian bones, if preserved with human industries may be of environmental importance.

As among plants, it is the animal species which are least adaptable to varied conditions that are the best indicators of particular environments. In Europe the wild pig and squirrel are exclusively forest animals. The reindeer, if present, certainly denotes an arctic or sub-arctic tundra environment. The hippopotamus indicates frostless winters, for it is a feeder on water plants, and these die off in winter in northern Europe today. Elk (moose, in North America) must connote forest, for it is, in Europe at least, in part a barkfeeder and cannot live without conifers.

With the Neolithic, both agriculture and the domestication of animals begin. Instead of simply collecting wild vegetable food and hunting wild animals, man had learned to cultivate plants and to keep herds of tame animals for slaughter as required. Just as the clearing of fields for crop-production represented interference with and modification of the natural environment, so, for instance, the fencing in of stock, or herding animals under the control of cowman, shepherd or swineherd at the forest-edges near the village meant continued destruction of tree-seedlings and the prevention of forest regeneration.

The history of the domestication of the common animals

which man has exploited for his own ends is still known only in outline. Only through the intensive study of domestic animal remains from archaeological sites will the detailed facts eventually emerge. A beginning has already been made, but a great deal more work is required in this field.

8. Time

Of all the factors influencing environment, time, only, can be expressed exactly by a single quantity—a number of years. Though we now have some 'clocks', in the form of radioactive isotopes, which can be used to measure geological time and give us dates in years, most of the methods are not, in practice, as accurate or reliable as archaeologists could wish, though they are, of course, better than nothing.

There are two kinds of dates used by geologists and archaeologists—relative and absolute. The former are basic to any kind of time-scale and show the true *sequence* of events, i.e. that event A must have occurred before event B. They are based upon the geological rule of stratification, which states that, *provided there has been no subsequent disturbance,* a stratum or layer in a geological or archaeological section which overlies another must be later or younger than one on, or above, which it lies. Thus, we can often, from the field-evidence, arrange a sequence of geological or archaeological events based on observation of mere stratigraphical order, without knowing how long in years any event took or how long ago, in years, it happened. Having the bare order in which events took place, the next question of course is: 'How many years does our sequence cover and exactly *when* did events A and B occur?'

Evidently, to answer this sort of question, we have to obtain a *countable* series of events, or measurable processes, associated with A and B and connecting their times with our own. Some ways in which this may be done are described in Chapter 9.

Time becomes a factor in the environment of man on two scores: first because in considering an ancient human group we are thinking of it at a point in past time, or over a period relatively short in comparison with that which has since elapsed; secondly, because the natural processes of formation of the environment at a state of balance or equilibrium take time.

The actual position, i.e. the relative date, of an archaeological event in the known sequence is an important feature of its environment. When this is known, we know also that certain natural and archaeological events, which may have great influence on the environment of the time or on the men we are studying, have preceded it and must be taken into account, while others, which we know to have happened later, clearly cannot enter into consideration at the point in time with which we are concerned.

One stage of Palaeolithic culture flourished in Britain at a time (some quarter of a million years ago) when the sea stood about 100 feet (33 metres) above its present level in relation to the land. Much has happened to the shape of our countryside since then—and all this we must *undo,* in imagination, before we can begin to visualize the geography and environment of that time. Certainly, the past appearance of the Thames Valley would not be recreated if the land were merely submerged, or sea-level raised, by 100 feet today.

Use and improvement of the natural advantages of any environment must depend upon the sum of human experience available to man, at that place and at that time. Thus, copper ores may have been present in the environment of Neolithic man, but they were not available, i.e. an *useful* part of that environment, until the knowledge of how to treat them was developed or learned.

This is obvious when we consider absurd extremes—that, for example, Mesolithic man had no knowledge of steam-engines. It is not so clear when we take a much more remote human invention, such as pottery making, and ask whether Mesolithic man was interested in clay as a raw material. We have, as yet, no certain Mesolithic pottery in western Europe, but the forerunners of the earliest Neolithic vessels of Denmark (Ertebølle culture) are unknown and the style *may,* possibly, be indigenous and have its roots in the local Mesolithic culture which just precedes it. We need a far more exact knowledge of the sequence of events in primitive technology before we can confidently make statements from negative evidence like this.

Finally, given sufficient time, the development of an environment under an unchanging set of formative factors eventually arrives at a 'climax', a balanced state of affairs which will be maintained without apparent further development until one or more of the factors is altered. Alteration in any of the factors brings about a renewal of corresponding changes in the direction of a new equilibrium-state or climax.

The over-all character of an environment, and whether it is still changing towards a climax state or has already reached it, depend on its former character and that of the new factors, on the one hand, and, on the other, on the time that has elapsed since that particular steady combination of factors was established. In the long run, speaking in terms of geological time, no factor is permanent or constant—all are subject to slow revolutions and changes. Since, however, the rate of growth of vegetation, for instance, is rapid in comparison with such periods, a climax may often be reached and apparently maintained for a geologically relatively short time. Whatever the causes of the Pleistocene glaciations, the place, climate, topography, soils, floras and faunas of most of the Northern Hemisphere have suffered several cycles from extreme cold, low sea-levels and continentality to temperate conditions, extended seas and more oceanic conditions, and back again, within the past one million years. As we count lifetimes and recorded centuries, the natural changes, because they are so slow, have seemed only of the slightest within historic times, being masked by the apparently still greater changes in natural environments brought about by civilized and numerous human communities. The natural changes, however, are doubtless still going on and will become, perhaps painfully, apparent to future generations, when history has been written for long enough for the altering geography and climates of our homelands no longer to be overlooked.

2

Place. The Emergence and Dispersal of Man

IF, IN detail, the origins of the human species remain some-what obscure, there can be no doubt that the earliest men lived amid tropical surroundings.

Man, as an animal, almost naked of hair and unprovided by nature with natural weapons of offence or defence, could only have arisen where living was fairly easy, with tempera-tures high enough at all seasons for comfort without any covering, and with vegetable food available for the picking.

We still do not know with certainty where the cradle of mankind was situated, but the tropical zone, extending 23° of latitude north and south of the Equator, certainly con-tained it. In the Far East this belt extends from southern China in the north through Indo-China and the Malay Archipelago to northern Australia. It includes peninsular India, southern Arabia, and the greater part of Africa from the mid-Sahara to the southern end of Madagascar. In the New World it comprises Central and South America from the tip of Lower California to Rio de Janeiro, and, in the Pacific, most of the islands, from Hawaii to New Caledonia. Since only the Old World has yielded human fossils of considerable antiquity, the Americas and the Pacific area seem very unlikely to have been inhabited until much later, and the tropical parts of Asia and Africa have hitherto alternated in favour with anthropologists as man's original homeland. At present, it looks as if Africa is leading, if only because a larger number and variety of fossil men and near-men are known from there.

One must always bear in mind that the Old World dis-tribution of human fossils, as of many archaeological relics, mainly corresponds with the areas of modern civilization and industry, which also provide scholars with the interest and opportunity to study remains of past ages. Large areas have hitherto yielded no evidence, probably mainly because they are scientifically unexplored rather than because the evidence does not exist. Many such discoveries are made by chance in road or railway cuttings, in excavating for the foundations of new buildings or in commercial excavations for gravel, brick earth, limestone and so on, so that where such works are not numerous the possibly fossil-bearing deposits are seldom exposed, even if there should be scientists on the spot competent to examine them. In the New World the case appears to be different. Men first reached the Americas across the Behring Strait from northern Asia, not earlier, it is generally supposed, than the end of the Last Glaciation, perhaps ten to twelve thousand years ago.

The physical remains of early men, in the form of skulls and skeletons, are rarities. This is not only because man was, in earlier times, rather a rare animal but also because for bones to be preserved, a body must be quickly buried or naturally covered by sediments. Being highly intelligent, man generally succeeded in avoiding death by drowning, while the remains of the larger mammals show that they were frequently caught by floods and their bodies buried in water-laid deposits. Dying in almost any other way the remains are soon scattered by scavengers and dissolved away by weathering processes. With the adoption of formal burial, human remains become quite common. The stone implements of early man, on the other hand, are commonly and widely found in Pleistocene deposits of the warmer parts of the Old World, dating back to some 500 thousand years ago, and, while these have been well known for at least the last half-century and have been the subject of new discoveries all the time since, nothing comparable has been found anywhere in the Americas, despite the most diligent search, especially in the United States.

Thus place, as a factor in the environment of Lower Palaeolithic man, means the Old World, and those parts of it which, at some time within the last half-million years, have enjoyed a tropical or warm-temperate climate (Fig. 2).

We presume, on current theory supported by the evidence now available, that man arose from an ancestral form common to him and to the living great apes, which lived probably at least as far back as the Miocene period of the geologists, between twenty and thirty million years ago. At

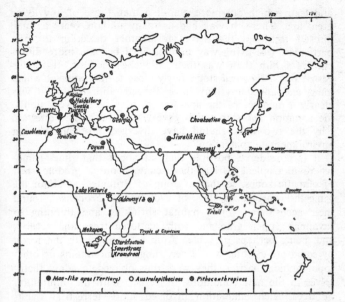

Fig. 2. Distribution of man-like apes, Australopithecines and Pithecanthropines. Note that the apes mostly belong to Tertiary times, when the climate was much warmer in the temperate zone.

that time the larger apes were only just becoming distinct from the monkeys. One fossil form, called *Proconsul africanus*, from Lower Miocene beds near Lake Victoria in Kenya, was a primitive ape, rather smaller than a chimpanzee. Though unquestionably an ape, it had a few features of the skull

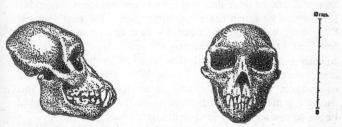

Proconsul

and teeth which are more man-like than those of any living great ape. These, having had as many million years as man himself to adapt themselves in another direction to their particular, tree-living way of life, have become more different from him than was their Miocene ancestor. It is suggested that *Proconsul* stood fairly close to the point at which man- and ape-stems may have divided, and, though it was clearly a member of the ape-branch, may be not very unlike the common ancestor which gave rise to both. The question why the two lines should have diverged probably has an environmental explanation.

It is considered possible that, at about that time, somewhere in tropical Africa, there came about a gradual shift of climatic zones, so that a group of Primates, at about the same little-specialized stage of evolution as *Proconsul,* found their accustomed forest habitat shrinking and thinning to savannah (open grassland with scattered trees and scrub), and, being perhaps prevented from retreating with the forest by some pre-existing wide river, range of mountains or other topographical barrier, they were thus obliged to adapt themselves to the new conditions, or perish. With the diminution of trees, such adaptation involved more terrestrial habits and the adoption of an erect stance, making the most of an ape's highly developed senses of sight and hearing, as opposed to the sense of smell, on which terrestrial mammals, as a group, more usually rely. Being without natural defences against possible enemies, they would be obliged to become both wary and cunning. Their upright stance, freeing the hands from any ordinary part in locomotion, made these available to grasp, manipulate and use inanimate objects—sticks and stones, for instance—as weapons and implements. Since, in their new and poorer environment, vegetable food would be much scarcer than formerly, the new ground-living apes would begin to acquire flesh-eating habits, killing for food at first any creatures—insects, birds, reptiles and rodents—small enough and slow enough to be caught and overpowered with the bare hands. With practice in the use of cudgels, stones, bones and horns to hunt swifter and stronger game, the larger herbivores of the open plains would be added to their list of food-animals.

All these activities distinguish the ways of life of primitive men from the usual habits of their cousins, the apes.

It has recently been shown* that, in the wild, chimpanzees do, on rare occasions, eat meat, small game presumably caught and killed by themselves, though this latter has not been proved by observation. In parts of Uganda, parkland and savannah border on the normal forest habitat of chimpanzees and they often frequent the more open country. Here they also catch and eat termites, showing that they are not as exclusively vegetarian, at least in this environment, as had always been supposed. In this latter activity, which has been photographed, they are tool-*users,* employing convenient grass-stems and twigs, carefully selected for the purpose, to probe holes in termite-mounds and to extract the insects, which are then quickly transferred to the mouth.

A captive chimpanzee family, suddenly faced by a chained(!) leopard, picked up sticks of various sizes provided for the purpose of the experiment among a mass of vegetable litter. These they waved and used to threaten, standing erect, and even threw them, without very certain aim, towards, if not *at,* the potential attacker. This behaviour has not been observed in the wild, but it seems likely that the adult individuals concerned, captured fully grown, had prior experience of leopards and were only exhibiting their normal reactions to such a situation. Without doubt, the potentiality for such actions, bordering on typically human behaviour, is already present in living higher Primates and may justifiably be presumed in their extinct forbears.

This exposition of the way in which the ancestors of man in time might have developed from ape-like creatures may seem highly speculative, but, in fact, remains of the Australopithecines, found in ancient cave-deposits at Taung in Bechuanaland and at several sites in the Transvaal, do suggest beings at exactly the stage of physical development, between ape and true man, just described. They walked upright on flat-soled terrestrial feet. The form of the pelvis was more man-like than ape-like owing to this change in posture. The poise of the head and the form and arrangement of the teeth were also human. Nevertheless, the skulls have small brain-cases and many remaining ape-like features. Two main groups of Australopithecines are distinguished—*Australopithecus* (ex *Plesianthropus*), small, light in build and per-

* At a Symposium on the Primates, held in April 1962 at the Zoological Society of London.

haps predominantly carnivorous, and *Paranthropus*, with enormous jaws and grinding teeth, more vegetarian. They may represent adaptations to slightly different environments, savannah and riverside bush respectively. The animal remains associated with the Australopithecines are those of open savannah with rocky kopjes. There is also some evidence of tool-using.

One thing only excludes them, so far, from a hypothetical role as the direct links between ape and man in the chain of evolution—their comparatively late date, probably, at most,

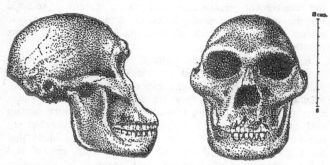

Australopithecus (ex Plesianthropus)

no earlier than Lower Pleistocene (late Villafranchian). The place of their discovery, far south and, indeed, just beyond the boundary of strictly tropical Africa, suggests that the Australopithecines were comparatively late-surviving relics

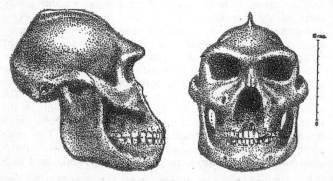

Paranthropus

of a type formerly more widespread and certainly of some much greater antiquity. This conclusion is also made in view of the very considerable morphological progress in the human direction which the extinct end-products present.

To transform an ape-like ancestor, not very different from *Proconsul,* into an Australopithecine such as *Plesianthropus* undoubtedly took millions of years in a very slowly changing environment. According to the geological time-scale, however, some 27-28 million years were available! That their general type was not confined to south Africa is shown by Leakey's recent (1960) discoveries (e.g. *Zinjanthropus*) at Oldoway in the Serengeti area of northern Tanganyika, within 3° south of the Equator, or 1,600 miles

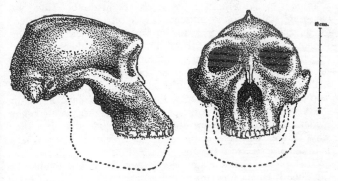

Zinjanthropus

farther north. This find seems to be of similar Lower Pleistocene date. An absolute figure, based on potassium-argon dating, of 1.75 million years was published in 1961 for the base of Bed I at Oldoway, but this is regarded as too high by many authorities.

While the making of stone implements by the south African Australopithecines is still regarded by most authorities as unproven, though there are certain indications at one site (Swartkrans) of roughly worked stones, there can be hardly any doubt that their equatorial representative, *Zinjanthropus,* did so. Numerous flaked pebbles, of a type everywhere accepted hitherto as of human workmanship, were found in the same well-sealed layer with his remains. It is further notable that the associated animals, on which he presumably fed and discarded the bones, were mainly small

—lizards, rodents, etc.—while those few representing larger species were invariably of young individuals and so within his small means and experience as a hunter to catch and kill.

From the next layer (Bed II) at Oldoway, appeared another skull, unnamed as yet by Leakey, of a youth who made and used more advanced tools—the well-known hand-axes of Chellean type—and hunted adult animals of the larger species. The making and use of tools seems to have arisen out of pressure of human competition with the large animals, accompanied by the acquisition of the carnivorous habit. *Zinjanthropus,* judging by his enormous molars, was largely vegetarian. The find has not yet been fully studied, but it is clear that we have here a true man, whose relationship, if remote to living human beings, is not in doubt. Thus, we can now point to the emergence, as our theory predicted, of a true tool-making man in tropical Africa, following if not directly derived from, an Australopithecine stage, in which only the beginnings of humanity, tool-making and hunting are observable. Whether this was the one and only such emergence is a far different matter. It would be an astonishing fluke, in that case, that we should have hit upon the very place where it happened. In the absence of other evidence, however, we are obliged to conclude that, in Oldoway Gorge, we have chanced on at least one place where man did emerge from the apes.

This makes Asia's claim less strong. In Asia, notably in the Sivalik Hills of northern India, there existed, in the Miocene and Pliocene periods of the later Tertiary Era, several kinds of apes, different from any now living but without many special resemblances to man. From this we may justifiably conclude that they are not any more closely related to humanity than their living representatives. The remains are, in any case, extremely fragmentary, consisting mainly of teeth and fragments of jaws, so that any conclusions from them could only be provisional, until we find more complete specimens. It has recently been suggested, however, that one of these Pliocene fossils (*Ramapithecus*) may prove to have been a true Hominid, a member of man's zoological family.

Another ape of large size, called *Gigantopithecus,* lived in south China, but at a date (Early Pleistocene) comparable with that of the far more hominid Australopithecines in Africa. These we have already agreed to regard as survivals of a probably much older type. At about the same time, however, south-east Asia, especially Java, could boast of some true men, about whose antecedents we at present know nothing. These finds further illustrate two points already made: first, that their position is fully equatorial (only 7-8° south of the Equator) and second, that Java, of all the islands in the Malay Archipelago, has been, under past Dutch administration, the most accessible, best studied

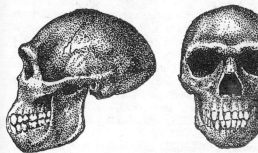

Pithecanthropus erectus

and technologically advanced. That we have human fossils at all, and those adequately known, is probably as much due to this circumstance as that Java was better suited to harbour a branch of primitive humanity than Sumatra, Borneo, Celebes or the Malay Peninsula of the Asiatic mainland. These are, geologically, largely unexplored and may yet give evidence relating to the problem.

However that may prove, it remains that, in the Early and Middle Pleistocene, there were several now extinct types of man living in Java. Related more or less to Dubois' original find, called *Pithecanthropus erectus* (1894) from Trinil, von Koenigswald's fossils (1936—40) represent a type on about

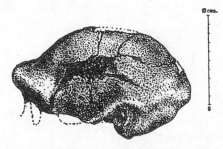

Chellean man (Oldoway, Bed II)

the same level of physical evolution as Leakey's Chellean Man from Bed II at Oldoway. They are of approximately the same date. *P. erectus* is assigned to the lower Middle Pleistocene, but *P. modjokertensis,* from the Djetis Beds, is somewhat earlier—late Lower Pleistocene (Villafranchian). Thus the last-named is probably at least as early in date, though morphologically a stage more advanced, than the Australopithecines. Unfortunately, we have so far no evidence of how the Pithecanthropines came to be in Java—whether developed independently in place or immigrant from elsewhere, perhaps ultimately from Africa via the tropical northern shores of the Indian Ocean. If the latter, we lack at present any geographically intermediate evidence of so long a journey. In view of the long stretches of time available, however, the journey is by no means impossible—perhaps a migration of only a few tens or hundreds of miles in each generation.

That the Javanese Pithecanthropines were not unique in Asia is well known, but the other occurrence of closely allied forms is in northern China, at Choukoutien, near Peking, where a further rich group of fossils, of a different species of the same genus (*P. pekinensis*), was discovered between 1930 and 1940. It was originally called *Sinanthropus,* but is now regarded as not being generically distinct from *Pithecanthropus.*

The immediately striking environmental circumstance of these finds is their relatively far northern position, in Latitude 40° N., the same as that of New York. In date, they are assigned, with *P. erectus,* to the early Middle Pleistocene, but, if falling within the same general period, it may be thought that, in such different surroundings, they should be distinctly later in date—better adapted to conditions of an environment which, today, is certainly not tropical, but of pronounced

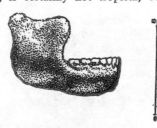

Heidelberg jaw

cool-temperature continental climate, with hard winter frost. However much milder the conditions at Choukoutien may have been during the First Interglacial of Europe, in that place they could scarcely resemble those of Java!

Heidelberg—near the site where the famous Mauer Jaw, of a man possibly at the same stage of physical evolution as *Pithecanthropus* and of similar date, was discovered—lies nearly 10° farther north than Peking. If the argument of better adaptation to a less favourable climate applies to the Peking men, it should, on the score of latitude, apply even more to the Heidelberg individual. Owing to its position, on the border between western and central Europe, however, and lying on the edge of the Rhine Rift, which today forms an island of almost Mediterranean conditions, Heidelberg has a far less extreme and more oceanic climate than Peking. The contemporary fauna associated with Heidelberg Man is distinctly warm-temperate in character, with animals like rhinoceros (*R. etruscus, D. merckii*), elephants (*Elephas meridionalis*) and so on which we now associate with a tropical environment. It does not follow, on that account, that the climate so far north was then tropical, nor have we much evidence that Heidelberg Man, of whom we have only the jaw, was at a stage of development comparable with that of *Pithecanthropus,* the latter group being mainly represented by skulls, with only fragmentary mandibles.

A further representative of mankind at the *Pithecanthropus* level of evolution is the probably slightly later *Atlanthropus,* from Ternifine, Algeria. The remains consist of two mandibles and a parietal bone of the skull-vault. The associated fauna, including, for example, hippopotamus, shows an environment with plentiful surface water, very different from that of the present day in north Africa. Hand-axes of Acheulean type occurred in the same deposits and were doubtless the work of *Atlanthropus.*

In the extreme west of north Africa, near Casablanca in Morocco, sandstones which represent ancient beach- and dune-sands have yielded a single jaw-fragment of an *Atlanthropus,* at the Sidi Abderrahman quarry, and numerous quartzite implements from various stages of the Middle Pleistocene, including both pebble-tools and hand-axes.

The Bed II find at Oldoway, Tanganyika, with Chellean hand-axes, referred to above as a successor of *Zinjanthropus,* seems, at any rate superficially, to compare morphologically with *Pithecanthropus,* though it appears also to have certain

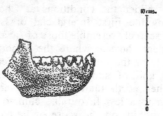

Alanthropus jaw

resemblances to *Homo rhodesiensis* (see below, p. 66), suggesting a possible genetic connection. It is possible that the *Telanthropus* jaw from Swartkrans, Transvaal, is another such. At least it seems to be at a stage more advanced than the Australopithecines.

Reviewing these finds, it is clear that the earlier Middle Pleistocene examples—the Java Pithecanthropines and the Oldoway Chellean Man—are strictly tropical. Probably slightly later are the *Atlanthropus* specimens and somewhat later still the much more northern Heidelberg and Peking finds. There is, as yet, no secure evidence for dating *Telanthropus,* but his sub-tropical situation would best equate him with the similarly placed north African fossils.

Heidelberg Man brings us up towards the time, some 300 thousand years ago, of the greatest European glaciation, called Mindel in the Alpine area and Elster in Germany (see Table p. 96). His relative date is uncertain, but cannot, on the geological evidence, be later than the Intersta-dial between the two phases (Mindel I and II) of the glacia-tion, and might fall at the end of the full Interglacial which preceded Mindel I. Chellean (Abbevillian) hand-axes from gravel-pits in the Somme valley, northern France, are attri-buted to this Interglacial and are associated with a warm fauna having some archaic survivals. This suggests that early man, of whose skeleton we have as yet no fossil example, inhabited Atlantic Europe at this time.

The southward advance of the ice-sheets covered, at their maximum extension, nearly all of the British Isles, Scandinavia and north Germany, as far south as the northern slopes of the Harz, Erzgebirge, Riesengebirge and Carpa-thians. The ice turned all of Europe north of the Pyrenees, Alps and Balkan mountains into a periglacial zone of tundra, loess-steppe and cold forest. Man evidently could not survive in these conditions at his then stage of cultural development and was obliged to migrate southwards with the temperate animals he was accustomed to hunt. The possible routes of such migration led into the peninsulas of Iberia, Italy and Greece, but for the greater part the Mediterranean barred further progress. It is doubtful whether, even so long ago, any actual land-connections joined Europe to Africa, though the sea-crossings were not, perhaps, as wide as they are today.

The extension so far south of the ice and its accompanying glacial anticyclone diverted the zone of westerly winds and rain-bearing Atlantic depressions further south, so that at this time north Africa and the Near East, deep into the present desert zone, were relatively well-watered and fertile lands. It was probably during this time that the Algerian *Atlanthropus* and the Moroccan makers of the primitive tools found near Casablanca flourished.

What may have been the effect of this shift of climatic belts on Africa south of the Sahara is still uncertain. Evidence exists of alternating relatively wet (pluvial) and dry (interpluvial) periods in the tropical zone, but nothing so far permits these to be correlated at all confidently with the European glacials and interglacials. Climatic fluctuations in tropical Africa there certainly were, involving some changes in the positions of the rainy and drier belts, but these changes have affected the African fauna as a whole very little, merely compelling migrations of species with the slow shift of the environments to which they were adapted, and this probably applied to man also. Africa is a single great land-mass, undivided by transverse mountain-ranges or other permanent barriers to animal or human movements—unlike Europe and western Asia, in which the east-west mountains represent serious obstacles, stretching over long distances, and the Mediterranean is a definitive barrier to further southward migration. While the European flora and fauna have undergone several distinct changes, with total loss of some of the more ancient species owing to the Pleistocene climatic fluctuations, those of Africa have easily been able to reoccupy their former territories when unsuitable conditions again became more favourable. Hence apes and elephants and lions, among many others which are no longer found in Europe, still occupy considerable areas of Africa.

Both ape and early human fossils are rather rare and, as we have seen, mainly confined to the warmer regions of the

Old World. In a few places (Oldoway Beds I and II, Terni-fine, Sidi Abderrahman near Casablanca) the finds are associated with pebble-choppers and primitive types (Chellean or Acheulian) of hand-axes. Some, notably the *Pithecanthro-pus*-group in Java and at Heidelberg, are not known to have made stone tools. The north China *pekinensis*-men are found in two quite distinct sets of deposits. The earlier of these contain rough chert pebble-tools, the later some rather undistinguished flake-implements of vein-quartz. The latter, by their technique of manufacture, are certainly later and even the pebble-tools may be so rough because of their technically difficult material and are not, for that reason, necessarily very early. The pebble-tools and more primitive hand-axes are therefore probably generally attributable to men at or about the *Pithecanthropus* stage of evolution, so that the

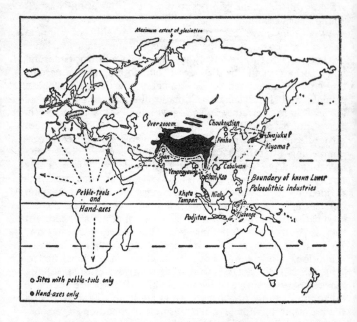

Fig. 3.   Distribution of Lower Palaeolithic implements, the known extent of the maximum glaciation and the central Asiatic plateau. The whole of Africa, south-western Europe and much of the Near East was occupied. Individual sites are marked only in the Middle and Far East.

known distribution in the Old World of the implements should show the former extension of their makers.

Hand-axes are widely distributed (see Map, p. 58) from the Cape throughout Africa. In Asia they are found in the Near East and in India, but not north of the Himalaya and the Tibetan plateau, which presented an impassable barrier. In Europe they extend from Spain to southern Britain and to the Rhine-Danube line, but are rare north of it. They are not known in the Balkans or Greece* and are found only in extreme eastern Asia Minor on the borders of Palestine. In Europe they belong exclusively to Interglacial periods, when the climate was at least as warm as it is today, then disappear during the intervening Glaciations. It is clear, therefore, that the hand-axe makers could not normally adapt their ways to cold, or even to cooler-temperate climates and, indeed, that their true homeland and preferred environment were in the tropical and sub-tropical zones. The pebble-tools, fore-runners of the hand-axe, are almost confined to Africa, north-west India and south-east Asia—truly tropical regions.

The inference is that hand-axes were developed in Africa, at a stage of which Oldoway, Bed I, is the type. It represents a moist-climate period (Kageran Pluvial of Africa) apparently equivalent in time to the first European glaciation (Günz of the Alps). In Asia, however, they generally occur in deposits of the next pluvial (the Alpine Mindel), though at Tampan, in Malaya, they are thought to be approximately contem-porary with the African pebble-tools. It seems, therefore, as if their makers may have spread from Africa to the extreme ends of Asia—Burma, Malaya and Indo-China. They also extend to north China, as far as Choukoutien, and to the islands of Java, Borneo, Celebes and the Philippines. In this large area there are, with the sole exception of Japan, no true hand-axes. These are confined, in Asia, to the central and southern parts of India, save in the Near East.

Oldoway Bed II yields the first African hand-axes, which, here at least, are clearly a later development than the pebble-tools. Some hand-axes of Lower Palaeolithic type are found in Japan, though their dating there is at present uncertain. In Africa, the only human remains associated with pebble-tools (*Zinjanthropus*) resemble the Australopithecines, while true hand-axes seem to be the work of men (Oldoway Chellean Man, *Atlanthropus*) at the *Pithecanthropus* state. At Chou-

* Greece (since the map was drawn) has now yielded hand-axes.

koutien, on the other hand, the pebble-implements seem to belong to *P. pekinensis*, and the Patjitanian choppers and flakes of Java (less certainly, and only by inference) to *P. erectus* or his descendants. We do not know what type of man made the Indian hand-axes.

Huge areas of southern Asia have so far yielded no fossil or archaeological evidence. Still, it is unlikely that it does not exist, in view of what has been found at these scattered points. The few spots that we so far have on our map do not enable us to arrive at more than the most tentative conclusions, but these are consonant with the environmental evidence.

No generally accepted evidence is yet known for the use of fire by hand-axe makers. Hoxne, in Suffolk, has yielded wide-spread traces of burning, but not hearths which would point to control of fire. The fire there might well have been natural. This evidently explains why the widespread Lower Palaeolithic cultures never reached the Americas. The sole land-bridge, or at least island-studded strait, between the Old World and the New is between north-east Asia and Alaska (see Map, Fig. 4). Even during the most genial of Inter-glacials, the climate so far north (50° N. even for Kamchatka and the Aleutians, more than 60° N. for the Behring Strait), was too boreal to be supportable for people who lacked fire. The mean annual temperature at Behring Strait is today close to freezing-point at sea-level and only reaches a monthly average between 50° and 60° F. in the month of July. For migration on foot, therefore, a deliberate journey north to Behring Strait and again south, over some 20° of latitude each way, would be required. Together with the nec-essary easting, this represents a distance between (say) the southern extremity of Kamchatka and Queen Charlotte Sound in British Columbia of between three and four thousand miles, ignoring some inevitable detours. It is now known that central Alaska was never covered by an ice-sheet and so could have afforded a half-way refuge for immigrants to the New World even at the height of a glaciation. The conditions there must nevertheless have remained very severe at the best of times. For whole families migrating into the unknown together, and with the necessity to hunt for their subsistence *en route*, the journey would be possible only to people equipped with fire, warm clothing, tents and adequate weapons, and accustomed to the hazards of overwintering in a frost-climate. As far as we know, men in the Old World reached that

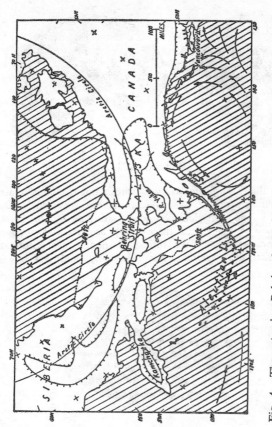

Fig. 4. The extensive Behring land-bridge, between Asia and America, afforded by a fall in sea-level of only 300 feet, as during a glaciation. Contemporary ice-margins are suggested and the retreat of the ice from the British Columbia coast, in view of the westerly wind-circulation in the North Pacific.

stage only during the Last Glaciation. They could not have attempted the crossing until at least a well-advanced stage in the Wisconsin glacial state of North America—and indeed we find their earliest traces in the Americas soon after that event.

Returning to early man at the hand-axe stage of culture, it is clear that his geographical range, even within the Old World, was limited by his modest equipment and his inability to survive in any but the more favourable environments. This was certainly the case up to the end of the Last Interglacial, perhaps a little over 100 thousand years ago.

By that time there had developed types of man more ad-

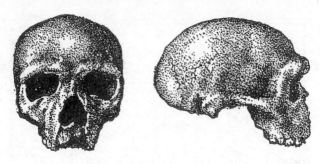

Steinheim skull

vanced than *Pithecanthropus,* foreshadowing the classic
Neanderthalers of the Last Glaciation, but very much more
variable in their physical characters. Judging by the known
distribution of their fossils, these people preferred warm conditions, for nearly all save three (Steinheim near Stuttgart,
Ehringsdorf near Weimar, East Germany, and Ganovče in

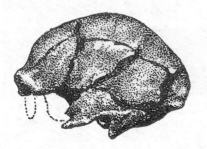

Ehringsdorf skull

Czechoslovakia) come from sites (see Map, Fig. 5) fairly
near the Mediterranean Sea, in Europe, north Africa and
south-western Asia, where their remains are associated with
warm-climate faunas. Whether any form of *Pithecanthropus*
was their direct ancestor is unknown, for fossils representing
intermediate stages, leading from 'ape-men' with a brain-
capacity of 900-1,000 c.c. to better-developed men with
1,300-1,400 c.c., are so far lacking. Their antecedents are
further complicated by the fact that, by the close of the Last
Interglacial (and perhaps even from the end of the Great

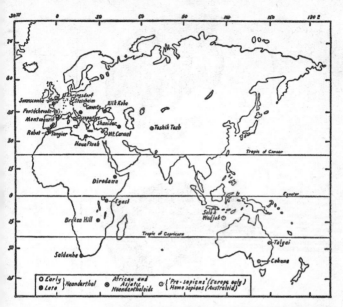

Fig. 5. Known human distribution from the Great Interglacial to the beginning of the last Glaciation. The dots within the broken circle show the distribution of the late Neanderthalers in their classic area. The concentration in the west is likely to be fictitious; this is the most closely explored area.

Interglacial) there were in existence men seeming to be scarcely at all different, as far as their remains go, from *Homo sapiens*. The evidence for this statement comes from Swanscombe (Kent, England, Great Interglacial) and Fonté-chevade (Charente, France, Last Interglacial) where skulls consisting only of the vault and back of the head and deficient in the important frontal and facial parts are still the subject of controversy, though recent work does suggest that they may have belonged to the Neanderthal-like group we are now discussing. The opposing view is also widely held and published expert opinions differ sharply as to whether or not the warm-climate early Neanderthaloids did or did not give rise to *Homo sapiens*. If Swanscombe and Fontéchevade are regarded as distinct 'Pre-sapiens' examples and not as Neanderthaloids, then the simplest derivation for *H. sapiens* is clearly from them. Since the date of Swanscombe is a whole glacial cycle earlier and that of Fontéchevade the same as

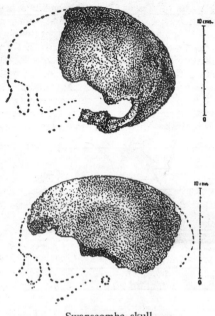

Swanscombe skull
Fontéchevade skull

for the warm Neanderthaloids, it would seem unlikely that the latter could have entered into the ancestry of *H. sapiens*.

There can be little doubt that they *did* lead on to the extreme, or 'classical', Neanderthal type, which alone seems to have occupied Europe and western Asia in the succeeding first stage of the Last Glaciation, only to be replaced more or less completely by incoming *H. sapiens* at its conclusion.

The fully developed, or 'classic', Neanderthalers represented a new departure in human history in their physical and cultural adaptation to a climate not merely cold-temperate or even cold, but positively arctic in character, at least in winter. In the region of south-western Europe, where both remains and Mousterian cultural relics are most plentiful, the environment must have resembled that of Lapland or Labrador at the present day, with reindeer, mammoth, woolly rhinoceros and a boreal cold-steppe or tundra vegetation. Survival in these circumstances depended on marked cultural advances—the adoption of caves and overhanging rocks for shelter, the use of fire and (though here we have as yet no direct evidence) the wearing of animal skins, perhaps as a mere cloak or poncho, for clothing. It is striking that, while hitherto the distribution of human fossils, and the associated stone industries, floras and faunas, had generally indicated settlements in the open, no use of fire and a tropical to warm-temperate climate, the Neanderthal human finds and the associated Mousterian industry are invariably sheltered and show hearths. Numerous in south-western Europe, the type is found sporadically through northern Italy, Jugoslavia, the Crimea, and even as far away as the highlands of Persia and the mountains of Uzbekistan. Greece has lately yielded a single specimen.

It seems as if, with the onset of the Last Glaciation, the already fairly widespread temperate-climate Neanderthaloids, instead of retreating southwards, as their predecessors had had to do when faced with a similar situation, had by now acquired the ability to adapt their way of life to the severer conditions and so were enabled, not merely to survive but to live successfully through cold winters with frost and snow. One favourable point in their environment, however, commonly escapes attention. If one assumes that the glaciation was caused only by changing climatic factors and not by polar shift, however near may have been the margins of the Scandinavian and Alpine ice-sheets, or intense the glacial anticyclones attending them, the low latitude of south-western France, for example, would have afforded even in the midst of winter a fairly long day and a sun at noon much higher than in the high circumpolar latitudes where alone such periglacial conditions exist in our day. For the same reason, the respite of a much longer and warmer summer must have made life more bearable to primitive cave-dwellers in Last-Glaciation France than it is in present-day Lapland or Labrador. The change from the previously supportable conditions for human survival was nevertheless marked. Henceforth, 'place' for mankind included the temperate and cold zones of the earth as well as the tropical and sub-tropical—a potential extension of range, under the present distribution of climatic zones, of some 20° of geographical latitude in both hemispheres.

After the maximum of the first phase of the Last Glaciation in Europe, a considerable, if short-lived, retreat of the ice-sheets took place (First Interstadial), during which the climate of at least the southern half of the continent reverted to a fully temperate condition. The homeland of the classic western Neanderthalers, hitherto more or less isolated from the rest of Eurasia by ice and by the inhospitable tundras and steppes which extended between central Germany and the north-Alpine foothills, appears to have been invaded, probably from the south and east, by fully-evolved varieties of *H. sapiens*. They were bearers of a superior stone-working technique based on the manufacture of parallel-sided, thin flint blades, skilled hunters and successful exploiters of a temperate environment which, if still cool, was not so severe as that to which the Neanderthalers had had to adapt themselves.

The attitude of the new immigrants towards their predecessors is unknown—it is only certain that, in western Europe, the Neanderthalers and their characteristic stone implements were within a comparatively short time replaced everywhere by the newcomers. It is not clear whether these newcomers actively exterminated the Neanderthalers, interbred with them and so absorbed them genetically in their own large majority, or merely displaced them economically, being more fitted to compete on advantageous terms in the new conditions. The fact of the disappearance of Neanderthal man as a recognizable ethnic and cultural group is well established. Henceforth through the two succeeding readvances of the ice, the intervening Second Interstadial and the final ice-retreat of the Postglacial period, different varieties of *H. sapiens*, with characteristic cultures, held the stage.

In less thoroughly explored and exploited parts of the world the transition to the dominance of *H. sapiens* over more primitive human types is not so clear. Even the homeland of

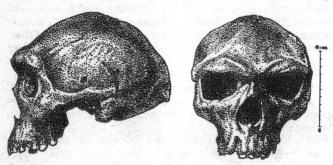

Homo rhodesiensis (Broken Hill) skull

the new species is unkown, for, appearing in Europe from the east, as it seems, the invaders might equally well have come straight from central Asia or, via the eastern end of the Mediterranean, from the south and some region of development in Africa.

In south Africa a species of man (*H. rhodesiensis*), having, like Neanderthal, some primitive characteristics, may have intervened in time between the earlier *Pithecanthropus*-type hand-axe makers and true *H. sapiens*. Unfortunately specimens are few (to date two only: Broken Hill [Rhodesia] and Saldanha [Cape Province]) and their dates and cultural equipment are too inexactly known for any firm conclusions. Culturally speaking, the hand-axes improve in workmanship by well-defined typological stages, which in a few places are found in a geological stratigraphic sequence. They are then replaced by flake-industries, having in common the Levallois tortoise-core technique of production, about whose makers we know very little, save that later users of these implements in Africa were certainly of *sapiens* type. Finally, the Upper Palaeolithic 'blade-and-burin' industries, often tending towards very small (microlithic) examples, superseded Levallois flakes and were still in use by Bushmen in south Africa at the time of the European colonization.

Asia, once more, lags behind in finds which might clarify the problem. Neanderthaloids here and there trace a long road from Near Asia to the mountainous south of the U.S.S.R. in Uzbekistan, seeming to be, in the widest sense, Last Glaciation in date, though here the finer temporal subdivisions of that phase possible in geologically well-explored Europe cannot be as reliably established. Middle Asia, including the Indian sub-continent, has yielded no single human specimen of any age. Choukoutien, near Peking, the *Pithecanthropus pekinensis* site, has yielded, from an Upper Cave,

Homo soloensis skull

some human remains of the *sapiens* type, associated with poor stone implements of an Upper Palaeolithic (blade) technique. Not only human fossils but even the Upper Palaeolithic types of stone-work are absent from India.

Java, again, with *Homo soloensis,* has given us an Upper Pleistocene (though not more closely datable) form somewhat akin to Neanderthal in skull-shape. Local continuity between *H. soloensis* and the *Pithecanthropus*-stem, though often suggested, has not been proved; nor do we know what relation, physical or cultural, these people may have borne to *H. sapiens*. In any case, it seems unlikely that Indonesia ever afforded a centre of evolutionary dispersion for man at any stage, but rather represented a marginal area in which favourable environmental circumstances permitted survivals of types developed more centrally on the mainland of Eurasia.

We are not yet ready, therefore, to do more than make a few tentative speculations on the evidence of a distribution-map so sparsely populated!

Since, in Europe, advanced *sapiens* men with a fully developed stone industry all at once replaced the Neander-thalers, with their less efficient equipment, we have no evidence of any but this transition, so that we must conclude that, if *H. sapiens* was anywhere developed from a Neanderthaloid ancestry, the process took place outside Europe. In the absence of easily negotiated land-bridges across the western Mediterranean, probability, as well as chronological evidence, suggests that the newcomers entered from western Asia, coming perhaps from a place of origin still deeper in that continent, or, via the Isthmus of Suez, from Africa. At the moment the evidence to determine the question is lacking, but the presence at Mount Carmel in Palestine of an early Neanderthaloid type, having clear indications also of anatomical affinities with *H. sapiens*, suggests that the latter species may have been differentiated in Asia rather than Africa. Further than this we cannot at present go.

Neanderthal man, in his final, 'classic' form, had been the first able to adapt his ways to a cold-winter environment, but up to the present the Teshik Tash find in Uzbekistan is the most eastern example of his species known. Thus, though they were potentially capable of the difficult passage from the east of the Old World to the New, via the Behring Strait, we have no evidence that they had yet penetrated as far, even, as the jumping-off point. Moreover, while the northern migration-route is difficult enough today, it must have been even more formidable during a major glaciation. It was therefore left to some group of *H. sapiens* to achieve the crossing at a later time, when he had himself undergone the experience of learning how to live under arctic conditions. Improving climate made the enterprise practicable only in some later stage of the Last Glaciation. Specialized dwellers in arctic environments today—Eskimo, Lapps, Samoyeds, Yakuts—are all members of one main subdivision of the uniquely surviving human species *H. sapiens* known as the Mongoloid. So too were, without exception as far as we know, the pre-Columbian inhabitants of the Americas, from Alaska to Tierra del Fuego.

So far, no trace of human occupation of the New World has been datable with any confidence to a time earlier than the early Postglacial period, beginning perhaps ten to twelve thousand years ago. The early peopling of the Americas thus seems to have taken place, perhaps by successive waves of immigrants, entirely across the Behring Strait (if we discount possible late castaways on Pacific voyages from Polynesia, who can never have contributed significant numbers) until the arrival from eastwards of European colonists in historic times, beginning with the Northmen in the ninth and tenth centuries of the Christian Era.

The place-factor is therefore closely bound up with climate and time. The first emergence of man evidently took place in the equatorial belt. His early spread as a hunter and food-gatherer at the hand-axe stage of culture was confined to the tropical and sub-tropical zones, or those parts of the cool-temperate zones which, at certain periods, enjoyed milder conditions than they do today. Adaptability to cool-temperate or cold climates was possible only when he had learned the use of fire, of protective clothing, and of both natural and artificial shelter. Only the later development of the whole complex of arctic equipment enabled him to travel, as well as merely survive, in the severe conditions presented by the northern transit from the Old World to the New.

The history of the peopling of Australia and the oceanic islands is not certainly known. Judging by their physical attributes, the aboriginal Australians must be an ancient branch of the species *H. sapiens*. They may have reached Australia by sea early in the history of the species and there have survived in comparative isolation until today. The Talgai and Cohuna fossil Australians have a primitive appearance, but are undated, though they apparently were contemporary with some extinct marsupials.

The spread of populations to New Zealand and the Pacific Islands must have waited upon comparatively advanced ocean navigation, which is certainly a fairly late technical development, even among maritime peoples. The genial and attractive climates of the tropical and sub-tropical seas and islands facilitated and encouraged rapidity of this spread once it became technically possible.

3

Climate

IT HAS been said that Britain has no climate, only weather. Though the saying implies a somewhat testy disapproval of the unreliable and almost unpredictable day-to-day meteorological conditions of a group of islands in the eastern Atlantic, it nevertheless makes clear the fundamental distinction between weather and climate.

Weather is the momentary state of the atmosphere in a particular place and at a particular time. *Climate* represents the average conditions experienced through the seasons of a year, over a considerable number of years—thirty is regarded by climatologists as providing an adequate sample.

On our tilted globe, zones near the Equator undergo but little change in conditions from season to season as the Earth revolves around the Sun. This attitude results in the more direct presentation to, and aversion from, the solar radiation of each Pole alternately, once every year. Thus, in polar and intermediate latitudes, more or less marked *seasons* are experienced, so that it is not so much the annual average of meteorological conditions as the winter and summer, or even monthly, averages that become important in describing climate.

The factors which, together, constitute both weather and climate are atmospheric temperature, barometric pressure, humidity, and amount of precipitation (rain, snow, dew, etc.) To these may be added observations of cloud-forms, amount of cloud-cover and duration of sunshine, of wind-force and wind direction. The measurement of these and the formulation from the date, generally of many observation-stations, of weather-predictions and climatic observations are the province of the meteorologist and climatologist.

The interactions of these elements are complex and they are intimately affected, for each point of observation, by the

71

main environmental factors of place, land-forms and, to a lesser extent, by geology, soils and vegetation. Time also enters into the assessment of both day-to-day meteorology and secular climatic changes.

The climatic factor in environment is thus seen to be perhaps the most important of all, mainly and directly controlling as it does the character and growth of vegetation, the animal inhabitants, large and small, and to a great extent the ways of man himself. By manual skill, foresight and the growth of technology and knowledge man has learned how, at least sometimes and locally, to modify the more disastrous effects of unfavourable climate. Still, the annual toll of damage to life and property and the disruption of human affairs in, for instance, the hurricane-belt of the United States or the 1952 floods in the Netherlands and Britain, show that we still have a good deal to learn in this department, even in modern times.

Viewed on the global scale, climate shows some systematic variations from zone to zone of latitude. These are due to the figure of the Earth and its motions, but the influence of place, apart from latitude—the distribution of land and water, topography and exposure—introduces differences within such major zones, not only from coast to continental interior but, very locally, as between one valley and the next or on two slopes of the same hill. The character of such *micro-climates* may be of considerable importance in determining the sites of human settlement and the consequent advantages or limitations to ways of life of the inhabitants.

Since the time-factor also inevitably enters into any study of the climatic environment of human cultures of the past, as archaeologists we have not only to investigate the climate of the site in our own day and time, but also to reconstruct that of the time of the ancient occupants, when they were living. Since we cannot employ our thermometers, barometers and rain-gauges to measure the elements of a climate of the remote past, we have to fall back on indirect assessment of conditions, by study of such geological and palaeontological evidence as may be associated with the cultural remains. Properly to evaluate such evidence, we need to be intimately acquainted with the geological and biological effects of the wide varieties of climate to be observed today in different parts of the world. Within human times, at any rate, it is a fair assumption that somewhere on our planet we shall today find conditions comparable with those enjoyed or suffered by the ancients, if not an exact match. Reference has already been made (p. 64) for instance, to the inevitable difference, due to latitude only, between the climate of (say) south-western France during a major glaciation and that of the present day in Lapland or Greenland. Our modern analogies must not, therefore, be stretched too far.

The causes of differences and changes in climate and weather go back to a number of fairly simple physical phenomena—the Earth's attitude and motions, the balance between heat-energy received by radiation, mainly from the Sun, and that lost to space by re-radiation. Unequal heating at different times of different parts of the globe sets up differences of atmospheric pressure, and winds are caused by the movements of air-masses tending to equalize these again. The origin and course of such air-masses, once set in motion, determine whether they are relatively hot or cold, moist or dry, light or dense in comparison with their surroundings. Since the oceans are also fluid their main currents, generated partly by wind-friction and partly, as with the atmosphere, by differing density under changing temperature, evaporation and salinity are also reservoirs or sinks for energy, whereby they greatly influence the climates of the adjacent lands. Since both atmosphere and hydrosphere have depth as well as extent in horizontal directions, these movements of bodies of fluid take place in three dimensions, of which the vertical is scarcely appreciable to an earthbound or seagoing observer without instruments for sounding, both in height and in depth. Aircraft, radio, sounding-rockets and artificial satellites all help us to appreciate the height-dimension in the atmosphere, while echo-sounding and other recently developed oceanographical techniques are beginning to lead to greater familiarity with the depths. We thus seek to understand the mechanisms of what we experience as climate and weather on the earth's surface and hence, perhaps, not only to predict coming meteorological events with more accuracy than heretofore, but to comprehend the secular changes through which our present-day climates have developed from those of the past.

The consequence of the receipt of radiation at the Earth's surface is to heat it. The amount of such heat is greater towards the Equator, less towards the Poles, the surface being most directly exposed to a vertical sun, more obliquely to one low in the sky. The heated surface then transfers, by conduction and convection, some of its heat to the atmosphere lying in contact with it. Hot air being less dense than cooler, a belt of air above the Equator is continually rising, moving polewards at height and being replaced by streams of sub-tropical air flowing in at surface-level from northerly and southerly directions, to fill the resulting belt of low pressure (Fig. 6). Conversely, at each Pole the dense, cold air forms a high-pressure cap with outflowing winds at ground-level and poleward streams of contrary direction replacing it at height.

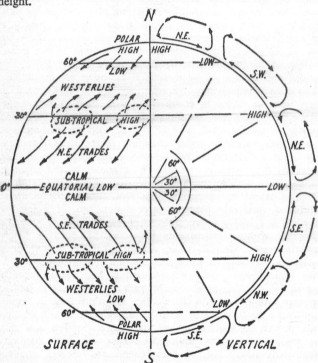

Fig. 6. Ideal global wind-circulation at an equinox. The vertical dimension is much exaggerated and the movements suggested apply only to the lower atmosphere.

In about 30° and 60° latitude, North and South, there are the sub-tropical high-pressure belts and the temperate 'lows', respectively, for which an explanation is not so obvious. They may be due to dynamic effects of the centrifugal force of the Earth's rotation. This rotation also has the effect of diverting all air-streams from their true courses, which they would assume in view of the causative pressure-gradients, in the Northern Hemisphere in a clockwise or right-handed direction, in the Southern left-handedly, or anti-clockwise. Thus, the winds escaping from the sub-tropical 'highs', if unaffected by the Earth's rotation, would flow due southwards towards the equatorial, and due north towards the temperate, 'lows'. Turned right-handedly in the Northern Hemisphere and left-handedly in the Southern, these air-streams form the north-east and south-east Trade Winds in the equatorward direction and the prevailing south-westerlies and north-westerlies of the North and South temperate zones, respectively, in the poleward directions (Fig. 6).

This picture of symmetrical pressure-systems and winds, is, even in theory, true only at the equinoxes, when Northern and Southern Hemispheres are receiving equal amounts of heat from the Sun. Owing to the alternating exposure during the year of the north and south hemispheres to a more vertical sun, the thermal equator migrates somewhat northward of the true Equator in the northern summer and southward of it in the northern winter, so that the pressure-belts and their resulting prevailing winds also suffer seasonal excursions in latitude.

On a featureless earth, these orderly seasonless systems of winds would continue to blow with predictable reliability. Continents, mountains and oceans, however, as well as islands and inland seas, are irregularly distributed over the Earth's surface. These interrupt the main planetary air-circulation owing to the different responses to heat of land and water. Not only is water a fluid, so that heat received at one part of its mass is relatively easily conveyed elsewhere by bodily movement of the medium, but it has also the largest capacity for heat of any known substance, taking it in and yielding it back slowly. Land-surfaces exposed to the Sun heat up rapidly to no great depth and as quickly re-radiate the heat they have gained when the source is cut off. Large areas of land, therefore, may experience extreme differences of temperature between one season and another, or even between day and night, whereas oceans warm and cool seasonally and diurnally through a much narrower range.

A well-known phenomenon is that of land- and sea-breezes, best seen in the nearly calm equatorial belt with its clear skies. Near a coast, the land heats up after sunrise more

quickly than the sea. The air over it is warmed, expands
and rises, forming a local area of low pressure, into which,
by the early afternoon, a cool sea-breeze begins to blow.
It falls calm again at or soon after sunset and during the night
the land under the clear sky cools to a lower temperature
than that of the sea, so that conditions are reversed and
the breeze blows from the land.

Exactly the same thing happens, on a much larger scale,
between continental areas and the adjacent oceans during
the changing seasons. In summer the hot centre of southern
Asia generates an intense 'low', towards which blow winds
from the Pacific and Indian Oceans, bearing moisture that
falls on the land as the monsoon-rains. In winter, the intense
cold of the continental interior results in a corresponding
'high', centred near Lake Baikal, from which cold, dry winds
blow outwards, so that only the eastern fringe of the continent, still within the control of the ocean, obtains any
moisture during the winter. This seasonal (monsoonal) wind-
system completely overshadows the general planetary circulation in the Asiatic region.

Since the largest land-areas are situated in the Northern
Hemisphere, the planetary circulation remains clearest in
the Southern, interrupted in middle latitudes only by South
America, the Cape of Good Hope and Australia. In the North-
ern Hemisphere it is disturbed to a large extent by North
America as well as Eurasia, so that the planetary winds, clear
enough in the open spaces of the North Atlantic and North
Pacific, tend to be much distorted near the continental coasts.

Owing to the easterly bent of the Trade Winds these blow
offshore on the western coasts of continents, so that, in
general, such coasts in the sub-tropical zone have a dry or
desert climate. Examples are: north-west Africa, northern
Chile and southern Peru. Conversely, eastern continental
coasts in the Trade Wind belt experience moist on-shore winds
which have crossed thousands of miles of warm ocean (e.g.
eastern South America and the Gulf of Mexico). The marked
monsoonal effect of the Asiatic land-mass on the Indian
Ocean and western Pacific is to repel these on-shore winds
through the influence of the continental winter 'high' and to
attract rain-bearing air-masses, even from the south-east
Trade belt, across the Equator, to fill the summer 'low'. In
crossing the Equator the south-east Trades are turned right-
handed almost through a right-angle to become the south-
west monsoon of Middle and Far Asia. A further effect

of this is to divert some (southern) winter rain, which would otherwise reach south-eastern Africa. It is now known that the monsoons are controlled by complex three-dimensional changes in the movements of air-masses at great heights, so that the above phenomena, observable at ground-level, are only a part of the story, which is not yet fully understood.

Similarly, in the temperate zones the prevailing westerlies bring plentiful rain from the oceans to western shores of continents (American north-west, western Europe, New Zealand, southern Chile), while the eastern coasts in these latitudes may be dry (much of Patagonia). The eastern part of temperate North America, however, is *not* markedly dry. This is due, in a lesser degree than in the case of Asia, to the continental monsoon-effect. A summer 'low' over the Great Basin draws rain-bearing winds far inland from the Atlantic Ocean and the Gulf of Mexico, while a winter 'high' that centres over the Dakotas is not large enough or intense enough to isolate the eastern states and the Maritime Provinces of Canada from oceanic influences. The great sea-inlet of Baffin's Bay and the presence of the Great Lakes accentuate the maritime effect.

The equatorial belt is continually moist. It shifts seasonally with the thermal equator over about 10° of latitude, so that the fringing areas to north and south have dry and wet seasons, often obtaining rain only in their local summer (Sudan, southern Congo).

The boreal and arctic lands, owing to low temperatures and consequently low evaporation-rates, are never really short of moisture, even if precipitation is, on the whole, small in total amount in continental areas, save within the reach of the temperate westerlies, which may penetrate a good distance northwards and inland. Great winter cold and shortage or (within the Arctic Circle) even seasonally total deprivation of daylight are the severest checks to human occupation. The South Polar regions as a human habitat interest only modern scientists and explorers. They have no history before the first expeditions and, so far as we know, no archaeology.

The greatest desert zone in the world straddles the Tropic of Cancer, extending right across north Africa from Mauretania in the west, through the Sahara, across Egypt and Arabia and north-eastwards into central Asia. The Thar Desert of north-west India, the deserts of Sinkiang and the Gobi Desert of Mongolia are outliers of it, cut off from moisture by mountain barriers, high plateaux, and mere distance from any ocean. The western and central third of Australia, lying in the zone of Capricorn, with its back to the Trade Winds, is in a like case in the Southern Hemisphere, as are the Kalahari of south-west Africa and the western coastal strip of South America, including Peru and northern Chile. The other major regions of almost perennial drought are in the Basin and Range Province of western North America and a narrow north-south strip of Patagonia between 25° and 50° South. These last are in 'rain-shadows' of the Rockies and the Andes respectively.

Mountains rising near windward coasts, as in the cool-temperate portion of South America, concentrate rainfall on and round themselves. The Andes of southern Chile rise to some summits of over 12,000 feet, while much of the range is above 6,000. The temperate westerlies, blowing across thousands of miles of the South Pacific and so saturated with moisture at a temperature between 50° and 60° F., meet this range and are forced to rise. Since temperature falls with increase in altitude by about 1° F. for every 300 feet, on an average, topping the mountains involves for the moist wind a fall in temperature of something like 20° F. Cold air has a much smaller capacity for moisture than warm, so that this forced fall in temperature as it were 'wrings' moisture from the wind and much rain falls, especially on the seaward slopes and summits. Descending again to lower levels on the eastern flank of the range, the air is again warmed, but now is far below saturation and dry, indeed is capable of taking up and away from the ground below any moisture that is already there. The result is an arid climate in the lee of the mountains and the dry area is called a 'rain-shadow'.

The wettest place in the world is Cherrapunji, at between 4,000 and 5,000 feet on the southern slope of the Khasi Hills of Assam. Here it faces the oncoming south-west monsoon, straight from the Bay of Bengal across the plains, and *averages* 450 inches of rain annually—the maximum recorded in a single year was just over double this figure! High mountains even on the Equator (Kenya, 17,000 feet; Cotopaxi, 19,600) have snowfields, so that their flanks are climatically zoned with height, from equatorial to glacial. All intermediates exist at the appropriate latitudes and elevations. It was, for example, the facility for officials to rest and recuperate in the pleasant and more temperate surroundings of hill-stations like Simla or Buitenzorg which made possible the continuance of European administrations in hot climates, as of the British in Delhi or of the Dutch in Batavia.

Existing climates have been variously classified, beginning with the classical 'torrid', 'temperate' and 'frigid' arrangement by zones of latitude. Analogously, the three stages of climate encountered in the same latitude in Mexico, depending only on differences in elevation above sea-level, are locally described as *clima caliente* (to 3,000 feet), *templada* (3,000 to 6,000) and *fria* (6,000 upwards)—hot, temperate and cold. The more modern systems become more complicated by taking into account, as far as possible, the other elements of climate as well as their seasonal distributions.

A. A. Miller's classification is adopted here. It has five main divisions bounded by stated levels of temperature:

A. Hot (annual mean above 70° F.)
B. Warm-temperate (no monthly average below 43° F.)
C. Cool-temperate (1-5 months below 43° F.)
D. Cold (6 or more months below 43° F.)
E. Arctic (no month above 50° F. in average)
F. Desert climates (dry—less than 10″ annual precipitation)
G. Mountain climates (as in the case of Mexico, a direct result of altitude)

Each main class is subdivided according to the seasonal distribution of rainfall, which is determined, as we have seen, by place and topography—position in relation to land-masses, oceans and prevailing winds. The 43° F. bounding temperature is chosen because means below this prevent plant-growth. An annual mean above it, as for A- and B-type climates, permits growth all the year round. Any month for which the mean temperature falls below this constitutes a true winter season.

A. Hot climates are subdivided as follows:
   1. Equatorial, with double rain-maxima (Congo and Amazon Basins).
   1m. Monsoon type of A.1 (Indonesia).
   2. Tropical-marine, with rain at all seasons (Caribbean, southeast Africa coast lands).
   2m. Monsoon type of A.2 (Philippines, Queensland coast).
   3. Tropical-continental, with summer rain (central Mex-

    ico, African savannahs, South American Pampas).

    3m. Monsoon type of A.3 (India, Indo-China).

B. Sub-tropical or warm-temperate climates:
1. Western continental margin, with winter rain only (Mediterranean, California, northern Chile, Cape Province southern Australia).
2. Eastern margin, with rain at all seasons (south-eastern United States, north Argentina, south-eastern Australia, North Island of New Zealand).

    2m. Monsoonal type of B.2 (south-eastern China, southern Japan).

C. Cool-temperate climates:
1. Marine, with rain at all seasons but winter maximum (north-western Europe, north-western Pacific Coast, southern Chile), South Island of New Zealand, Tasmania).
2. Continental, with summer maximum of rain (central Europe, central and eastern United States).

    2m. Monsoon type of C.2 (Manchuria, Japan).

D. Cold climates:
1. Marine, with rain at all seasons (Alaska, Iceland, central Norway).
2. Continental, with summer maximum of rain (central Canada, central Siberia).

    2m. Monsoon type of D.2 (eastern Siberia).

E. Arctic climates (Alaska and northern Canada, Greenland, northern Siberia).

F. Desert climates:
1. Hot desert (southern California, northern Mexico, Sahara, Arabia, Iran, north-west India).
2. Mid-latitude desert (Great Basin, Turkestan, Gobi).

G. Mountain climates. Those which differ from the base-level climates of their latitude because of high relief, as in Mexico, above. In comparison with other types, G-climates occupy only a small area of the globe, save for the central Asiatic plateau and two long strips of the Rockies and Andes. Wherever there are high mountains, however, climates of this type, often only of slight areal extent, will be found. World distribution of these climatic types is shown in the map (Fig. 7).

    The most direct effect of climate on man is to expose him, in the primitive state, with little natural means of protection, to its worst extremes. The human response to exposure has been to find or devise some form of shelter against inclement conditions. The form which such shelter takes—hollow tree, cave, brushwood windbreak, tent, igloo, hut or house—depends on the degree and permanence of protection needed, on available materials, and on technical knowledge and skill.

In equatorial climates of Types A.1 and A.2, where temperatures are constantly high and seasonal changes only slight, exposure is generally less a threat to life than a minor

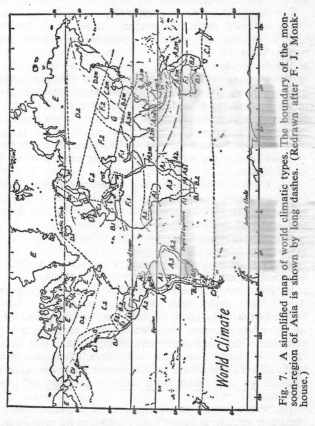

Fig. 7. A simplified map of world climatic types. The boundary of the monsoon-region of Asia is shown by long dashes. (Redrawn after F. J. Monkhouse.)

inconvenience. A naked savage in tropical jungle may face many hazards, but exposure is not among them. Direct sun is easily avoided in the forest shade, rain may be enjoyed or ignored where the discomfort of wet clothing is not a consideration, and only a tropical storm with violent convectional

winds and its chances of injury by lightning or falling trees
will make some temporary shelter advisable, such as a convenient space beneath a fallen log. At a higher, but still fairly
primitive, level of civilization, the Indian Yucatecans of
today live in houses of daubed hurdle construction with
roofs of palm-leaf thatch, exactly like those portrayed in
ancient Mayan temple-reliefs.

The A.3 types, with a marked dry, as well as a rainy,
season, make for more open country, so that at certain times
of the year and day shade is attractive, if not absolutely
necessary. In the dry season, if of long duration, many trees
of the savannah are leafless, and thus practically shadeless,
so that a prominent rock would seem to afford a grateful
natural shadow. This could be no more than temporary, save
in an exceptional case, for open country is the preferred
habitat of large herbivorous animals and these are hunted by
the greater carnivores—lion, leopard, etc.—which threaten
man also if he allows himself to be approached unawares.
At night, during the long dry winter and under a clear sky,
the temperature may fall sufficiently to make a shelter a
comfort, but the prime need of a house and a thorn-fenced
enclosure is for protection against wild beasts rather than
against weather. Where equipment exceeds what can be carried with and on the person, shelter against rain for family
and prized possessions is a necessity, at any rate during the
wet season.

Changing seasons may demand a change of habits, not
only because of shelter requirements but, for hunters and
collectors, according to the availability and changing location of water, game, fruits and other foodstuffs. The Australians of Arnhem Land, in the Northern Territory, studied by
D. F. Thomson, have six different seasons of activity in
their year. During the north-west monsoon, from late Decem-
ber to late March, they live in wet-season houses, but for the
rest of the year they make moving camps in the open and use
shade-houses only during the greatest heat, in September and
October.

The tribal farmers and pastoralists of Africa, in the A.3
climate zones, live in lightly built thatched mud or grass huts,
often within a thorn zareba, or enclosure, to keep predators
at a safe distance. Clothing is light. The Masai (Tanganyika)
kaross, a loose skin robe, is typical. In the Nilotic Sudan or
Central America loose cotton garments are worn with an
additional woollen blanket or poncho for cold-season nights.

Houses, where required by more advanced peoples, may be of mud-brick (adobe), timber and thatch, or of stone, according to available materials, but are of open construction with verandas or patios for coolness in the hot weather.

Climates of sub-tropical (B) character, though having no true cold season on the average, can suffer winter conditions of a certain discomfort with at least short periods of really low temperature. Snow and frost, though uncommon in the Mediterranean region, for example, are not unknown, as the combatants in Italy during the latter part of the Second World War can testify.

This, the western margin type (B.1), is the more equable, with an average annual temperature range of perhaps no more than 20° F. (e.g. Gibraltar: 55°-75° F.). On the eastern margin of Asia, however, where the winter monsoon effect is felt most strongly the range may be much wider (e.g. Chungking: 50°-85° F.). In either of these cases some winter shelter would be essential for primitive man, even at the present day—more so when a glaciation was in progress—so that at Gibraltar and at Mount Carmel in Palestine Middle Palaeolithic man lived in limestone caves and used fire. Today the courtyard-house gives shade in summer heat, but unless the house is adequately heated, it is not well adapted to the occasional spell of raw, wet weather. In the B.1 type, with hot dry summer, shade and coolness are the most desirable features of shelter. Winters are on the whole mild, but protection from northerly winds blowing from less favoured lands, such as the *mistral* of southern France, has been sought by all Mediterranean inhabitants from the Upper Palaeolithic onwards, whether the dwelling concerned was a limestone cave or a Riviera villa. The comparable New World conditions are found in Southern California.

Before modern building methods were developed or imported, the mud-brick or adobe house with flat roof was the world-wide traditional style. In moister climates thatch or shingles and wide eaves are necessary to protect such building materials from driving rain. They have, in any case, a short life, even in semi-desert, on the margins of the B-climate zones. Dr Braidwood, discussing the life of a mud-brick house in the prehistoric town of Jarmo, in Iraq, estimates some eleven years only before it required rebuilding.

Climate Types B.2 and B.2m, those of the Gulf States or of maritime eastern Asia, with rain at all seasons and, in the case of the Asiatic region, much colder winters, call for stouter roofs, often of steep pitch and tiled, as in the Far East. Summer clothing may be relatively flimsy, but winter demands indoor heating and warm, weatherproof outdoor garments. The cave-dwellers used fire wherever they are found. Sedentary cultures of the Near East, from the Neolithic on, built their houses of mud brick and, where available, reed thatch or matting. Timber is never plentiful in that environment, especially in the form of sizeable logs for building.

The C (cool-temperate) climatic regions were, and are, far less easily colonized, though in modern times they have harboured the most enterprising civilizations. The difficulties of the early European colonists of the eastern United States, even coming as they did from homelands with a high civilization and with many established crafts and techniques denied to more primitive settlers are an historic example.

C.1, the oceanic or martime subdivision, is typified by north-western Europe, which has a climate relatively equable in respect of temperature owing to the proximity of the ocean and the North Atlantic Drift, a warm current assisted by the prevailing south-westerly winds, which has a marked thermostatic effect. This may be more clearly realized when we consider that the latitude of London is the same as that of the northern tip of Newfoundland. The chief feature of the cool oceanic type of climate is the unreliability and changeability of the weather, which makes necessary preparedness for relatively uncomfortable outdoor conditions at any season. Summers are seldom hot or winters extremely cold, though the occasional temporary diversion of air-streams from the subtropics, on the one hand, or the arctic, on the other, may bring unseasonable warmth or chill, generally only for short periods. There are sudden overnight reversals, calling for rapid change of habits on the part of the population.

Cave-dwelling must have been a severe exercise in adaptability, and, indeed, in the more northern parts of western Europe the poverty of the surviving equipment of the earliest inhabitants suggests that they were somewhat marginal examples of their kind. South-western France and northern Spain have to show the famous painted caves of the later Palaeolithic, which prove the existence of a culture that was, if not easeful, at least fully viable and in equilibrium with its environment.

Shelter, apart from caves, has in this zone from prehistoric times taken the shape of the durably built thatched timber house. A well-known prehistoric example is the Little Woodbury (Wiltshire, England) farm-house dating from the Early Iron Age, excavated in 1939 by Bersu. Only the post-hole plan was preserved, but from it it was possible to deduce the probable design of the wooden superstructure in some detail. Where the materials were available, such houses were later replaced by buildings of stone and brick, often, however, retaining the timber framework to support the main weight ('half-timbering').

The house was invariably centred round a capacious open wood-burning hearth, for house-warmth in winter is a necessity and may be desirable in summer also in colder, wetter spells.

Clothing in temperate to cold climates in prehistoric times was chiefly of skins, furs and leathers, but later warm woven stuffs, of sheep's wool replaced these. Formerly home-spun and woven, modern materials of similar make still clothe the countryman of today. Protection outdoors from wet has always been desirable at all seasons, but was seldom attainable in practice until the advent of rubber and plastics for weatherproofing, save by the heroic use of hair-felt, linen canvas or tar and linseed oil applied to lighter fabrics, as in seamen's oilskins. The grass skirt or palmleaf raincoat would have sufficed in warmer climes.

The cool-continental climatic type (C.2) covers most of the northern and eastern United States, and central and eastern Europe. Its monsoonal variety obtains over north China, Korea and northern Japan. It has a hot summer, during which occurs the main rainfall, within which all agricultural activity must take place, and an extremely cold winter, with fairly thin snow-cover and hard frost. The winter cold is the main limiting feature for humanity, especially in the more primitive stages of culture, but plenty of timber for buildings and fuel and furs for clothing make it supportable. Life necessarily has to go into hibernation to a large extent and only modern civilization, with sufficient energy resources, can widen the areas of living-space made tolerable by artificial heating and lighting and enable social and industrial activity to continue unabated. Daytime sunshine and the dry cold facilitate vigorous outdoor activities, but the winter days are short. While in the more oceanic regions winter agricultural operations can at times continue, lumbering is almost the only outdoor productive activity possible in extreme continental conditions. This type of climate does not exist in the

Southern Hemisphere, owing to the absence in the corresponding latitudes of extensive land areas.

D and E, the cold and arctic climates, are tolerable for
primitives only by those who, like the Lapps or Eskimo, have
developed cultures especially adapted to them. In summer the
economy is tied to the hunting of reindeer (caribou) or musk-
ox, and fishing from boats. In winter seals provide most of
the meat and fuel. Housing is in skin tents or earth-houses
in summer, in snow igloos through the winter. Clothing is
highly specialized (e.g. the Eskimo parka and trousers with
sealskin boots) to withstand the prevailing cold. Even modern
civilized man can survive, beyond the timber-line, only by
importing his materials for shelter, protection and subsistence
from more favourable climes—or by 'going native' and
adopting in detail the ways of the indigenous peoples.

Another consideration, intimately connected with climate,
which has a direct influence on human occupation of any
tract of country is the water-supply. It scarcely arises in the
colder climates where, even if precipitation is only slight, the
rate of wastage by evaporation is slow, so that surface-
water, or snow and ice which only need to be melted, are
readily available. It becomes most urgent in the world's
truly desert regions, under an F-type climate, but may be
supremely important in any area where there may be a
possibly prolonged seasonal shortage. This applies to large
areas of the hot and warm-temperate climatic zones having
a long dry season (Types A.3 and B.1) and where total
rainfall is rather slight, as in the most extremely continental
C.2 regions.

Of rainwater falling on the land a proportion soaks into
the soil, and of this some percolates into the subsoil rock to
join the ground-water, which largely feeds the streams. Part
runs off directly into streams and lakes and part is soon once
more lost to the atmosphere by evaporation from the soil,
vegetation and free surfaces of water-bodies. Availability
depends on the balance of total precipitation and these losses
(Fig. 8).

In warmer climates, the hot sun soon dries the ground
after rain and shrinks streams and pools that have no perennial underground supply. Even deserts are not often permanently dry, though they may sometimes go for several years
without rain, but when rain does fall it is sudden and heavy,
so that torrential run-off forms gullies and extensive shallow

lakes in undrained depressions, and as much as does not find its way underground is soon re-evaporated.

Desert and semi-arid country will thus only permanently support a sparse, shifting population of hunters, collectors and nomadic herdsmen travelling from water-hole to water-hole. Such, at the present day, are the Bushmen of the Kala-

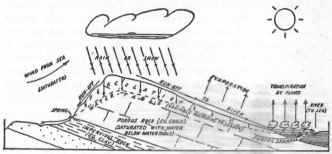

Fig. 8. The hydrographic cycle, with some geological features affecting water-supply.

hari, the Australian aborigines, at the hunting stage; many pastoral peoples of north Africa, the Near East and central Asia among the stockkeepers. Settled agriculture is impossible under these conditions and brief squatting for a few weeks by passing nomads, sowing and harvesting a catch-crop in one place when an unexpected rainstorm has moistened the region, is the only cultivation.

In many semi-arid lands of north Africa and the Near East, artificial catchments and underground storages for surface water were constructed by the Romans and are even today still in use, but most of the ancient, as well as the modern, settlements are by springs or in places where relatively shallow wells will reach a reliable supply of groundwater. Such underground water may occur in an area superficially desert, where the run of porous geological strata enables them to accumulate rainwater falling, perhaps on mountains, some distance away.

Jericho, the most ancient town known in the world, grew up beside a perennial spring called Elisha's Well or 'Ain es-Sultan. It was continuously occupied from some time before 8000 B.C. up to its final destruction and banning by Joshua about 2000 B.C. Though the ancient city-mound is now desolate, the same warm, clear water continues to gush out at its base and supports the modern town of Jericho some distance away. Modern irrigation-channels, fed from the same supply, maintain a productive wide green oasis amid the grim dry hills of Jordan. There are many other such local centres of historic civilization in the desert zone.

Though much less rainy than the Petén, northern Yucatán is not desert, since it receives eighteen to forty inches of rainfall a year. Apparent aridity is due to the fact that the region is a low-lying platform of porous limestone under a very thin cover of dominantly red residual soil. Rainwater quickly sinks into the ground leaving only a few lakes and small streams which are little more than arms of the sea. Underground, water descends through cracks and cavities, collects in caverns, and flows sluggishly through tunnels largely excavated by solution. In coastal lowlands the water table lies less than fifteen feet below the surface, though this figure increases inland as the elevations rise.

Modern man responds to this situation by drilling wells and fitting them with pumps, powered by wind, petrol or rarely by electricity. Mérida, capital of the state of Yucatán, is about eighty-two feet above sea-level. The city is famous for its abundance of wind pumps, or *veletas* ('windmills' in the United States, whence most of them were imported), which provide water for both dwellings and business buildings.

Where the water table lies near the surface, the ancient Maya dug wells into the limestone or enlarged solution cavities. Elsewhere, water usually was—and still is—obtained from *cenotes,* which are caverns whose roofs have collapsed. The great religious centre of Chichén Itzá (it was not a true city) was built around two cenotes whose water is now about sixty-five feet below the surrounding surface. One cenote provided for everyday needs, but the other became the famous and sacred Well of Sacrifice.

In the Puuc Hills, southward from Mérida, elevations approach 300 feet. Here ground-water lay beyond the reach of ancient Indians, but the Maya devotion to ceremony demanded a chain of temples including those of the great Late Classic centre of Uxmal. Priests as well as visiting pilgrims obtained water from cisterns dug into bedrock or into filled areas. Plaster-paved courts caught rainwater and channelled it into these cisterns, which were also lined with plaster to prevent leakage. Some ancient catchment-courts and cisterns are still used by custodians of ruins which, unlike Uxmal and Chichén Itzá, are far from villages and hotels.

Great rivers, having their springs in rain-catching hills, often supply desert regions and enable towns and cities to arise on their banks. Egypt thus owed its early civilization to the Nile; Assur, Nineveh and Babylon to the Euphrates and Tigris; Harappa and Mohenjo Daro to the Indus system. Modern dams all over the world provide power and water for irrigation from such rivers, in places where earlier peoples without our technical resources could do comparatively little to mitigate a dry climate.

Too much surface-water was as inimical to primitive human life as too little. Only in historic times have swamps and fens, marshes and bogs been drained so that they afford land and a way of life suitable for settlement. The Dutch have been the leaders in this branch of civil engineering, where the encroaching sea is as much their enemy as freshwater floods. In ancient times the few inhabitants of such country, whatever the climate, were isolated, a race apart from their neighbours, their territories valueless, save for fishers and fowlers, inaccessible and a barrier to communications. Disease, especially malaria, was rife. The Ma'dan of the Lower Tigris marshes, Iraq, are a surviving people of this kind.

Seasonal climatic differences have at all times and in most regions had great influence on the ways of life of man. Seen from the point of view of our modern society, based firmly on food-production by settled agriculturists and stock-raisers, the round of the seasons naturally seems to fall into times for ploughing, sowing, caring for the growing crop and harvesting—or an appropriate sequence of seasonal operations in the breeding, fattening and marketing of animal stock. It is hard to put ourselves in the position of primitive people wholly dependent on hunting and gathering, but it is clear that they must, during their year, have ranged far from one place to take advantage of seasonal migrations of the mammals, birds and fishes on which they lived and the seasonal availability of particular vegetable products— foliage, bark, seeds, roots, fibres, fruits—at the appropriate places and times of year. The particular annual routine evidently differed greatly from region to region and from culture to culture, according to the desirable products to be had and the means at hand for obtaining them.

The Upper Palaeolithic hunters of Moravia apparently

gathered in numbers to hunt the migrating mammoths, which passed through the so-called Moravian Gate to their summer pastures on the north-European plains, after wintering perhaps in Hungary. Sites such as Prĕdmost and Vĕstonice to the south of this mountain gap, bestrewn with bones of mammoth and few other beasts, are perhaps the temporary camping places of a few weeks in each year—certainly not permanent settlements. Modern river-fisheries, the grouse-shooting season in Scotland, and the deer-hunting season in North America are vestiges of these essentially seasonal occupations, now followed for pleasure rather than for essential victuals.

Thus, in studying an ancient site the archaeologist should always have in mind its possible character as the scene of an only seasonal activity, often, perhaps, forming only quite a small and subsidiary part of the total economy of the people concerned.

Nomadic stock-breeders obviously follow the feed with their flocks and herds, perhaps not in any systematic way from year to year; but more settled animal-keepers might, as do the Norwegians and Swiss even today, shift their homes from valley to mountain pasture to valley again during spring, summer and autumn.

The modern farmer's life is governed as much as ever it was in earlier times by the weather and the seasons, in view of the needs of his crops and his obligation to stand by them to weed, to water, to fence and protect from marauders, predators and pests. Even a townsman's year may be directly affected by his close connection, in early times at least, with the economy of the near-by countryside. Some Londoners even today migrate annually for a few days or weeks to Kent to help with seasonal fruit-picking and the hop-harvest. Doubtless it is for them a pleasant working holiday, but their help is greatly appreciated by the growers, who would otherwise be hard put to it to find the necessary casual labour at the right time. During the Second World War, Civil Service office-workers were given special extra leave to help with the cereal harvest or potato-lifting, at a time of great shortage of man power on the land and in view of the need to make the most of home-grown food, not making demands on valuable shipping space. This was only a return, under stress of wartime conditions, to a situation that formerly arose every year, before Britain developed manufacturing industries and came to depend for foodstuffs more and more on imports from overseas.

For past periods of thousands and tens of thousands of years there have been slow changes of climate and environment, chiefly affecting the temperate zones, where, over vast land-areas, conditions have oscillated during the last million years at least four times between warm-temperate and sub-arctic. The causes of these changes are not yet certainly known, but the facts, as elucidated by both geological and palaeontological evidences, are well established in their main outlines, though there is still plenty of controversy about the interpretation of details.

From the point of view of one wishing to establish the causes of glacial periods, one of the puzzling features of Ice Ages is that they seem to be uncommon events in the earth's geological history. The Pleistocene group, which witnessed the rise and development of man, is not unique, but the preceding major glacial phase—or group of phases, for our information is incomplete as yet—seems to have affected chiefly the Southern Hemisphere, in south Africa and Australia in particular, and took place as long ago as the end of the Carboniferous and the beginning of the Permian geological periods, something like 200 million years ago. In the intervening ages there is no evidence of anything like this; in fact, world climate seems generally to have been much more genial and uniform than it is today. It has been suggested that the (geologically!) recent Alpine outburst of mountain-building, which took place in the later part of the Tertiary Era and gave rise to the American Cordillera, the Alps, the Himalaya and other young folded mountain systems, has made the Quaternary (Pleistocene and Recent periods) an era of unwontedly high relief and climatic diversity. During the greater part of the geological record land-areas have been much smaller than those of today and the oceans, by their balancing and thermostatic effect, have prevented great extremes of climate. The Permo-Carboniferous glaciations also followed an intense phase of land-uplift and mountain-building.

Though this theory may explain, at least in part, the cause of an ice age as a whole, it does not make clear why, within our latest period of glaciation, the ice should have advanced and retreated several times in a periodic fashion. For this the geological evidence is now firmly established. It seems, then, to call for some periodic changes, superimposed on the conditions making glaciation possible, to account for the periodic oscillations of the glaciers.

One of the most favoured theories to explain the internal periodicity of ice ages is that of Milankovitch, who invokes changing maxima and minima of solar radiation received at the Earth's surface to explain the alternating advances and retreats of the ice. There are several 'perturbations' of the Earth's motions, slight in themselves and having known periods of variation running into tens of thousands of years each, which, when acting together in one sense, would appreciably affect the amount of radiation from the Sun falling on particular zones of latitude. This is not the place to go into the theory in detail, but since these slow minor changes in the tilt of the Earth's axis in relation to the plane of its orbit, secular variation in the ellipticity of the orbit itself and a slow conical movement of the axis due to gravitational forces acting on a globe not perfectly spherical can be separately computed and their conjoined effects in terms of radiation-changes during the last million years or so be calculated, it is possible to find out in theory what changes in radiation have been experienced by the Earth during that time and to compare the results of these astronomical calculations with the series of actual events observed to have taken place by the geologists. In fact, the correspondence between the two quite distinct sets of phenomena is astonishingly close, even to minor details. Geologists had long thought of the Ice Age as consisting of four main glacial advances, separated by three Interglacial ages, during which the climate returned to something like what it is today. Of the glaciations, they concluded that the second and third were the largest in intensity and that the Interglacial between them was the longest of the three and also the warmest. Some workers were inclined to think that each of the glaciations had been marked by double maxima, with a short, milder interval separating them, save only the last, which had *three* maxima and two such 'Interstadials'.

Now Milankovitch's theory stated that it was during these times when minimum amounts of radiation were being received in high latitudes during the summer that increase of glaciation would be favoured, for a cooler summer would mean less melting of the ice and snow which had formed during the preceding winter. His published curves, the result of years of painstaking calculations, showed just the same sequence of summer minima of radiation as the geologists had found of ice-advances—four major minima, each of them double, save the last which was triple; three intervening periods of increased summer radiation, of which the middle one was by far the longest (Fig. 9). The results of Emiliani, working with deep-sea Foraminifera (see p. 225), are also shown. Such correspondence in detail of results gained by the study of three such different sets of phenomena can scarcely be fortuitous. If we still do not fully understand the underlying *causes* of glaciation, there must be some connec-

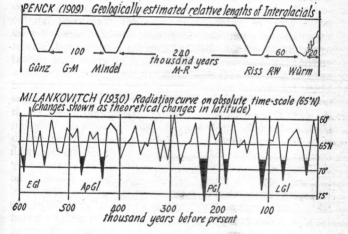

Fig. 9. Curves, obtained from three entirely independent sets of data, agree surprisingly well with each other in distinguishing and dating climatic changes during the Pleistocene. (Redrawn, at a common scale for the time-axes, after Zeuner [1959].)

tion between its oscillations and those of summer radiation intensities. Since the astronomical results are bound up with a time-scale and extend back with a fairly high degree of accuracy for at least something over half a million years and with rather less precision for an entire million, the 'radiation-dates' can with some confidence be applied to the geological events, at least as a basis for discussion until some more reliable method of dating is devised. The figures and some of their implications will be discussed when we come to consider the Time factor in environment.

Whatever its causes, glaciation resulted at four different times in accumulation of vast ice-sheets, like those of Greenland and Antarctica today, centred in northern Scandinavia, the Alps and Pyrenees, in Europe; at two centres, in the Keewatin Territory north-west of Hudson's Bay and in the Labrador region of north-eastern Canada; there was also a subsidiary centre in the Cordilleran chain. Thence the ice spread into lower latitudes and into the plains, reaching at its greatest extent beyond the 40th Parallel in North America and as far as the 50th in Europe (Figs. 10, 11).

Fig. 10. Europe, showing the maximum extent of Pleistocene glaciation and a corresponding sea-level lowered by 600 feet, to the edge of the existing continental shelf. Note that, even at this maximum marine regression, there were no land-bridges between Europe and Africa, save by the eastern end of the Mediterranean.

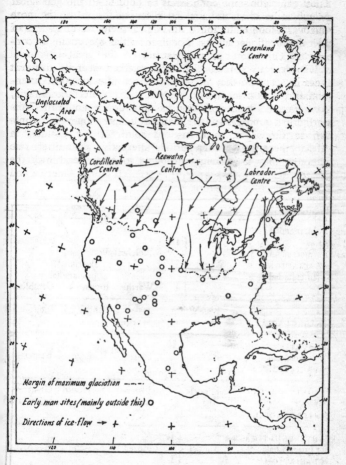

Fig. 11. North America, showing the centres of ice-origin, the maximum extent of Pleistocene glaciation, the unglaciated 'bridgehead' in Alaska and the known sites of early human occupation, for the greater part outside the glaciated area.

The result of ice-advance was to give to the climates of the present cool-temperate lands in both continents an arctic or sub-arctic character and push far to the south the cool- and warm-temperate zones. In Africa there were, of course, no widespread glaciations, though the Atlas Mountains formed a local ice-centre and the glaciers of the great equatorial volcanoes, Kenya, Elgon and Kilimanjaro, descended to much lower levels than they do today. The southward shift of the climatic zones brought relatively humid Mediterranean (B.1) conditions to much of what is now desert and drove the northern boundary of the Sahara deeper southwards into Africa. Elsewhere, as in regions south of the Equator in Africa, there were wetter periods alternating with drier, but, although they are thought probably to correspond with the

General	Alps	North Europe	North America	African Pluvials
Interstadial **3** **LAST** Interstadial **GLACIATION 2** Interstadial **1**	Würm {III, II, I}	Weichsel (III, II) Warthe (I)	Wisconsin Peorian Interstadial Iowan	Interpluvial Gamblian
LAST INTERGLACIAL	Riss-Würm	Saale-Warthe	Sangamon	Interpluvial
PENULTIMATE 2 Interstadial **GLACIATION 1**	Riss {II, I}	Saale	Illinoian	Kanjeran
PENULTIMATE or GREAT INTERGLACIAL	Mindel-Riss	Elster-Saale	Yarmouth	Great Interpluvial
ANTEPENULTIMATE 2 Interstadial **GLACIATION 1**	Mindel {II, I}	Elster	Kansan	Kamasian
ANTEPENULTIMATE INTERGLACIAL	Günz-Mindel	—	Aftonian	Interpluvial
EARLY 2 Interstadial **GLACIATION 1**	Günz {II, I}	—	Nebraskan	Kageran

northern glaciations and interglacials respectively, this still remains to be proved.

The four glaciations have both general and local names, of which the probable correspondences are shown in the Table on p. 96. A fairly generally accepted provisional correlation of the African Pluvial sequence is also given.

The final retreat of the ice opened what we call the Post-glacial period, though, for all we know, we may be living in what may prove to be only an Interglacial or Interstadial period, so that the next few thousand years may witness the beginnings of a readvance to full glacial conditions. It seems likely, however, that we are, in fact, only in the earlier stage of an Interglacial, if such it is, and that our descendants for a good many generations may look forward to some further degree of warming of climate in the temperate zones, before any deterioration again sets in. Climatic changes in the Postglacial have been of only minor intensity, but have yet had important influences on the human cultures subjected to them. The succession of events for Europe follows the classical scheme of Blytt and Sernander and roughly corresponds as follows with the human cultural stages. The American terminology (due to Antevs) for the climatic stages is also given:

Type of climate	Europe	America	Human cultures in Europe
Cooler { more oceanic more continental	Subatlantic Subboreal } Medithermal		Early Iron Age to present Bronze Age
Warm-oceanic	Atlantic	Altithermal	Neolithic
Cool-continental Cold sub-arctic	Boreal Preboreal } Anathermal		Mesolithic
Arctic	Late Glacial		Late Palaeolithic

The Ice Ages saw man in Europe at the hand-axe stage of Palaeolithic culture and drove him southward, save during the milder intervals between glaciations. Middle Palaeolithic man learned to overwinter even in arctic conditions. The end of the Last Glaciation left Upper Palaeolithic hunters a problem in adaptation, faced with a steadily warming climate and changing vegetable and animal environment. Mesolithic man, still a hunter and collector, had learned a new way of life, hunting new game and fishing in sea, river and mere. The Postglacial climatic optimum, Atlantic or Altithermal, coincided with the arrival of new peoples from the East, bearers of New Stone Age culture and the arts of agriculture, stock-rearing and the habits which go with the former at least, including settled habitation. Through the early Metal Ages up to the present day, technology and command of animate and inanimate Nature have advanced at ever-increasing speed. At first the plaything of his climatic environment, man now carries his preferred atmospheric conditions, within doors at least, along with him, to the Equator or the Poles and even, briefly, to the bed of the sea in a bathyscaphe, or right outside the Earth's atmosphere and climates in a rocket-propelled space-capsule.

In the earlier years of this century, geographers studying the various environments for man presented by different regions of the Earth arrived at the conclusion that environment, and in particular the climatic factor, absolutely determined the form of culture developed by the men living in it, and not only the culture but the character and psychology of the different races and people concerned. Geography was thus thought to hold the whole key to history. There is without doubt a 'geography behind history',* but it is not the whole story and few students of mankind today would go so far in deterministic faith.

A more modern view of the situation is 'possibilistic': man is presented by his environment with a certain set of situations and materials, from which he is at liberty to make a selection according to his knowledge and skill and to evolve the form and culture, society and attitude to life which best please him among the various possibilities. One environment may afford more varied possibilities than another, but it is the men themselves who decide how they shall use what Nature has given to them.

* Gordon East, 1938, *The Geography behind History*, London, Nelson, 200 pp.

4

Land-Forms
and Topography

EVERY FIELD-ARCHAEOLOGIST needs an 'eye for country' if he is to visualize the people whose cultural remains he is studying in their proper natural setting. The farther removed in time that their day is from ours, the less will the shape of their countryside resemble the one we see today, for even the 'eternal hills' are so only on the scale of human lifetimes and generations, while less permanent features of the landscape, such as lakes, the courses of rivers and lines of coast, are sometimes seen to change considerably even in a single lifetime—let alone some centuries or millennia. When we contemplate our homelands today and try to see them as they may have been during the Last Interglacial, or at some even remoter stage of the Pleistocene, it needs a great effort of imagination and considerable local geological knowledge to undo the work of sun and wind, water and ice, which has been steadily going on during the intervening 150 thousand years, with several major climatic changes superadded.

Without putting ourselves to such exertions, it will be worth while to consider the influence of present-day topography (or something very like it) on the lives of the inhabitants of our world during the last few thousand years only.

The Earth is very ancient. A recent estimate of its age stands at about 4.5 thousand million years. During the greater part of that time there was no life of any kind, but the forces of inorganic nature had been at work to break up, wash away, re-deposit, re-consolidate, over and over again to re-shape and destroy the modelling of the Earth's face. For at least 2,000 million years—probably many more—some forms of life, at first only lowly ones, have been the witnesses, and in a small way the collaborators with the inorganic world, in these processes of change. Mostly they inhabited the seas at first, where bottom-sediments were forming from the comminuted remains of pre-existing land-masses. In time, these hardened and were upheaved once more from under the sea, to meet again sun and air, rainwater and frost, which in further ages would reduce them to pebbles, sand, silt and clay for building of yet newer continents.

Beneath its mantle of weathering rock, soil and vegetation the Earth's crust, our solid land, on the surface of which a greater part of human activity goes on, is therefore a layer-cake of different rocks of many ages, the layers tilted, folded, broken, faulted, rifted, over-thrust and re-levelled by newer deposits, injected by molten magma from deeper down and even, in places, broken through by volcanoes, which throw up their ashes and pour out their lavas still. The 'bones' of the countryside are its underlying geological formations, so that the shapes of the continents and the contours of their mountains and valleys, the courses of their rivers, the extent of their plains is in part determined by the underlying structures. Most of the more prominent of these, though young on the geological time-scale, are exceedingly old as men count time, so that, for example, the world's most recently-formed folded mountains were complete and already somewhat worn before ever man had evolved to marvel at them. Among them are the Rockies, the Andes, the Pyrenees, Alps, Caucasus and Himalayas.

A glance at the physical map of the world will show how clearly land-outlines of some parts of it depend on structure.

The chain of narrow islands studded with volcanoes forming the southern boundary of the Malay Archipelago is, even to the ungeological eye, manifestly a fold of the crust, cracked and weakened by the volcanic forces which upraised it, to which corresponds a down-fold in the adjacent ocean bed, forming a long, narrow 'deep' immediately to the south. On the smaller scale, many familiar promontories and sounds may be similarly explained. There is something solid in the appearance of the huge mass of Africa, with its comparative lack of mountain ranges and deeply indented coasts. In fact its nature as a primaeval continental block, its fundamental architecture largely unaltered by later geological events, is borne out by structural studies.

Imposed on the geological structures is the secular etch-

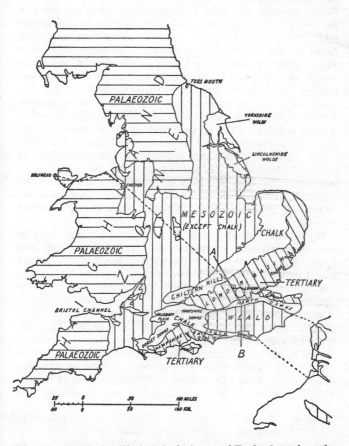

Fig. 12.   Much simplified geological map of England, to show the
Highland Zone based on Palaeozoic rocks, the outcrop of the
Chalk, the line of the Section shown in Fig. 13, and how a journey
from London to Holyhead traverses strata representative of nearly
the whole of the geological column. The continuation of the
Wealden anticline across the Channel is also indicated.

ing, fretting and shaping produced by the agencies of denudation—especially water, weather and wind. It is, in fact, a comparative rarity for the summit of a mountain or the bottom of a valley to correspond respectively with an up-fold or a down-fold of the strata of which it is composed. Peaks like the striking pyramid of the Matterhorn have often been carved by weathering out of a series of strata whose complicated structure bears little or no relation to the present surface. The Grand Canyon of the Colorado River has clearly been cut by running water through a most regular, horizontally bedded sequence of sediments and, as a valley, it owes nothing to the arrangement of those strata. On the other hand, the buttes and mesas of the Western Badlands, which are clearly remnants isolated by intense erosion, as evidently depend for their present shape on the same regular bedding of the rocks of which they are composed, the harder layers showing flat tops and steep or vertical faces while the softer form undercuts or gently sloping scree-slopes of eroded material.

On a less imposing scale, and less obviously, because close vegetation-cover masks the rocks themselves, the gentler hills of south-eastern England, all less than a thousand feet in altitude, owe a good deal of their shape to folding and sub-surface structures on which denudation has for long ages been at work.

A geological map (Fig.12) shows the present surface-distribution of the Chalk in southern and eastern England. It forms a prominent belt trending roughly north-east from Dorset to the north coast of Norfolk, continuing, beyond the break made by the Wash, into a lesser, narrow, rectangular area with its long axis almost at right-angles to its former direction, in the Wolds of Lincolnshire and Yorkshire. The

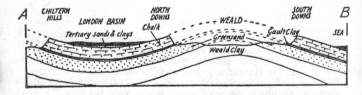

Fig. 13. A north-south section along A-B (Fig. 12) across the London Basin and the Weald, to show the relations of the Chalk ridges with overlying and underlying strata.

main outcrop gives off a branch extending almost due east, close to its southern end, and this divides into two narrow strips passing to north and south of a somewhat truncated long-oval area (the Weald of Surrey, Sussex and Kent) and terminating in the cliffs of Dover and of Beachy Head respectively. This curious irregular outcrop is readily explained by introducing the third, vertical, dimension by means of a north-south section drawn approximately through London (Fig. 13). The Chalk has been forced from the south into two gentle folds, domed up over the Weald (anticline) and dipping down into a basin (syncline) beneath London. The northern rim of the basin is formed by the rising limb of the latter fold in the Chiltern Hills, the southern by that of the North Downs, and both show steep scarps, where the whole thickness of the Chalk has been cut through by erosion. In the Weald, all save the two descending limbs of the anticline has been eroded since the folding, so that the North Downs

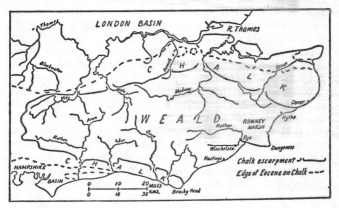

Fig. 14. The Weald, to show the pattern of the drainage, superimposed from the former Dome, the position of the Chalk scarps, broken by numerous water-gaps and the build-up of new land, at and near Dungeness, since historic times (p. 122).

scarp is faced by that of the South Downs some thirty miles distant, the beds there dipping away beneath the Channel to meet the Chalk of northern France on the other side.

Below are exposed the older underlying sediments of the Wealden series, which take their name from the Weald, or forest (an Anglo-Saxon word), lying on the sands and clays between the jaws of the broken Chalk.

The present pattern of the rivers draining the Weald (Fig. 14) tells how all this vast mass of material has been cut away. They began as streams draining radially from the summit of the newly upraised Wealden Dome to the London Basin northwards and to the depression of the Channel southwards. Their action was accentuated by 'rejuvenation' through the sea's retreat during the middle Tertiary periods. In the late Pliocene the sea again advanced briefly to a height of 600 feet above its present level, cut benches into the flanks of the dwindling dome and left slight gravelly deposits near the summits of the present North Downs. Since then, sea-level seems to have been falling steadily, save for the minor eustatic oscillations imposed by the Pleistocene glaciations, with the result that the rivers have been continually provided with a sufficient gradient to continue their down-cutting. This rejuvenation has enabled them to keep pace in cutting into the surrounding Chalk scarps, so that today almost all leave the Weald through deep gaps in the scarps, to empty, as they have always done, to north and south, into the Thames Basin and the Channel, and not by the route which now seems more obvious, eastwards, where there now remains no rim of Chalk to impede them.

Westwards, the Wealden anticline was never so high or so steep. At the Hampshire border with Surrey the Chalk arches gently over without a break at its summit, and in the Berkshire Downs and Salisbury Plain the great anticline fades out into several minor up-folds, so that the Plain represents a fairly high continuous rolling plateau of Chalk, with only the summits above 500 feet, here and there intersected by the deep valleys of the Avon and its tributaries. Salisbury Plain and the Marlborough Downs thus form a sort of focus for the whole Chalk system of England.

Since Chalk is very porous, it affords relatively light dry soils and, whereas the valleys between the eastern Downland ridges and plateaux are floored by London and Wealden Clays and carried thick oak forest and swamps in prehistoric times, the Downs themselves were probably never closely wooded, though doubtless they were not then the wide tracts of open country which they mainly present today. Neolithic, Bronze Age and later Iron Age invaders from the Continent found the Chalk ridges not only affording almost the only practicable routes of penetration, but providing the fairly open pasture and easily tilled land to which they were accustomed on the loess-lands of Europe. Since Salisbury Plain, the focus, offered a wide expanse of such land in contrast with the high and relatively narrow ridges of the Downs and Chiltern Hills, this became the centre for their successive cultures and the ridges their highways. Not until iron tools became common, and especially until the iron-shod ploughshare was developed, could prehistoric men clear the thick forests on the heavy soils and begin to exploit the lowlands. The distribution of Neolithic and Early Bronze Age funeral monuments and settlements is mainly confined to the

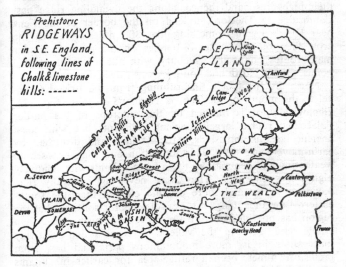

Fig. 15. The main lines of prehistoric communications in south-east England, following the Chalk and other limestone ridges.

Chalk, though in the Bronze and Iron Ages the rivers themselves were in use as lines of communication, even if the land of their immediate valleys was unsuitable for settlement.

Along the Chalk ridges run the prehistoric trackways—today grass-grown and long abandoned for the easier valley roads. Of them perhaps the Ridgeway and the Icknield Way are the best known, though branches criss-cross the high tops in all directions.

The Ridgeway (Fig. 15) begins near the mouth of the River Axe, in eastern Devonshire, climbs on to the Dorset

Downs and follows their crest, eastwards and northwards, to the neighbourhood of Salisbury, where the ancient river-crossings may be guessed but have been obliterated by historical and modern developments. North of Salisbury a network of ancient tracks covers the Plain, but a main branch points towards Avebury from Stonehenge. Near Avebury it crosses the infant Kennet, climbs on to the Marlborough Downs and follows their northern edge and that of the Berkshire Downs, now nearly due eastwards, to Goring Gap, where the Thames cuts through the Chalk. From Goring it becomes the Icknield Way and follows the scarp of the Chilterns, but below their high crest, and thence, along the dwindling ridge past Cambridge to Thetford, to end on the border of the Fens near King's Lynn—something like 300 miles in all as the crow flies, but closer to 400 miles on the ground. Similar main routes connected Avebury with the Channel at two points, via the North and South Downs ridges.

North and west of a line running from the Bristol Channel to the mouth of the Tees is Highland Britain (Fig. 12). Geologically, it is marked by the outcrops of the harder Palaeozoic rocks, largely ancient sediments but with local ancient igneous intrusions. Much folded and disturbed by earth-movements since their formation and long exposed to weathering and denudation, these form uplands with relatively high ridges and hills. They were never agriculturally rich, having a wetter and more oceanic climate than the southeastern Lowlands and, on the whole, poorer soils, so that the region has provided pasture for cattle and sheep rather than arable land, save in the valleys. It is wild and relatively inaccessible in its more mountainous parts and has, from prehistoric times, been a refuge-area for earlier inhabitants retreating before successive waves of continental invaders, each of which, in turn, occupied the more desirable and profitable Lowlands.

Across the sea again, Ireland, largely lowland in character, received various prehistoric immigrants, who appear to have been more or less peacefully absorbed. The inhabitants never suffered Roman conquest, repulsed the Northmen and were with difficulty subjugated by English Kings of Norman ancestry.

Lowland Scotland is divided from the mountainous Highlands by a rift-valley—a wedge of late Palaeozoic sediments, including the Coal Measures, which feed the modern industrial areas, faulted down between two blocks of earlier rocks. Here is the 'waist' of the country, where the outermost frontier of the Roman Empire, Antoninus' Wall, joined the Firths of Forth and Clyde and divided civilization from barbarism for a short while in the early centuries of our Era. North of the Highland Boundary Fault lies nothing to attract a conqueror and little of modern economic importance save sheep, hydro-electricity, whisky distilleries, new forests, and the haunts of red deer, salmon and grouse that elsewhere in these Islands have been driven out of their natural surroundings by the pressure of human economy. The scenery, the field-sports, the surviving culture and history of a proud, virile, talented and hard-working but poor people form the principal attractions to numerous modern tourists. Outlying position, mountain and moor, river, loch and island made Highland Scotland what it was and is, despite the hand of man, which elsewhere has so altered landscapes with towns and factories.

Other mountain peoples come to mind for comparison. Not so isolated geographically as the Scots, the Swiss have always been surrounded by potential enemies. Their economy, again, was chiefly pastoral until modern precision instrument-making, international banking and tourism gave them new directions in which to extend their genius. The twenty-two Cantons, at various times subject to their more powerful neighbours, were finally federated into a nation only in 1848, though more or less united by common interest into a League from the end of the fourteenth century. Even today, three languages —French, German and Italian, as well as local variants of them—are predominantly spoken in the parts of Switzerland most in contact with the homelands of those tongues.

A large part in this minute subdivision of even so small a country must have been played by its mountainous character, whereby each valley-system, cut off from its neighbours by ranges that could only be crossed by high passes, developed a culture of its own. Since they hold the Alpine passes over which, since prehistoric times, has flowed the land traffic between the Italian peninsula and central Europe, the inhabitants of Switzerland have always been at a focal point of communications.

To all but local mountaineers, high peaks and ranges have always presented formidable obstacles and objects of terror and superstition. Did not the Greeks locate the home of their gods on Mount Olympus (a peak under 6,000 feet high and easily climbed)? How much more would the Alps, with their snowfields and glaciers, unpredictable weather, avalanches, falling stones and other natural hazards intimidate primitive peoples obliged to pass through them? The enjoyment of mountains is a quite modern development, due largely to nineteenth-century alpinists and their successors.

Another notable prehistoric route, greatly in use from the Early Bronze Age (say 1500 B.C.) onwards and marked by finds of amber ornaments, is known as the Amber Route (Fig. 16). It ran across Europe from Jutland, where the fossil resin was found, by way of the major river valleys (Elbe, Vltava, Danube, Inn), crossing the Alps at the Brenner Pass and ending on the Adriatic Sea at the mouths of the Po, whence the amber traffic went by sea to the Mycenaean centres of Bronze Age civilization in Crete and the Greek mainland. The prized material and ornaments made of it doubtless passed from hand to hand between one intervening tribe and its neighbour all along the route, which was probably never traversed by any one intermediary in its entirety.

Fig. 16. The main trade-routes of central Europe, from Early Bronze Age to Iron Age times. (Redrawn after V. G. Childe.)

The contrast with the Chalk Ridgeways is striking, this route lying mostly across the predominantly east-west 'grain' of the geology, whereas the former followed an outcrop in its course across country. For the Amber Route, the river-valleys afforded the only practicable paths across largely mountainous country, as they do for roads and railways today.

The traffic was not all one-way. In Early Iron Age times, during the last few centuries before the Christian Era, the classical Greeks established trading-posts at numerous points in the central and western Mediterranean, of which Massilia, the modern Marseilles, is perhaps the best known. Through these, they exchanged wine in pottery amphorae and figured vases from Attica, bronze vessels, red Mediterranean corals and other products of a southern city-civilization with the barbarous Celtic tribes of the hinterlands of western and central Europe. From the coast the goods travelled northward by the Brenner and other, even higher, Alpine passes from the Adriatic and by the Rhone valley from Massilia to the Rhine. With them, as in commercial penetrations of later times by Europeans in Africa and elsewhere, doubtless went some notions of the parent civilization, even if mainly material in nature.

Examples could be multiplied of routes of communication dictated by topography, which can be shown to have served the traffic of mankind from very early down to modern times.

If mountains divide peoples, valleys thus often afford both pathways for the diffusion of culture and local climates suitable for habitation. Structural valleys, owing their form to synclinal folds in the surface rocks, are rare. They occur in the French Jura. Others, called rift-valleys, due to the subsidence of a block of country between parallel faults, leaving high shoulders (horsts) of rock on either hand, are also comparatively uncommon. The vast majority of valleys is due to erosion, largely by streams of water cutting their beds down into the underlying rocks and following the steepest gradients of the country.

Of rift-valleys, that of mid-Scotland, a very ancient example now almost levelled, and that of the Rhine, between Basle and Mainz, have already been mentioned. The largest rift-system in the world (Fig. 17) begins in Palestine with the Jordan Rift, running south to the Gulf of Akabah. This and the Red Sea are flooded rifts, dividing the ancient, north-east tilted block of Arabia from its parent mass, the African Continent. From the Red Sea, the fault-system bears south across

Fig. 17. The Great Rift Valley. (Redrawn after F. J. Monk-house.)

Ethiopia and, separating into two branches which rejoin at Lake Nyasa, passes through eastern Africa to the lower Zambezi valley—about 50° of latitude, more than 3,000 miles in all. The course of the faults may be followed by the chain of long, narrow lakes which here and there occupy their deepest parts.

These rifts may greatly affect local climate. The Rhine valley between the Vosges and the Black Forest forms an area in central Europe of almost Mediterranean climate. In Palestine, the Jordan valley away from the river is practically waterless desert between hills with a certain amount of winter rainfall—whence the importance of the rare permanent springs, such as the 'Ain es-Sultan at Jericho. In Ethiopia, the rifts provide strips of forest and savannah between high, dry steppes and, in the equatorial belt, revert to desert. Along their length they are thus, today, alternately favourable and unfavourable to human occupation. The situation in the past has not always been so. Former lake deposits in areas now perennially dry (as at Oldoway, northern Tanganyika, for example) show that, at various times in the Pleistocene, there must have been wetter periods and plentiful vegetation.

The commonest valleys are those cut by water, sometimes, in higher latitudes, greatly assisted by frost and glaciers.

Even where rainfall is insufficient to maintain permanent streams, water action due to seasonal storms often dissects the country by the formation of steep-sided gullies, which are a feature of many desert and semi-arid regions. The absence of continuous vegetation assists the formation of these whenever sufficient rain falls for run-off to be considerable. They are variously called canyons, barrancas, wadis, dongas, nullahs, according to the part of the world in which they occur. These gullies are of invaluable assistance to both the geologist and archaeologist by providing extensive natural sections, in their walls, of sub-surface strata and ancient occupation-levels, which are often lacking in lands with a close carpet of vegetation and only subdued relief. Under these latter circumstances stream erosion is very slow.

Given sufficient time, however, running water alone is, even in the most temperate lands, a potent agency in the formation of landscape. The former Wealden Dome, already described, first upheaved early in the Tertiary Era, has been almost entirely levelled between that time and the present day —a matter of sixty million years at the most. The present gentle-seeming rivers are the direct descendants of the streams which have achieved that great task of earth-moving.

Rivers and their valleys have, from the earliest times, afforded many advantages for human settlement—water, fish and wildfowl, lines of communication by raft, canoe or boat and positions of easy defence within sharp bends and at the confluences of tributaries with the main stream. The implements of Lower Palaeolithic man in Europe are almost confined to waterside sites, mainly rivers, though that of Hoxne in Suffolk or of Lehringen in Hanover were located by now-vanished lakes. The earliest known human beings in the Mexico Basin, the men of Tepexpan and Peñon, hunted mammoths near the beaches of a formerly much more extensive Lake Texcoco. The dwellers by an ancient lake in Tanganyika are now world-famous since their remains have been exposed in the walls of the Oldoway Gorge, a great stream-gully in country now waterless, in most years at least.

Hand-axes and other implements occur in the ancient terrace-gravels of many rivers, among which the Thames in England, the Somme in Northern France, the Vaal in South Africa, the Aniene near Rome, and the Manzanares near Madrid are representative examples. The tools are known in their hundreds of thousands from river-valleys, while mere dozens have been found at sites away from water, or where water used to be in their time.

The archaeologist, therefore, who aspires to understand these finds in their environmental context must closely study the habits and developments of river-systems, the evolution of their profiles, terraces, knickpoints, periods of aggradation and downcutting and the relation of these phenomena to changing climates and sea-levels. This is not the place to go more fully into these matters, for they have been exhaustively treated in many works on geomorphology, physical geography and Pleistocene geology. They afford means of dating the earliest human industries as well as explaining the environments in which their makers flourished.

Mesolithic man was also a lakeside, riverside and seaside dweller, but unlike Lower Palaeolithic man, he was not confined to such places.

Particularly in Switzerland, lake-villages built on piles over shallow water or marshy margins were constructed and occupied from Neolithic to Iron Age times. Defence and security apart (perhaps main considerations in this specialized type of settlement), a lakeside affords many natural advantages—

building-space without preliminary forest clearance, transport by towage for constructional timbers, reed-thatch, fish, flesh and fowl in plenty and constant water for man and beast.

Owing to silting by tributary streams and growth of vegetation, lakes comparatively rapidly pass through the stages of swamp, marsh, bog, brushwood-carr and forest, becoming dry land admirably suited, when cleared, to agriculture. The peaty Yorkshire 'carrs,' for example, and many level valley-floors in hilly or mountainous districts owe their origin to silted lakes.

From the earliest times, rivers have given rise to important settlements. London lies at the lowest readily fordable or bridgeable point on the Thames, whose valley has afforded an important thoroughfare certainly since the Bronze Age. With agriculture and growing trade, a river links together its whole catchment-area with a network of tributaries and leads, in later times, towards principal markets at main confluences and perhaps to a seaport at its mouth. Before the days of metalled roads, water-transport was little slower and far easier than by routes across country, even if less direct. The first city-states of the Near East were made and maintained by the rivers on the banks of which they arose, and widespread agriculture became possible through water diverted for irrigation to areas some distance from the main stream.

Sea-coasts, the other form of waterside environment, share with rivers and lakes the advantage to primitive peoples of land unencumbered with forest. After the last retreat of the European glaciations, the open steppes of the periglacial zone, with their roaming herds of large herbivores, gave place to forest, becoming ever denser as climate improved. The human inhabitants had to accommodate their habits to the new environment, or to migrate with the northward retreat of the old. No doubt some of the more specialized hunters chose the latter alternative, but behind them a different sort of culture grew up, still based economically on hunting, fishing and gathering but adapted to the new conditions. Instead of the mammoth, bison, horse or reindeer of the open country, the Mesolithic peoples preyed mainly on the forest elk, red deer and wild pig, among the larger mammals, and, to a much greater extent than before, on smaller rodents, birds and fish. Inland, their settlements are found in drier, sandy areas and other places where the forest grew less thickly, and by rivers, lakes and bogs, where they could find at least a strip of open country. Coasts afforded them similar conditions with the added advantage of plentiful sea-food—fish and molluscs—and other, more seasonal delicacies, such as the eggs and unfledged young of the numerous sea-birds. In the islands of Scotland and northern Europe generally this latter harvest provided an important part of the human dietary right up to recent times.

Since the sea-level was, in the time of the European Mesolithic peoples, considerably lower than it is today, owing to the vast volumes of water still tied up over the continents in the form of land-ice (eustatic effect), a very wide area of the shallow seas now covering the continental shelf was then land —if not dry land, at least low-lying marsh, fen and delta, not yet closely forested. It is known, for example, that some at least of the sandbanks in the North Sea, which today form favoured fishing-grounds, were then exposed, for the fish-trawls not infrequently bring up masses of 'moorlog'—peaty material consisting of remains of freshwater and land vegetation. One such dredged mass, from the Leman and Ower Bank, off East Anglia, yielded a deer-antler barbed harpoon of Maglemosian (Mesolithic) type, doubtless lost by some fenland fisherman when that part of the North-Sea bed was still land.

In Scandinavia the Early Postglacial coast-lands often stand well *above* the present sea-level, not below it. While the world-wide sea-level has there risen to the same extent as elsewhere, with the melting of the ice the land itself has been rising faster yet. An ice-sheet, such as that in Greenland today, perhaps thousands of feet in thickness, bears down on the land with such weight as to cause it to sink slightly into the underlying layers of the globe. When this weight is removed by melting of the ice, the continent, like an unloaded cork in water, recovers a few feet in compensation and, nearest to the ice-centre, where the load and degree of depression were greatest, the subsequent recovery (isostatic effect) is most marked. The relation of sea-level to land level depends on the relative intensity of these two contrary effects—in southern Britain, the eustatic, farther north, as in Scotland, the isostatic movement has been more marked. It is striking, therefore, that in Scandinavia the known Mesolithic settlements of that time occur well inland from the present coasts, but close to the raised beaches marking the former coastlines before the land rose again.

Rocky coastlines are often marked by steep cliffs and the formation at high-tide level of sea-caves, due to wave-erosion of local weaknesses such as faults in the rock. When the land

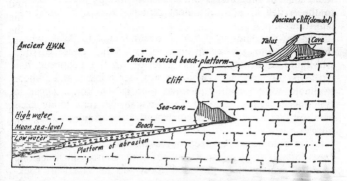

Fig. 18. Modern sea-beach, cliff and cave, showing remains of such features indicating a former high sea-level.

rises or sea-level falls, these caves are left high and dry, well above high water, and then afford most desirable ready-made seaside residences for any home-seeking human inhabitants (Fig. 18). Not only in Europe, but everywhere, such caves have yielded evidences of prehistoric and later habitation. Those of the Near East and of South Africa are well-known extra-European examples, which could be multiplied on other coastlines all over the world where conditions have been suitable.

Inland caves, of course, were equally used as habitations at times when the rest of the environment was favourable, but here their occurrence is almost confined to limestone districts, for they were principally formed by solution of the rock in carbonated water along the channels of former underground watercourses. Long after they were abandoned by their streams, now flowing at deeper levels, erosion of the landscape exposed some of their passages in the valley-sides, where at least the outer parts were used for shelter from Palaeolithic times onwards. Their deeper recesses may have been visited from time to time by the ancient inhabitants for ceremonial purposes, or as refuges in times of danger, but were never occupied from day to day as dwellings. The darkness and dampness of such retreats, alone, make this understandable!

Some modern peoples, as in the loess-zone of China and in a local deposit of loess-like sediment in Tunisia, live in artificial caves dug into the sides of the vertical-walled gullies which are characteristic of this material. It is possible that more ancient inhabitants did this also, but no case is known to the writer of archaeological remains found in these circumstances.

For the rest, natural caves do occur inland in lavas, where they are due to gas-expansion cavities or the release of their still-liquid contents after the exterior of the lava-flow had hardened on cooling. They are not uncommon and, where available, were certainly at times used as dwellings. Those in the archaeological 'zone' at Teotihuacán, Mexico, today used as a restaurant for the convenience of visitors, are striking examples.

More common than deep caves are the overhanging rock-faces, often found in the valleys of watercourses in limestone country, which have provided most of the classical 'rock-shelters' of Palaeolithic archaeology. Their distribution is worldwide, but the best known and most numerous examples are found in the Dordogne Département of south-western France, where the modern houses of the village of Les Eyzies, for instance, are largely built against them at the present day, using the living rock as a back wall. Some of these sites have probably been continuously inhabited since Upper Palaeolithic times.

While limestone most usually provides suitable conditions for their formation, any slight overhang, in whatever rock, would be suitable. Obviously, in cooler climates, rock-shelters having a south-facing aspect (in the Northern Hemisphere) would be preferred, as affording the maximum sun and warmth especially in winter. Recent work in southern Australia, however, in about Latitude 35°S., has shown that such shelters were (and are) frequented by the aborigines more for shade in summer than for shelter from wind or rain, so that a southern aspect was here preferred also, as being as *little* as possible exposed to the sun!

A rather special environment is provided for their inhabitants by islands. They vary in size from barely habitable off-shore skerries to vast land-masses far out of sight of their mainland. There are two main types: the continental and the oceanic. While the former belong structurally to the main land-masses of the world, being separated from them only by fairly shallow seas, oceanic islands, such as the Azores in mid-Atlantic and most of those of the central Pacific, are volcanic in origin or are based on volcanic platforms, rising steeply from ocean deeps, and so are independent of any other land. The latter have played no important part in early human history and, indeed, have mostly been colonized and inhabited by seafaring peoples and only at a fairly late date as an overflow from the continents. Thus, radio-carbon dates for early occupations suggest a time about the middle of the first millennium B.C. for the first colonists, probably from south-eastern Asia, in western Polynesia.

Continental islands, on the other hand, throughout history and before, have occasionally been important foci of civilization. One need only cite Minoan Crete as an example of an early island civilization, of apparently indigenous development which had enormous influence in its time on the surrounding lands of the eastern Mediterranean.

While the distribution of land and water has not, apparently, changed in the last few thousand years, if we take only smaller and later geological spans of time into account it is clear that many continental islands have not always been so. We have already noted that England was last united to the European continent during the period of lowered sea-level (perhaps as much as 100 metres, or 330 feet) which accompanied the maximum development of the Last Glaciation. The deepest soundings in the Straits of Dover are little over thirty fathoms (180 feet) so that about half of the Last Glaciation maximum depression of sea-level would enable men to cross the Chanel dry shod on a wide front, avoiding only a few shallow lakes. This situation persisted until about ten thousand years ago, and had doubtless existed during the retreat-stages of earlier glaciations than the Last.

The Irish Sea, on the other hand, is deeper than the Channel. Only two narrow land-bridges, between Anglesey and Dublin and the Lleyn Peninsula and Wicklow Head, respectively, would have emerged briefly at about —50 fathoms (—300 feet) at the last glacial maximum. To all intents and purposes, therefore, Ireland has been an island since the Penultimate (Riss of the Alps) Glaciation, when the sea-level may have fallen to —200 metres (—660 feet), i.e. to below the line of present-day 100-fathom soundings. There is, however, no known Lower Palaeolithic colonization of Ireland, so that it may be thought that, during its necessarily short junction with the mainland at glacial maxima, the conditions were too severe for any human group to contemplate the crossing.

Even such a low sea-level would not create complete land-bridges across the Mediterranean. At —600 feet, Sicily would just be united with Calabria, in the 'toe' of Italy, and with

Malta, but there would still be forty miles of water between the western extremity of an enlarged Sicily and Cap Bon, in Tunisia, and nearly ten miles in the Straits of Gibraltar (Fig. 10, p. 94).

Large areas of the continental shelf would emerge all along the eastern coasts of America (Fig. 19), from Labrador to Cape Horn, but only Trinidad, among the major Caribbean islands, would lose its identity. Alaska, on the other hand, would then be completely joined to north-east Siberia, the peninsula of Sakhalin to its mainland, southern Japan to Korea, Formosa to China, and the Yellow Sea and East China Sea would largely disappear. These sea-level changes and the resulting land-bridges and extended coastal lowlands are of crucial importance for the history of man in the Americas. If Lower and Middle Palaeolithic peoples were

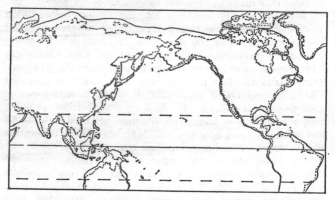

Fig. 19. Pleistocene land-bridges and coastlines, if world sea-level were lowered by 600 feet, as was probably the case at the maxima of major glaciations. Note the side connections between Asia and North America and between Australia and New Guinea. The modern coastlines are dotted.

not yet culturally adapted to life in Latitude 60°N., the Upper Palaeolithic hunters of the Old World possessed tailored skin garments and all the necessary knowledge and equipment to cross into the New World. During the greater part of a glaciation, so wide a bridge (Fig. 4) would exist between northern Asia and Alaska that the crossing could easily have been made much farther south than in the present Strait. Even at the maximum of the Last Glaciation (as suggested by the ice-margins sketched in the map) neither Siberia nor central Alaska was covered by continuous ice-sheets, so that the latter would be afforded an adequate 'half-way house' for hunters from Asia. With even slight glacial retreat, the temperate westerly winds prevailing in about Latitude 50°N. would soon have opened an ice-free coastal corridor along the shores of southern Alaska and north-western Canada, permitting the newcomers to enter the American Continent proper and to spread southwards into more favourable environments (Fig. 4, p. 61).

Some archaeological evidence has long existed to support this theory, though it has scarcely been admitted by American anthropologists until quite recently. Hrdlička's persuasion that man in the Americas was only of Postglacial date has been hardly superseded.

The most striking changes, however, would show in south-eastern Asia and the Malay Archipelago. Indo-China, Malaya, Sumatra, Java and Borneo, at a time of low sea-level, would form one land-mass with the complete disappearance of the Strait of Malacca, the southern half of the South China Sea and the Java Sea. Celebes and the eastern islands of the Sunda chain would remain as islands, but New Guinea would form a separate island-continent with Australia on a front of 1,000 miles between Timor and Cape York. A narrow junction would, in fact, be effected here by a fall in sea-level of less than 100 feet (33 metres). It is across this land-bridge, in all probability, that Australia was originally populated, though at present little serious excavation has been undertaken there and almost everything about the prehistory of the aborigines, extending up to the time of Captain Cook, still remains unknown.

Much more work is needed on the extent of the worldwide eustatic lowering of sea-level during the various glacial phases. This will have to be based on detailed and accurate submarine surveys of the continental shelves to detect submerged coast- and beach-features, which should be found marking the major stand-stills of the sea-level. Numerous profiles obtained by echo-sounding, where possible (down to —100 feet) checked by free diving with modern equipment, will be necessary to effect this. We shall then be in a position to show, with some probability, where and when in the past floras, faunas and human cultures were enabled to colonize lands which are today isolated by wide sea-channels.

Such isolation from mainland influences has evidently happened many times and in many places all over the world. It results, in the case of human beings, in changes, whether of evolution or impoverishment of culture, which are dependent only on the local environment (itself frequently poorer than that of the adjacent mainland) and on the innate genius of the people themselves. The end product is something peculiar to the island and, after long separation, frequently so different from mainland developments as to be difficult to trace to its proper origins, especially in a case where chronology is still deficient, as it is in Australia. The aborigines there (those, at least, untouched by modern Western civilization) are technically still at a palaeolithic stage of culture, having no knowledge of cultivation or domestic animals, save the dog, and not even using the bow and arrow for hunting, but only the extremely ingenious and characteristic boomerang and spears propelled by a thrower as missile weapons. Nevertheless, they have some complicated beliefs, ceremonies and social customs which make it seem that they must have had some contact in the past with more sophisticated peoples. Possibly these were seafarers or castaways who provided at least occasional social novelties from the outside world.

Boats, in the shape of dugout canoes, were in use in Europe, at least by the Mesolithic coastal hunter-fisher communities, as far back as Early Postglacial times, some ten thousand years ago. The eskimo, lacking much timber, had skin boats, the *kayak* and *umiak,* framed with drift-wood, bone or baleen. All were certainly propelled by paddles. In the Mediterranean the first regular seafarers seem to have been the Phoenicians, followed by the Greeks. Ships and coastwise trade, at least, certainly go back to the Mediterranean Bronze Age, as witness the Finike ship, wrecked off the south coast of Turkey in the fourteenth or thirteenth century B.C. The ship was laden with copper ingots, amongst other goods. An international party of divers and archaeologists, organized by the University of Pennsylvania Museum in 1960, was the first to apply scientific survey and excavation-techniques to a submarine site.

Most early navigation was necessarily coastwise, or confined to short sea-crossings, guided by observation of stars or other heavenly bodies, but major voyages beyond sight of land, voluntarily undertaken, are a feature of comparatively late times. Those of the Norsemen to Iceland, Greenland and the American mainland in the ninth and tenth centuries A.D. are the most famous. The peopling, even of eastern Polynesia, probably via Melanesia from south-east Asia, however, seems to have taken place some centuries before our Era, according to recent researches supported by carbon dates. The Egyptians are credited by Herodotus, on hearsay, with the first circumnavigation of Africa, in the reign of Necho (*c.* 600 B.C.), but as far as distant islands are concerned, it is clear that only chance castaways in primitive boats or on rafts are likely to have contributed much to their seaborne colonization before the last millennium B.C. The Polynesians had the very seaworthy outrigger canoe and double-hulled ships, stabilized on the same principle, for their astonishing ocean voyages, in which they ultimately reached Hawaii, Easter Island and New Zealand, at the three corners of the Pacific.

If, in the absence of seagoing craft, islands cut their inhabitants off from the mainland, peninsulas do so only partially. Their role as refuge-areas for primitive cultures retreating before the pressure of others technically more advanced has already been indicated above.

The rough 'stratification' of differing peoples and cultures is well seen in the Indian sub-continent, though modern communications and political unification have, to some extent, blurred the outlines. Land-access is barred to the north and east by the Himalayas and the mountains of Burma; on the west, by those of Afghanistan and Baluchistan. Invaders by land have all entered by the same routes—the Khyber and Bolan Passes, both on the North-West Frontier. The aboriginal inhabitants, the dark-skinned Dravidians, are confined to the south and east of the Deccan plateau, while successive conquerors occupy the more desirable coast- and river-lands of the north and west. Among these were Hindu Aryan nomads from the Kirghiz Steppe, the raid of Alexander's Macedonians through the Punjab, Turks and Mongols and Persians, down to the seaborne European incursions of modern times.

Unlike the southward-pointing peninsulas of America, Africa and India, beyond which lie only oceans, that of Malaya, with its associated string of islands, leads towards the northward-pointing peninsula of Cape York, in Australia. This, as we have seen, is likely to have been the bridge over which the island-continent was mainly populated by its pre-European inhabitants, though their backwardness indicates that the bridge has long been closed, cutting them off from further Asiatic influences of great cultural consequence.

Until the day of the bulldozer and other mechanical juggernauts, man had had little direct influence on topography. The outstanding examples have been the Dutch land-reclamations, still continuing; but in ancient, as well as more modern, times, extensive deforestation has had important effects in the form of soil-erosion, sometimes accompanied by corresponding deposits of sediments elsewhere to form new land.

About 3000 B.C. the rivers Tigris and Euphrates reached the sea independently at 'Amara and Ur respectively. The combined deltaic silts of these rivers, with those of the Karkheh and Karun, draining into the Persian Gulf from the mountains of Luristan to the north, had, by Roman times, met at the site of Basra, cutting off the head of the Gulf as a great lake, Lake Hammar. Today, all four rivers meet in the Shatt-el-Arab, the mouth of which is already 80 kilometres south-east of Basra. The head of the Gulf has thus apparently retreated some 300 kilometres in the last five thousand years. Deforestation and agriculture are probably largely responsible for the changes. Recent geological work has suggested, however, that the Lake Hammar area is a tectonic basin, still sinking, which has received most of the river-sediments for thousands of years past, and this would mean that the delta has *not* greatly extended.

On a much smaller scale the twenty-five miles of coastal level between Hastings in Sussex and Hythe in Kent, known as Romney Marsh, running out into the Straits of Dover in the shingle-point of Dungeness, is a largely modern accretion. An eastward tidal scour collects the sediments of all the southward-flowing Wealden rivers and deposits them here. Forest clearance from Roman times on, to provide fuel for the Wealden iron-smelting industry, has increased run-off and river erosion, so that Winchelsea, Rye and Hythe, which were seaports in the fifteenth century, are now some way inland (Fig. 14, p. 103).

5

Rocks and Minerals

IN THE preceding chapter we saw the influence of geological structure and topography on human environment. We shall now have to consider some of the commoner and more essential materials composing the Earth's crust, their direct expression in the environment, and their contribution as materials of use to early man.

The geologist calls 'rock' not only the stones which we understand from the term in common usage, but all materials of the Earth's crust, whether hard stone, plastic clay or loose gravel and sand. Rocks are composed of minerals—often of several, or many, different kinds, as in granite; occasionally of one predominant mineral with only small amounts of others, as in limestone. As for 'rock', so for 'mineral'—the term has a much wider sense in geology than its common, restricted meaning of 'economically valuable mineral', as in the phrase: 'the mineral wealth of the country'. The mineral kingdom embraces the whole of inanimate Nature, with the solid part of which we are here concerned—the lithosphere, as contrasted with the liquid hydrosphere and the gaseous atmosphere which envelops it.

Minerals are not always pure substances, in the chemical sense, but mixtures, generally of related substances, sharing a common crystalline form—what the crystallographer calls 'isomorphous' substances. For instance, one group of felspars (see below)—the plagioclases—are mixtures in infinitely variable proportions of isomorphous aluminosilicates of sodium and calcium, ranging from the pure sodium mineral (albite) to the pure calcium plagioclase (anorthite). There are four arbitrary intermediate stages, according to the relative proportions of the two bases present, which have been given names of their own, but all grade imperceptibly into one another over the whole range.

Both the chemistry and crystallography, even of many common minerals, are rather complicated and details will not be mentioned here, save in passing and in the simplest terms.

The commonest chemical elements forming the rocks of the Earth's crust are, in order of abundance, as follows:

> Oxygen, silicon, aluminum, iron, calcium, magnesium, sodium, potassium.

These, between them, form about 99 per cent of all rocks. The first two are non-metals, the last six metals which combine with oxygen and silicon to form oxides and silicates. A further 0.9 per cent is made up by the six elements next in order of commonness:

> Titanium, hydrogen, carbon, phosphorus, manganese, sulphur.

Of these, titanium and manganese are metallic, the rest non-metallic. The remaining elements, including those forming many of the industrially valuable minerals, make up the rest of the 0.1 per cent, and are, therefore, comparative rarities.

From this it is clear that the common rock-forming minerals must consist, chemically, overwhelmingly of oxides and silicates, with a few less common salts, of the more frequent metals, those in the first list above. Silicon itself forms a very common dioxide, silica, SiO_2, so, in rock-analyses, the constituents are generally expressed as a list of the oxides present, in the following groups:

1. Silica, SiO_2
2. Alumina, Al_2O_3; ferric (iron) oxide, Fe_2O_3
3. Magnesia, MgO; ferrous (iron) oxide, FeO; lime (calcium oxide), CaO
4. Potash (potassium oxide), K_2O; soda (sodium oxide), Na_2O; water (hydrogen oxide), H_2O
5. Subsidiary oxides; Titania, TiO_2; phosphorus pentoxide, P_2O_5; carbon dioxide, CO_2; manganese dioxide, MnO_2, sulphur trioxide, SO_3

In general, oxides of non-metals are acidic in nature, those of metals basic. (The metal gives the *base* of the chemical name of a substance, e.g. *sodium* chloride; the other part of the name is the acid radicle [root], e.g. *chloride*, the radicle of hydrochloric acid, hydrogen chloride, HCl.)

Common minerals are those which are most widespread as rock-formers, and may be grouped as follows:

1. Quartz
2. Felspar group
3. Ferromagnesian minerals
4. Accessory minerals

1. *Quartz* is the must usual form of free silica, SiO_2. When pure, it occurs in colourless, water-clear crystals, which, if freely formed, assume the shape of beautiful hexagonal prisms, each terminated by a pyramid. In this form it is called 'rock-crystal'. The vast majority of quartz-crystals, however, are of irregular shape, having been formed in confined spaces among other crystalline minerals, to the shapes of which they have been obliged to conform. Small amounts of metallic impurities give crystalline quartz characteristic colours, when it may be sought after as a gemstone (cairngorm, citrine, amethyst, etc.), or it may be smoky, contain small bubbles of fluid or be milky and translucent. It occurs in acid igneous rocks, in veins injected under pressure into other rocks, both igneous and sedimentary, and as the most important component of many sediments, such as sands. Quartz is very hard—the hardest of the commoner minerals, being numbered 7 in Moh's Scale, inferior only to topaz, corundum and diamond (Nos. 8, 9 and 10, respectively). For this reason, and because it is almost insoluble in water at ordinary ambient temperatures, it is almost unchanged by chemical and weathering processes and retains its identity when nearly all other minerals have decayed. It is somewhat soluble under tropical conditions and in thermal springs.

2. *The felspars* are a group of complex aluminosilicates of the bases potash, soda or lime, or mixtures of these (see above). Distinguishing them from one another is a matter of crystallographic and optical tests on microscopical thin sections. One or other of them is present in most igneous rocks, save those, called 'ultrabasic', in which the content of silica is unusually low. In the hand, felspars are generally milky white or only faintly coloured, and show well-defined planes of natural cleavage. In hardness, they come next

below quartz in Mohs' Scale (6), i.e. they may be scratched by quartz or any harder mineral crystal, but will not scratch these. Felspars are more easily decomposed by weathering than quartz, and on long exposure the crystals often show signs of decay and disintegration. Completely weathered, they give rise to clay-minerals (finely divided aluminum silicates with combined water), the original bases being dissolved out and washed away.

3. *The ferromagnesian minerals* are silicates, mainly of iron magnesium and calcium, in very varied proportions. Among them are the micas, the hornblende group, the augite group and the olivine group. All these tend to be darkish brown, green or black in colour owing to their content of iron. The micas are especially characteristic, owing to their ready cleavage into thin plates, the plane surfaces of which reflect incident light and glitter conspicuously. Most ferromagnesian minerals, save the white mica, muscovite, are readily weathered, olivine especially so, giving rise to hydrated magnesium silicates, soft, amorphous minerals like talc, steatite (soap-stone) and serpentine, which have a characteristic soapy feel.

4. *Accessory minerals* in rocks are seldom present in any important amount, but are seldom altogether absent. They tend to include compounds of the rarer elements. Their names and kinds are many and their compositions varied, but they are important as providing small amounts of material with particular properties, often weatherable only with difficulty. Among them are zircon, garnets, spinels and many others, mostly present in microscopic grains only, but when available in larger crystals valued as semi-precious and precious stones. They are very important to the petrologist for distinguishing between similar rocks and tracing sediments to their source.

Rocks

Rocks are divided into three main groups, according to their mode of formation:

1. *Igneous* ('fire'), rocks crystallized by cooling from a molten 'magma' originating in the Earth's interior.

2. *Sedimentary,* laid down mainly by settling from suspension in water, though there are wind-formed sediments also. Sediments originate through breakdown, by weathering, of igneous rocks.

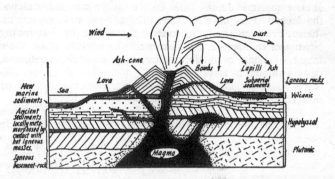

Fig. 20. An ideal section to illustrate the occurrences of the different classes of rocks. Stippling indicates contact-metamorphism. (Re-presentation of the ideas in a figure by F. E. Zeuner.)

3. *Metamorphic* ('altered') rocks, whether of igneous or sedimentary origin, in which the constituent minerals have been changed and recrystallized by heat, pressure and shearing during earth-movements, or by all three (Fig. 20).

Igneous rocks are classified in two main ways: (*a*) as to whether formed at great depth below the surface, intermediately, or ejected *at* the surface by volcanic action; (*b*) according to their content of acid (silica) or basic (metal-oxide) constituents.

Those formed at depth are called *plutonic* (after Pluto, the Classical god of the Underworld). Since large masses of magma (molten rock-material), injected into the solid crust far below the surface, cool only slowly, they tend to form large mineral crystals and to be completely crystalline.

Rocks ejected at the surface, *volcanic* rocks, are either blown out of a vent by an explosion as fragments of all sizes—bombs, scoriae, lapilli, ash and dust—or are poured out more or less quietly in the liquid form as flows of lava. Still very hot as they emerge from the volcano, they are quickly cooled by air, water or cool surface-rocks with which they may come in contact. If crystalline, the mineral crystals tend to be small, or even microscopic, and some part of their constituents may have been cooled and solidified so fast as to have had no time to crystallize at all, but remain as a glass.

Rocks formed from smaller masses of injected magma, or

at intermediate depths, are known as *hypabyssal* ('above the deeps'). They have lost their original heat more rapidly to the surface or their cool surroundings than the plutonic rocks, but not as suddenly as the volcanics. Largely crystalline, with mineral crystals of moderate size, they may also contain a certain amount of amorphous glass.

Igneous Rocks

Classified according to depth, with examples of each group

	Acid (SiO_2 80-70%)	Intermediate (SiO_2 70-60%)	Basic (SiO_2 60-50%)	Ultrabasic (SiO_2 50-40%)
Plutonic	Granite	Syenite Diorite	Gabbro	Peridotite
Hypabyssal	Quartz-porphyry	Porphyry	Dolerite	Peridotite-porphyry
Volcanic	Rhyolite Obsidian (all glass)	Trachyte Andesite	Basalt	Ultrabasic lavas (rare)

Arranged according to their chemical composition, four main classes of igneous rocks may be recognized:

1. *Acid:* Rocks containing much silica, SiO_2, the principal acidic rock-forming substance. If silica is present in such amount as to exceed that required to form silicate minerals with all the bases present, the excess will crystallize out as relatively pure silica, generally in the mineral form of quartz. Acid rocks, therefore, always contain some free quartz, felspars, which are high in silica combined with soda, potash or lime, and only small amounts of ferromagnesian minerals. Since both quartz and felspars are usually colourless, or only pale in colour, while the ferromagnesian minerals are dark, a generally pale igneous rock is sure to lie near the acid end of the scale.

2. *Intermediate:* Rocks without free silica (quartz), with plentiful felspars and rather more dark-coloured ferromagnesian minerals. A medium blue-green or brown colour is usual. There are no free iron ores (especially magnetite, which

is black and opaque) but occasional olivine (an olive-green, clear ferromagnesian mineral).

3. *Basic:* Rocks in which felspars are less important than before and with plentiful ferromagnesian minerals of darker colours, including much olivine. Free magnetite and other iron-oxide minerals show the presence of an excess of iron over the available silica.

4. *Ultrabasic:* Rocks with few felspars, which may consist almost entirely of iron/magnesium silicates with much free iron oxide and iron-rich minerals. They are invariably dark-coloured and may be almost black.

If, then, we arrange a number of typical rocks in a table with three lines and four columns, representing the above seven categories, those higher in the table will be of coarse texture, those below, fine, and those in the bottom line, with only microscopic crystals, more or less glassy. Those to the left will be colourless or pale in colour; those to the right highly coloured and very dark and heavy owing to their high iron-content. Since the composition of the parent magmas and the circumstances of their crystallization vary by infinite degrees, no hard and fast lines can really be drawn between these classes, which are quite arbitrary and show smooth intergradations in both directions, vertical and horizontal. The rocks named are taken as typical examples of their class. The names are mere labels, having no exact descriptive significance.

Beyond this rough description of igneous rocks we cannot go without becoming deeply involved in mineralogy and details of microscopic petrology, which are matters for specialists. Though they are far from irrelevant to the study of man's environment, the archaeologist must take the advice of a specialist when seeking to evaluate evidences in this field of knowledge. In order to comprehend his specialist adviser, he should, however, possess at least this bare minimum of knowledge about the subject.

Sedimentary rocks consist originally of particulate materials produced by the agencies of denudation and weathering of land-surfaces acting on pre-existing igneous rocks. Sun, wind, rain, frost and thaw, ice- and water-erosion and the chemical attack of solutions containing dissolved gases and other corrosive agents all combined, through the ages, to break up and wash away rocks exposed to their actions. Though most sedimentary mineral particles ultimately have an igneous origin, many are far from their first source and have, in the meanwhile, formed part of more ancient sediments from which they immediately derive.

Once carried away from their parent bedrocks by wind and water, the particles continue to be weathered, broken and abraded, so that from the state of rock-slabs and boulders they are gradually reduced to cobbles, gravel, sand, silt and clay. Particles of the finer sediments often consist only of individual mineral crystals, without any aggregates representing the original rocks. In the process of comminution, the more easily weathered minerals, such as dark micas and other ferromagnesian minerals, tend to decompose completely, giving soluble mineral salts and finely divided clay particles of sub-microscopic proportions.

The ultimate destination, given time, of all such rock and mineral sediments is the sea, whatever their intermediate vicissitudes. Once there, they are carried to some distance off shore until slackening waves and currents allow them to settle to the bottom, where, in time, they may form important accumulations. After some further long stretch of time these loose, wet sediments, compressed by the weight of overlying layers, have their excess water squeezed out and are consolidated into new hard rocks, the individual grains becoming cemented together by secondary minerals, often silica or iron-salts, deposited from solutions gaining the interstices between them. Later, fresh earth-movements may raise them once more to form part of a new land-mass and allow their destruction down to the ultimate particles to begin over again.

Sedimentary rocks, like the igneous, are extremely variable in particle-size and composition. A first rough division is into sediments of coarser and finer texture. Consolidated angular scree material or gravel is called *breccia*; if consisting of water-rounded pebbles, *conglomerate*. Particles of progressively finer grade form *gritstones, sandstones, siltstones* or *mudstones* and, finally, *clays* or, if hardened, *shales*. Since quartz and other forms of silica are both hard and long wearing and resistant to chemical attack, the final products of sediment-formation tend to be largely siliceous, and, though a conglomerate may contain pebbles of any sort of rock, some little weathered and containing fresh igneous minerals, even a conglomerate may be predominantly quartzose. This is even more the case down to sand and silt grain-sizes. When we think of sand, it is a *quartz* sand that we first picture, though sands may be of any substance and in oceanic islands in the tropical zone, for example, generally consist of little but grains of broken coral and molluscan shells. In the mud- and clay-rocks, the aluminous clay-minerals, still containing combined silica, become the most important constituents.

Among sandstones, quartzite is an important member. One kind of quartzite is a sand secondarily silicified by a weathering process under tropical climatic conditions. The secondary silica completely fills the interstices between the original sand-grains and is deposited as quartz in optical continuity with them. As a result the rock is extremely tough as well as hard and was used for making implements. A well-known quartzite of this character is the sarsen stone (Reading Beds, Lower Eocene) of the Marlborough Downs in Wiltshire, used in the construction of Avebury and Stonehenge circles. Some quartzites are metamorphic (see below).

A very important class of sediments is formed by *limestones*, consisting mainly of calcium carbonate, with more or less siliceous and aluminous impurities. The lime derives ultimately from the breakdown of lime-felspars and other calcium minerals in igneous rocks and is conveyed by streams to the sea, largely in solution as the bicarbonate. From solution in sea water it may be directly precipitated chemically. It is also taken up by animals to form their hard parts—shells, corals, etc.—as well as by numerous smaller organisms. Where such creatures are numerous, in places far from waterborne sediments from the land, the sea bed may consist of little else but an ooze formed by their skeletons and fine calcareous mud derived from the comminution of these. The Mountain Limestones of the Lower Carboniferous and the Chalk were thus formed. Dolomite rock is often an original limestone in which part of the calcium has been secondarily replaced by magnesium from sea water. The Magnesian Limestone (Permian) of north-eastern England is one such; the rock of the Dolomite region of the eastern Alps another.

Chemical sediments

Dripstone and travertine. Fresh water containing carbon dioxide from the atmosphere in solution is able to dissolve calcium carbonate, which may be redeposited when the water evaporates. This happens especially where the country rock is a limestone, so that percolating water charged with calcium bicarbonate emerges into the free space of a cave or into the open air, where evaporation can take place. A more or less dense crystalline deposit of calcium carbonate is formed, in caves known as dripstone, often giving the well-known stalactite and stalagmite formations there found. In the open air, as where a calcareous stream or spring emerges from under ground, the same substance is known as travertine or calc-sinter. Mosses and other plants, by extracting CO_2 from the dissolved bicarbonate, here contribute to its formation. The same reaction also takes place in lakes fed by calcareous water, where freshwater limestones, including shells of molluscs, may be formed. If contaminated with clayey sediments, the resulting rock is known as *marl*.

Salts. Besides calcium bicarbonate, sea water normally contains some 3 per cent of several other important salts—chlorides and sulphates of calcium, sodium, potassium and magnesium, with small amounts and traces of many others. Solid deposits of minerals containing these substances are formed where land-locked seas are subject to sufficient evaporation, generally under a hot sun. Though water-soluble, these beds may be preserved if subsequently sealed beneath impervious strata, such as clays, which prevent later percolation of water. When evaporation has proceeded to the extent of reducing the solution to a little less than two-thirds of its former volume as fresh sea water, calcium sulphate is first precipitated as gypsum. After removal of 93 per cent of the water, sodium chloride comes down as halite (rock salt). At 98 per cent evaporation, even the very soluble magnesium and potassium salts begin to be precipitated.

Salt is a valuable commodity to primitive people living far inland and on a largely vegetable diet, as do many cultivators. It may be obtained by trade from the coast but becomes a centre of mining and export where deposits are discovered inland. Salzburg in Austria is in a region where salt has been mined continuously since the Bronze Age at least. The properties of salt as a preservative of meat and fish were doubtless also known. Even the discarded skin clothing and wooden equipment of the ancient miners have so been preserved from decay from their time to ours.

Ironstones. Iron, in the form of soluble salts, is set free by weathering of original ferromagnesian minerals and may be concentrated locally, sometimes in lakes as beds of ironstones (ferric oxides and carbonates) by a variety of chemical processes both inorganic and organic. Limonite (hydrated oxide) and siderite (carbonate) are the principal minerals formed in this way. Haematite is the anhydrous oxide.

Siliceous sinter. Where there are hot springs or geysers, as in volcanic districts, the hot water is able to dissolve silica from rocks through which it passes on its way to the surface. When cooled on emergence into the open air, the water is unable to retain more than a fraction of its silica content, so that this is deposited round and near the orifice in an amorphous, hydrated form, often, as in Yellowstone Park, as handsome basins and terraces.

Chert and flint. Many limestones contain nodular bands and beds of silica, sometimes primary, sometimes due to a secondary process of silicification, known as chert. The material now consists of a close lattice of exceedingly fine quartz crystals with some interstitial amorphous silica which is hydrated, i.e. contains some combined water. This latter is possibly a former condition of the whole, having originated as a mass of silica gel, which has since lost most of its water of hydration and assumed the chalcedonic form. Specialists still disagree as to the exact way in which cherts were formed, whether at the bottom of the sea or in the limestone since its uplift as land. The chert found in the Mountain Limestone occurs in dense, hard black nodules. The variety occurring in the Chalk—probably not essentially different—is known as *flint*. It is extremely pure and homogeneous and is well suited to the manufacture of cutting implements. A smooth, black rock known as Lydian Stone, basanite or touch-stone, is an altered (silicified) shale or mudstone, not in its final form essentially different from chert, but tougher. It was used as a material for Neolithic polished stone axes. From early Classical times it was used by goldsmiths for testing the purity of gold by comparing the colour of the metallic mark made by rubbing on it an unknown sample alongside that made by a sample of known pure gold (hence 'touchstone' and 'basanite'—Greek: test or prove). The stone came to Africa immediately from Lydia in Asia Minor but seems in this particular case to have originated in India. It is not uncommon in western Europe and other places where there has been metamorphism of fine siliceous sediments.

Pyrite and marcasite. These iron-sulphide minerals may form important ore-bodies when they occur as metalliferous veins in older rocks. They are also found as concretionary nodules, with a characteristic radiating internal structure, in the Chalk, where they are probably due to reduction of ferruginous solutions by decomposing sulphur-containing organic matter. Until the invention of matches, pyrite was used with steel in tinder-boxes and strike-a-lights to give a hotter spark than flint in making fire.

Carbonaecous rocks

Free carbon in rocks is probably invariably of original organic (generally vegetable) derivation. Coal, cannel, jet, lignite and peat are all fossilized plant-remains of varying degrees of alteration and carbonization. Many ancient carbonaceous mudstones, shales and clays laid down in earlier times testify to a former organic content, due to remains of contemporary living things. From more recent periods up to the present day, organic muds, both of freshwater and marine formation, are not uncommon. They contain organic matter still incompletely decomposed (not carbonized) and give off gases like methane (marsh-gas). They often contain recognizable pollen-grains and remains of microscopic animals, which are useful indicators of the natural environment at the time of their deposition.

Metamorphic rocks

These are rocks which have undergone internal changes in their original constitution, having been subjected to heat or mechanical stress. The term 'metamorphism' is generally confined to effects due to these particular agencies, though there are others, notably weathering and chemical changes induced by injected solutions and vapours (metasomatism), which also cause alterations, though of rather different character. Weathering changes are mainly of decomposition and removal of some constituents; metasomatism involves addition of materials not originally present. Metamorphism proper consists of alterations and rearrangement, both chemical and physical, of the rock-substance itself, without either addition or subtraction.

Thermal metamorphism (by heat) takes place either by sinking of a rock-mass below overlying younger deposits, to a depth at which sub-crustal heat and pressure is increased far enough to effect changes in its constitution, or by contact with an injected mass of hot magma at lesser depths. In the former case, the metamorphism affects the whole mass equally; in the latter, the effect is localized, being most intense close to the source of heat and decreasing with distance from it, so that all stages from the unaltered rock to the product of the most intense heating can be observed. The actual changes produced depend very much on the materials present in the original rock. A rather pure quartz sand or limestone, for example, consisting only of silica or calcium carbonate, respectively, will suffer little or no chemical change but merely some recrystallization and densification, whereby the one will become a quartzite and the other a crystalline marble. Mudstone or shale, on the other hand, containing a variety of minerals with organic matter, may be unrecognizably changed into a hornfels, a pale-coloured massive rock without crystals or structure visible to the naked eye, but extremely hard and tough. An example of this is the Mynydd Rhiw (North Wales) hornfels (p. 143). Thermal metamorphism

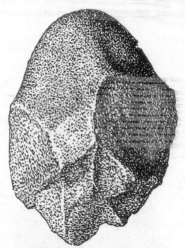

Lava pebble tool (Oldoway)

of igneous rocks, as opposed to the sediments referred to above, consists in formation of new minerals from the original constituents, in equilibrium with the new conditions of crystallization—temperature, pressure and duration of heating. Basic rocks are more radically affected than the more acid types. Recognition of such changes is a matter for a skilled petrologist. *Dynamic metamorphism* (by pressure and earth-movement) is frequently accompanied by frictional heat also. Great pressure results in the formation, where possible, of minerals occupying less space than their predecessors and re-orientation of others—micas, for examples—in planes at right angles to the direction of pressure. The result, in the case of a stratified fine-grained sediment, may be a slate, with foliation imposed in an entirely different plane from that of the original stratification, or, in a coarse-grained rock, of banding and flow-structures like those seen in schists and gneisses, which are rocks of this class.

All this mineralogy and petrology may seem to have little bearing on the study of human environment. Nevertheless, man has, from the beginning, been largely dependent on his inorganic environment for useful raw materials—in the first place for suitable rocks for the manufacture of cutting tools, in the Stone Ages; in the Bronze Age for ores of copper and tin; in the Early Iron Age for sources of iron-ore, and fuel wherewith to smelt it. From the Neolithic on there

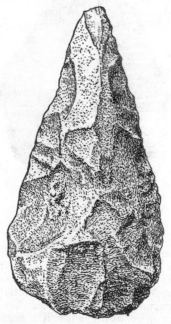

Quartzite hand-axe (Oldoway)

has been needed clay for pottery, various stones for special purposes and inorganic building materials, and ever since, there has been a demand for a widening variety of minerals and rocks to supply man's advancing techniques and industries.

Naturally-fractured sharp stones must, for long ages, have been used as cutting tools before the idea occurred to some contemporary genius to produce the required edge by means of deliberate fractures by blows from another stone held in the hand. Oceans of ink have been used among archaeologists in attempting to secure the general acceptance as implements of particular series of fractured stones, found in many widely separated parts of the world. Many of them may well have been so—indeed, numbers bear the unmistakable marks of having been broken by force—but to prove them as tools is, and will remain, as impossible as to disprove them, short of their discovery in the hand of a contemporary skeleton! It is not until an intentional *form* can be recognized, as well as an usable edge, that one can be sure that such stones were deliberately flaked as implements. Pebble-tools represent the first such recognizable type—water-worn pebbles from which two or three flakes have been struck by sharp blows with another stone so as to produce a more or less continuous, if zigzag, working edge.

The earliest undoubted artificial implements are the pebble-tools found in Bed I at Oldoway and elsewhere. They represent the first known attempts of man to improve on the unadapted chance fragments provided by Nature. The materials used at Oldoway were quartzite and a basaltic lava—neither of them ideal, because granular in texture and so tough as to be hard to work by flaking, but nevertheless giving a reasonably sharp and durable edge for rough cutting or chopping work. In Bed II appear the first hand-axes, pear-shaped with two edges converging to a point, and in successive levels these progressively improve in technique, even though the available rocks were not of the best.

The ideal materials for flaked work are barely granular, hard (i.e. siliceous, or high in silica), brittle and therefore readily flaked, and preferably available in masses of several pounds weight, for the amount of waste worked away in preparing, for instance, a hand-axe is enormous. All over the world, wherever they occur, flint or chert best answer these desiderata. In north-western Europe chalk-flint was used at all periods, almost to the exclusion of other materials, and where it does not naturally occur, either the best local substitute was used or flint itself was carried considerable distances. In midland and northern England, for example, there is the Carboniferous chert of the Pennines, but on the whole, some inferior material such as vein-quartz or quartzite had to serve unless flint was fetched from the Chalk lands and the valleys of rivers which drain them. There the flint was to be found in the gravels. Thus, the location of the flint no doubt influenced to a considerable degree the habits of the peoples to whom it was a valuable raw material.

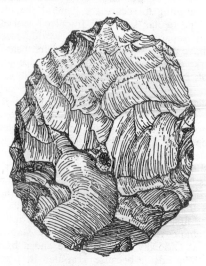

Swanscombe flint hand-axe

In Neolithic and later times it was found that the working properties of flint taken directly from the Chalk, so that nodules were fresh and unweathered, were much superior to those of flint found at the surface or in river-gravels and beach-shingles. At Grimes Graves in Suffolk, Cissbury Hill in Sussex, and in many other less well-known places in the Chalk area, there was, from the Neolithic onwards, a regular mining industry to win flint of the best kind from particular levels, often at a considerable distance from the surface. The pits sunk for the purpose often passed through, and ignored, other flint-bands which were of inferior quality.

Flint-mines are also known in Belgium, France, Sweden, Portugal and Sicily.

Where flint was absent, some cherts were found to be almost as good. Palaeolithic implements from Kharga Oasis and throughout Lower Egypt were often made of a fine-grained honey-coloured chert. In the Sudan, where the country rock was often a granite—far too coarse in texture for good cutting tools—vein-quartz or even rock crystal served for implements, but many of the smaller were of chalcedony, a form of crypto-crystalline silica occurring in rather small pebbles in the Nile gravels, often many miles away. Jasper, an often highly coloured and ornamental opaque silica, was also used there. Farther south, in Rhodesia, a variety of siliceous materials was employed, in the absence of anything better—fossil (opalized) wood, 'silcrete', a nodular concretionary siliceous material, and so on.

Kenya obsidian blade and core

Perhaps the finest material of all, but only locally available in regions of fairly recent volcanic activity, was obsidian, a natural acid volcanic glass, generally translucent and of a dark olive or bottle-green colour, appearing quite black in thick pieces. In Europe only the Mediterranean volcanic islands yielded it; there are also sources in Asia Minor and East Africa, where Kenya obsidian was in use from the Upper Palaeolithic onwards. Obsidian is, of course, plentiful in Mexico, where it was still in use as the principal material for fine tools and weapons up to the end of Aztec times in the sixteenth century A.D. with the arrival of the Conquistadores and their metal-using civilization. In the western United States there were various sources of obsidian. One in Wyoming is thought to have supplied mound-builders in the Ohio valley, over 1,400 miles away.

Another material closely resembling obsidian in the hand, and much used for implements in (for example) the southwestern United States, is *ignimbrite* ('fire-shower-stone'). It is distinguishable from obsidian by being almost opaque, even in thin pieces. In origin it is a mass of small flakes and shards of volcanic glass partially remelted by volcanic heat after its accumulation as a tuff, whence its other name, 'welded tuff'. In thin slice under the microscope, its original character as a loose mass of glassy particles is easily seen.

The nature of the raw materials governed to a considerable extent the finish that could be obtained on completed

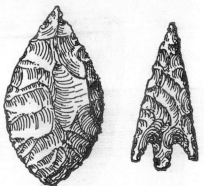

Neolithic flint arrowhead and Bronze Age flint arrowhead

implements. Some of the Middle and Late Acheulean hand-axes, in flint, of western Europe are beautifully and evenly flaked all over and, to anybody who has himself ever tried to work flint by flaking, are real masterpieces of workmanship. Implements from a similar technical level in Africa or India, for example, where only quartzite or igneous rocks were available, look rough in comparison, but are really equally admirable in view of the material and the difficulty of shaping it at all.

The nature of the raw material applies with even more force to the workmanship of Upper Palaeolithic industries, where an even higher degree of precision was necessary to produce the thin, parallel-ribbed blades from which the great variety of different tools was worked by further retouch. Nevertheless, some of the blade-cores, and the blades struck from them, attributable to later industries, are veritable jewels, showing a precision of intention and skilful achievement which has seldom been equalled anywhere. Many of them are of the rarer materials such as jasper, obsidian, or rock crystal, which were only obtainable in smaller pieces.

By Neolithic times, in Europe, flint or its substitutes were still the main materials for cutting tools, but the types on which most care was lavished had changed. Thin, leaf-shaped arrowheads are often beautifully worked, but one of the principal tools was the axe-head, or celt. Here an advance in

Ground flint axe

technique was introduced, for even a well-flaked axe has still rather rough faces which interfere with its smooth entry into the cut. The Neolithic people had, by now, learned the advantage of grinding at least the edge and the parts nearest it to a smooth finish. This can be done with flint by grinding it with sharp quartz sand and water on another stone, but is extremely slow and laborious, for the hardness of flint itself is little inferior to that of the abrasive. In the flint area, at any rate, sands and rocks containing any appreciable amounts of minerals harder than quartz are rare. Perhaps glacial sands, in part derived from igneous rocks in Scandinavia, would have provided small amounts of garnet, zircon and so on, which would have speeded the grinding. Another solution was to find a softer, but tougher, material than flint for axes—flint being so brittle and easily broken by a mis-hit

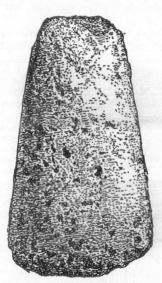

Ground axe

blow. Here the fine-grained igneous rocks were found to be suitable and, whereas flint had been mined for export, now axe-factories arose in the Highland Zone, based on outcrops of suitable tough, fine-grained igneous and metamorphic rocks which were roughed out by flaking and then ground and polished all over. The actual sites of several of these factories, in Northern Ireland, Wales, Cornwall and Cumberland, are known, and scattered examples of their products are found all over Britain.

As one instance: a site at Mynydd Rhiw, in the Lleyn Peninsula of north Wales, has recently been shown to have

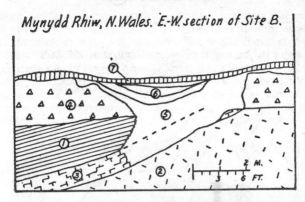

Mynydd Rhiw, N.Wales. E.-W. section of Site B.

Fig. 21. (1) Country-rock: Unaltered shale (laminated mud-stone) of Ordovician age. (2) Dolerite mass: igneous rock intruded into shale in a molten condition, solidifying *in situ* and intensely heating a zone of the country-rock near the contact. (3) Zone of heat-alteration of shale, 1 metre or so thick, in which the rock has been converted into a dense, tough, fine-grained hornfels, without laminations, but with joints at right-angles to the former bedding. (4) Boulder-clay: the product of an ice-sheet traversing the site, containing erratics, including all the foregoing rocks. Among these the pieces of hornfels were recognized by Neolithic Man as desirable material for the manufacture of axes, and pre-sumably led to a systematic quarrying of the rock *in situ*. (5) Neo-lithic quarry-excavation, showing extraction of nearly all the ac-cessible hornfels. When this zone had been followed to a depth at which the overburden to be removed became excessive, quarrying was continued laterally (at right angles to the plane of the sec-tion) and the waste from the new pit was dumped into the old, forming the primary filling. (6) Layers of filling, mainly natural, formed after the abandonment of the site. (7) Recent peaty soil. (Redrawn after C. H. Houlder.)

been both a mine and an axe-factory. The material here was a hornfels, formed by injection of sizeable masses (dykes) of dolerite into beds of carbonaceous shale which had been locally altered by the heat of the intrusion. The shale in con-tact with the dyke and up to quite a little distance from it had been converted into a dense, pale, hard and almost amorphous rock, admirably suited as a material for axes and taking a high polish (Fig. 21).

Among the finest materials for the manufacture of axes were various 'greenstones' including jadeite or pyroxenite, which were very hard, tough, almost grainless and capable of being polished and made to look very ornamental. Their

Fig. 22. Distribution in Britain of Neolithic axes of a single kind of stone, produced in Westmorland. The concentration of the most important market for the product, in the Upper Thames valley and in Wessex, is very striking. A route for the trade via south Yorkshire and the Midland Plateau is suggested. (Redrawn after J. F. S. Stone, 1950.)

known natural sources in Western Europe (in the Piedmont Province of north-western Italy for jadeite and Jordansmühl in Silesia for the similar-looking but mineralogically different nephrite, which is an amphibole) do not seem likely to have produced the British examples. It may be suspected, there-fore, that they come from glacial erratic pebbles found by chance by Neolithic man in drifts deriving, perhaps, from Scandinavia, where at present, however, no known outcrop of the material exists. The jade of China, famed for its exquisite workmanship in hard stones, comes from a rather small area near Khotan, in Sinkiang, north of the Karakoram. Another source is the Upper Chindwin basin in Burma, where nephrite occurs. Nephrite is also found in Mexico, in the

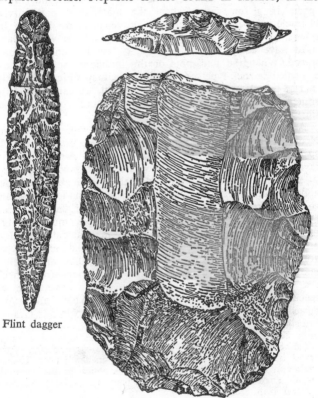

Flint dagger

Grand Pressigny core

Oaxaca region, and in New Zealand. These are practically the only localities known in the whole world.

Some of the Neolithic jadeite axes may have been traded far from their places of origin, but whether we know all the possible sources today is doubtful, and perhaps even more so is whether the Neolithic peoples knew all of those we know, even in Europe.

In Britain, at least, polished Neolithic axes have been closely and systematically studied. Thin sections have been prepared from hundreds of specimens in museums and private collections to identify the rocks of which they were made. In a few cases, where the material is particularly characteristic, the exact sites of provenance are known; in others, at least the general area or areas from which they must have come can be guessed; a few remain quite untraced. When the find-spots of the individual specimens of a particular rock-type are plotted on a map (Fig. 22), with that of the place of origin of the material, we can often gain some idea of the communications and trade-routes of the time.

As well as arrows and axes, other favoured types of Neolithic and Bronze Age stone weapons were the leaf-shaped spearheads and flint knives and daggers. A particularly favoured material was the yellow chert of Grand Pressigny, in western France. Not only was this obtainable in large nodules from which the proper form of prismatic blade-core could be prepared, but it was very pure and flawless. The blades struck off these cores were often as much as 12 inches long and up to 2 inches wide—magnificent examples of manufacturing technique. The used and exhausted cores are found there in numbers today, where they are locally known as 'livres de beurre'—pounds of butter—from their characteristic appearance. This again must have been a specialized industry, employing skilled workmen and supported by a well-organized distributive trade. Nor was Grand Pressigny the only centre. The high point of flint-working skill

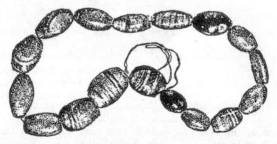

Cambay beads

in Europe was reached in Denmark during the Early Bronze Age, when thin, leaf-shaped daggers, pommelled handle and all, were worked in flint to resemble metal prototypes known from bronze-using areas farther south. The material was presumably obtained locally.

Flint and other stones for cutting tools have greatly preoccupied archaeologists because, not only are cutting instruments a primary requirement of savage existence, but the materials themselves are practically indestructible and so are

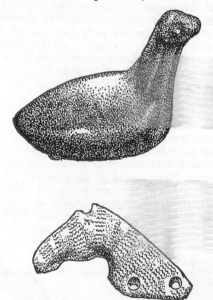

Mesolithic amber figurines

preserved to tell their story when almost everything else has perished.

With the invention of the ground axe abrasive materials became important, whether sands or stones containing some minerals harder than quartz. Abrasives were needed to drill beads of hard and brightly coloured stones and minerals. While a fine flintpoint had served well enough to pierce the string-hole in shells, wolves' teeth, or pieces of jet or amber to be used as necklace-beads, rock-crystal, carnelian or jade were a different matter. Armed with an abrasive powder like emery (corundum, crystalline alumina, of hardness 9 on Mohs' Scale) even a wooden, bone or soft metal drill-point would cleanly pierce quartz and other siliceous minerals. Deposits of such hard minerals, or sands derived from them, were early known in Egypt and the Near East, where, apart from pierced beads and pendants, even engraved seals of hard minerals appear in early dynasties.

In later dynastic times the Egyptians produced carnelian beads in quantity as trade goods, for exchange with less civilized peoples whose products they wished to obtain. These are often quite roughly finished and have the appearance of mass-produced goods. From the early centuries of our Era the agate beads of Cambay, in Gujerat, north-western India, were carried all round the western shores of the Indian Ocean and up the Red Sea by Arab traders. They have been found at early sites in the Sudan and in east and south Africa. They are still being made today.

Amber has already been mentioned in connection with trade-routes (p. 108). It is a fossil resin of Tertiary age, found at various places in the Baltic region and also in Sicily. It was a prized material for beads and ornaments from the earliest times. The first known amber artifact is a carving of a horse's head, from Isturitz cave in the Pyrenees, of Palaeolithic age. Mesolithic figurines in amber are not uncommon in Denmark. An Early Bronze Age cup, cut from a solid lump of amber, from Hove, Sussex, is another famous piece. The resin was valued in part because of its supposed magical properties.

The Hove amber cup
Mixtec obsidian earring

Coral is properly an organic, rather than a mineral, material, though chiefly consisting of calcium carbonate laid down by the polyps. Red Mediterranean corals, obtained from some depth by diving, were traded from Early Iron Age times to central Europe as ornaments for brooches and jewelry generally. The red colour, the colour of life, probably had some magical significance also.

While we are on the subject of ornaments, mention must be made of the Mixtec/Zapotec earrings of obsidian, from Monte Alban and elsewhere in the Oaxaca region of Mexico. These are jewels of infinite skill, care and patience, reel-shaped, some one and a half inches in diameter with a central hole of half an inch, cut from a solid discoid of flawless volcanic glass by painstaking hand abrasion (for no pre-Hispanic Mexican people had the wheel or the lathe).

Flint sickle

The finished article is as thin as blown glass, no more than 1-2 mm. thick, and as brittle. They were worn by priests or men of rank in the distended lobes of the ears.

Alongside flaked arrowheads and daggers, ground axes, adzes, chisels, and hoes, flint sickles for reaping straw-crops and querns for producing meal from the grain, appears with the Neolithic that all-important material for the archaeologist —pottery.

How pottery was first discovered is still a matter for argument among students of primitive technology, but the fact remains that at some early stage of the Neolithic of the Near East—at Jericho, for instance, perhaps as long ago as six to eight thousand years B.C.—vessels and objects of fired clay appear, replacing those laboriously produced by pecking, grinding and polishing blocks of hard stone.

Clay mixed with water is plastic and easily shaped by hand into the desired form, which it retains rigidly on drying. Mere drying in air or in the sun is not sufficient ro render the form permanent, for, if once more wetted, the material regains its plasticity and may disintegrate altogether in the presence of excess water. If, however, once dry, it is heated for a short time to a moderate temperature (no more than a low red heat) the clay minerals lose their chemically combined water, an irreversible change, and the material no longer softens when wetted or loses its rigidity. It is now pottery, and, short of reduction to powder, is practically indestructible, though brittle and easily enough broken into sherds.

Clay is not a primary mineral but generally a mixture of secondary minerals, formed by the chemical decomposition, chiefly by weathering, of primary silicate and aluminous minerals like felspars. In the process of alteration the original mineral loses, by solution, alkalies and bases (potash, soda, lime, magnesia) so that the residue is an extremely finely divided aluminous silicate containing usually some iron with the addition of some chemically combined water. The submicroscopic particles are platy in shape and so, when wet, glide upon each other without separation, giving a moist clay its plasticity. Once dispersed in water, the extremely fine (less than 0.002 mm.) clay particles may remain in suspension even for weeks. During that time they may be carried long distances by even slow-moving currents, and so be separated from coarser sediments of the sand (2.0-0.06 mm.) and silt (0.06-0.002 mm.) grades before being deposited in still, deep water.

Such pure clays are of little use to the primitive potter, for they are too plastic and do not retain the desired shape when wet, the pot having a tendency to 'squat' between forming and drying. Moreover, in drying, pots of very pure clays shrink a great deal as the water is withdrawn from their minute interstices, and so may crack before ever they meet the fire. The difficulty is overcome by adding a quantity of 'filler'—grit, shell, 'grog' (crushed fired pottery) or calcined flint—which stiffens the clay and, not itself shrinkable, prevents too great shrinking on drying of the body as a whole to which it has been added. Some natural clays evidently may contain enough grits of coarser grade to be usable without artificial additives, and these would soon have become known as superior materials to early potters who had not yet learned to 'temper' available clays which were naturally too plastic.

Thus, among mineral products necessary to the economy of pottery-using peoples, suitable clays must always have come high on the list of desiderata which their immediate environment should, if possible, afford. Especially would this be the case before they had advanced so far as to be able to modify suitably whatever they chanced upon conveniently close to their settlements. Later on, with the development of thinner, finer, lighter-coloured wares, fired at higher temperatures in closed kilns, the nature of the clay itself, its low content of bases and other undesirable impurities became of prime importance, so that specialized pottery industries would tend to arise near the best clay-beds.

Just as a thin section of a polished axe, studied microscopically, may lead to identification of its place of origin, so also with prehistoric pottery, the natural mineral grains in the clay, and especially any artificially added filler seen in the section of a sherd, may suggest where it was (or was *not*) made. This is a valuable indication when the archaeologist suspects that some particular group of sherds found at his site was imported, or at least not made just there, but some miles away. This method is at present only in its infancy as applied to pottery, but it has, for example, already shown conclusively that a number of early Neolithic sherds from Windmill Hill, in Wiltshire, contain fresh minerals from igneous rocks—felspars, olivine, etc.—which are not found in the local clays of the Chalk region, and so must have reached the site from places at least some tens of miles away, in the Highland Zone to the west and north, where such minerals naturally occur. It has not been possible to pinpoint the place, or even the most likely general area of origin of the foreign pottery-clays. This may follow in due course, but in the meanwhile it is certain that these few pots, or their clay at least, do not belong at Windmill Hill, though the bulk of the pottery there is evidently of local manufacture. Whether this means that the pots (or their contents?) were traded or that their owners travelled with them from the Highland Zone to the Lowland Chalk, is so far uncertain, but the proof of some human traffic is there for the archaeologists to think about!

A further use for mineral materials is for building. Clay was used either in the form of mud plaster (wattle-and-daub) for walls, as mud-brick (adobe) for construction, or shaped and fired as bricks and tiles.

Ancient plaster is usually of lime (burnt limestone or chalk) slaked with water to a paste and mixed with a sandy filler. Gypsum, also first burnt in later times to make 'plaster of Paris', was at first merely mixed with water, spread and burnished with a pebble. This method was employed in making the beautiful plaster house-floors of the Jericho pre-Pottery Neolithic. The setting plaster is naturally superior. Cement was obtained by the Romans by firing together ground 'cement-stones' or marls (naturally occurring mixtures of clay and calcareous matter). Portland cement is nowadays made on the same principle.

The local stone where suitable was an obvious building material, at first laid 'dry' (without mortar), the crevices being filled with earth or clay, but by Roman times public buildings demanded decorative, as well as merely utilitarian treatment, and though the walls might be made of the country rock or of roughly mortared flints, they would include tile-courses and be smoothly plastered and gaudily painted internally. Ornamental stones would be imported for mosaic floors and decorative wall-facings. Many were brought from long distances for this purpose—Purbeck shelly lime-stone (called 'marble') from Dorset and even continental stones for sculpture and statuary. Alabaster (a massive form of gypsum), soapstone (steatite), travertine, marbles, granites, porphyries and lavas, used for smaller objects, were perhaps not of British materials but imported ready manufactured to serve the Roman way of life in far-off Britain.

Minerals provided most of the pigments for the painted decorations, as had haematite, limonite, chalk, manganese dioxide, etc. from Upper Palaeolithic times.

The knowledge of the use of metals in the Old World seems to have originated in the Near East. Metals of antiquity are few in number: gold, silver, copper, tin, lead and iron. Both mercury and antimony, however, were known to Classical metallurgists.

Gold is usually found in the metallic state ('native') so

that its properties were obvious. Opinions differ, however, as to whether it, or copper, was the first known metal. Both appear about the 4th millennium B.C. Gold was lavishly used in the Royal Tombs of Ur in the 3rd millennium. One of the several coffins of Tutankhamun (late XVIIIth Dynasty of

The Rillaton gold cup

Egypt, 1300 B.C.) was of solid gold. About the same time the Bronze Age Mycenaeans had beautifully worked gold vessels and ornaments (e.g. the Vapheio embossed cup) and even in distant Britain the Early Bronze Age chieftains of Wessex were using it (Rillaton gold cup, etc.). The use of the metal as currency in Western Europe derived from the gold stater of Philip of Macedon (4th century B.C.) of which copies, more and more debased in design with distance and time from the originals, were locally minted in immediately pre-Roman times in Gaul and Britain (B.C./A.D.).

In the New World gold was the principal metal known to the pre-Hispanic Aztecs and Incas, though silver and copper were also produced in smaller amounts (Tomb VII, Monte Alban, Oaxaca, Mexico).

Gold is widespread in ancient metamorphic rocks, where it is generally associated with quartz-veins and intrusions, but though sometimes found in considerable 'nuggets' it is usually dispersed in very small grains. Once weathered out of the parent rock it tends, owing to its weight, to be concentrated in pockets in stream-gravels and may be recovered by panning with water (alluvial gold). This was thought to be the source of most of the gold of antiquity but there is increasing evidence that alluvial 'placers' were panned in order to trace the metal to the source in the original reef. The metal is very soft and malleable when pure and can be worked cold, melting at a bright red heat without being changed in contact with air. Silver and copper are common natural impurities and deliberate alloying metals.

Silver was much less common until later times although, as at Ur, it was used for drinking vessels. Sometimes, though not commonly occurring 'native' in the Old World, it was in use as early as gold, but most commonly occurs with the lead ore, galena, from which its separation is a fairly advanced metallurgical operation. It may be worked without heating when pure and has a slightly lower melting-point than gold. Both gold and silver were used for ornamental purposes only and were of little economic importance until their use as currency. Much of the New World silver occurs native.

Much more important is copper, which apparently less often occurs native and in usable masses. These may have been worked out in antiquity. Considerable masses of native copper have been found in the New World, so that the metal may once have been available in this form, to a larger extent than is usually supposed, in the Old World also. It may be significant for the history of metallurgy that the ancient Egyptians used both powdered malachite (a copper mineral) and galena (a lead ore) as eye-paints for cosmetic and prophylactic purposes, so that these minerals are well known long before their use as sources of the metals. Copper ores are numerous and, though widely distributed, rather local in occurrence. One of the commonest primary ores is chalcopyrite, a sulphide of copper with iron. This occurs in veins in ancient rocks, but where these are exposed near the surface the original mineral is often altered, by weathering, to form oxides, carbonates and sulphates by loss through oxidation of its sulphur-content. These secondary products include the minerals cuprite, malachite and azurite, which are coloured bright red, green and blue respectively and would strike any inquiring mind as something unusual and interesting. Chalcopyrite itself has a brassy, metallic lustre, and another sulphide-ore, bornite, often shows iridescent colours, so that men conversant with native metals might well experiment with these apparently related minerals.

Native copper was known in Egypt and the Near East in the 5th millennium B.C. and the metal was being smelted from its ores in the 4th millennium. Cyprus was an early centre of its production, and it was doubtless with Cypriote metal that the Finike ship (p. 120) was laden. Another well studied area of ancient copper production, here a regular underground mining industry, was active in Upper Austria from the Early Bronze period of Europe, early in the 2nd millennium B.C.

Bronze (copper + tin) first appears in the Near East about 3000 B.C. It was presumably first produced by the smelting together of copper and tin ores. These are known to occur together today in Turkey, Cornwall, Bohemia and China, so that unless the old metallurgists (as seems likely) had other sources, now worked out and unknown to us, only the first of these seems likely to have been the source of the first bronze.

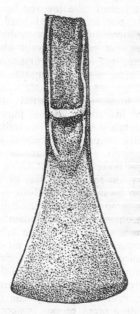

Bronze palstave

Cassiterite, or tinstone, tin oxide, is generally found as pebbles and dark heavy grains in alluvial deposits, like gold, and is recovered in the same way. Bronze with 10 per cent tin was found to be so greatly superior as a metal to pure copper for axes, swords and other cutting implements, that when the local tin deposits in the Near East were exhausted search was made for it far afield and it was traded over long distances to the manufacturing centres. It occurs with gold in northern Spain, Brittany and Cornwall.

Lead was also used to alloy with copper, but lead-bronze is supposed to be a very inferior metal for tools in comparison with the alloy with tin. Most Old World bronzes, from the Late Bronze Age on, contain more or less lead, however, which is known to improve the soundness of castings. Its brittle qualities only appear under modern workshop conditions. Galena, lead sulphide, the principal ore, was known in early times, being another showy heavy mineral with a bright silvery lustre. It generally contains a small proportion of silver, recoverable from it at a low red heat. As an industrial metal lead was not largely used until Roman times, though much of the silver of antiquity probably came from galena. The Romans were great hydraulic and domestic engineers and, with them, lead for piping first came into its own.

Iron, as we have seen, is a very common and widespread metal occurring, though not in workable quantities, in very many rock-forming minerals. Weathered out of these, it may be concentrated in beds of almost pure iron ore. The most important minerals are haematite (red ferric oxide), magnetite (ferrosoferric oxide), and limonite (hydrated ferric oxide). Workable occurrences of these are not uncommon and there are various other useful ores.

Not only, however, do most iron ores of themselves give no hint that they can be made to yield an useful metal, but the ores themselves, ground to powder, had been familiar to the ancients, time out of mind, as pigments. Moreover the smelting temperature is fairly high (some 1,200°C.) so that a proper closed furnace and a forced air-blast continued for hours are necessary to reach it. The difficulty is to raise the furnace-temperature sufficiently to soften the iron to welding point without admitting an excess of air and so preventing reduction of the ore. Primitive wrought iron was never more than pasty. The melting point proper is about 1,400°C., so that cast iron comes only later. Prehistoric metallurgy had to develop into a highly specialized craft, therefore, before it could devise means to overcome the technical difficulties of winning iron from the earth. Once the basic knowledge had been gained from the practice of bronze-metallurgy, the working and use of wrought iron spread rapidly and afar, so that the new metal soon displaced bronze for many purposes and, because it was common, began to find new uses never before contemplated.

Wrought iron for implements, hardened by 'cementation' (repeated heating and hammering) whereby it took up some carbon from the fuel to become a form of steel was produced in Armenia from early in the 2nd millennium B.C. Thence the knowledge spread both to the west and the east. Italy had it by 1200 B.C. and it reached even the extremes of Europe, in Britain and Norway, by the last few centuries B.C.

6

Soils

THE SOIL may be defined as the layer of material covering
the less precipitous parts of the land-surface, derived from the
underlying rock as a result of the physical and chemical
actions over some period of time of weathering, and of those
involved in the life-processes of its inhabitants, both vegetable
and animal. Among other definitions, this may be preferred
as including mention of each of the several factors which
have brought the soil into being and which influence its development: parent rock, climate, exposure, soil-colonists and
time.

Weathering and soil-formation

Weathering has already been referred to many times, in
general terms, as the principal cause of destruction and denudation of rocks. From the moment that a fresh rock-surface
is exposed to the open air, it begins to undergo changes
which, if to us seeming very slow, given time-spans of geological magnitude, are adequate to plane down whole landscapes to sea-level.

Weathering actions fall into two divisions: physical and
chemical. Among the physical are changes, especially sudden
changes, of temperature, due to sun-heating, followed by
cooling through re-radiation of the heat, or its removal by
convection through wind or water. Most silicates are rather
poor conductors of heat, so that under a strong sun rock surfaces may become extremely hot, while a few inches below
the surface the body of the rock may remain comparatively
cool. The sharp difference in temperature within a short distance sets up stresses through differential expansion of the rock
and, while these may not be enough to cause a fracture at
once, after years perhaps, and the repetition of the stress thou-

sands of times, the rock will give way and crack. Isolation, as this process is called, is most effective in places like hot deserts, where the sun is powerful by day and night temperatures are low, with rapid daily transitions from one to the other and back again. It results in the slow cracking of large slabs down to cobbles, to gravel, to sand, to silt.

Frost, next, is an even more rapid worker of physical weathering, but to be effective there must also be moisture. Mere low temperature is not enough. Water finds its way into porous rocks by capillarity, into the interstices between the grains and into the most dense rocks, eventually, by the hair-cracks caused by insolation or along natural joints and fissures. If, now, it should freeze there, it will have a powerful wedging action, for ice is nearly 10 per cent more voluminous than an equal weight of water. The ice-wedge widens the cracks and, when it melts again, the water penetrates even farther, to re-freeze on another occasion and again exert its expansive force. Ultimately the stone cracks right through and a loosened fragment may fall off. Where there is daily, or even more frequent, alteration between frost and thaw, this is going on all the time. In any steep mountain region subject to frost-action, falling stones and the scree-covered slopes below exposed rock-faces are witness to the efficiency of the process.

A third process of physical weathering is due to strong winds. Wind alone may suffice to dislodge already loose fragments of rock in steep situations, but its direct erosive effect is slight, save where, as on beaches and glacial outwash-fans, for example, loose sediments of finer grade —sand or smaller—are exposed to it. Where sand and dust are available to be wind-driven, the air acquires 'teeth' and the sand-blast effect in undermining, etching, fretting and polishing standing rock-masses is very marked. When the process, as in many exposed desert and sub-arctic situations, with only a sparse plant-cover, or even none at all, continues, day in, day out, for centuries and millennia, almost without intermission, the total effect in wearing away and breaking up the rocks becomes considerable. Not only standing rocks, but the abrasive grains themselves, are worn away.

To physical comminution is added chemical attack. Water is the almost universal solvent and while at ordinary atmospheric temperatures silica and many silicates are practically insoluble in pure water, yet even very slight solubility, of the order of a fraction of one part per million, becomes significant when the solvent, over long periods of

time, is plentiful and constantly renewed as the saturated solution is removed by gravity. Rainwater, however, is far from
'pure' in the chemical sense. In particular, it contains small
amounts of dissolved gases, oxygen and carbon dioxide from
the atmosphere and traces of nitric acid formed by combination of nitrogen and oxygen during lightning-discharges. Even
so, there are dry spells when the greater excess of surface-
moisture is re-evaporated, but in deeper rock-crevices the extremely dilute solutions normally percolating may be brought
by slow evaporation to much higher concentration and solvent potency. Over much of the earth, however, evaporation
greatly exceeds precipitation most of the time, so that, here,
it is likely that many chemical reactions, using such little
moisture as may be available from overnight dew, for instance, take place in rather concentrated solutions.

The effect of mere solution and of dilute acid attack by
rainwater on most rock-forming minerals is first gradually
to remove the more easily soluble alkalies (soda, potash) and
later the more resistant bases (lime, magnesia and even iron)
in the form of their bicarbonates, carbonates and nitrates, leaving a residue of silica and the more resistant silicates, such
as clays and some of the very stable accessory minerals.

In a granite, for example (being an acid rock, one of the
less easily attacked), the felspars and dark micas will first
decay under chemical weathering, leaving loose quartz grits,
white mica (which is less soluble than the dark varieties), an
impalpable powder of clay-particles from the felspars,
mixed with some brown iron oxide left over from micas and
other ferromagnesian minerals. Accessory minerals, like tour-
maline, may also be present as distinct crystals in the resulting sediment.

We have still not reached the stage of soil. Physically
broken and chemically decomposed rock is only the mineral
substrate. Soil requires, in addition, living colonists and the
products of their life-processes—organic matter.

Colonization by microscopic plants and animals begins at
an early stage in the formation of soil from the parent rock.
It certainly need not wait upon the degree of chemical decomposition described in the preceding paragraph, but develops with, assists and is assisted by it. Plants are probably
the first-comers. Everybody is familiar with the bright
green coat of microscopic algae which soon clothes any surface
of rock which is fairly constantly damp and well exposed to
daylight. To these are added invisibly small bacteria and

innumerable tiny protozoa, animals of the unicellular group, of which pond-dwelling *Amoeba* is perhaps the most familiar. After these lowly inhabitants have subsisted for some time on the mineral solutions of what we may now properly call the soil, and on each other, and have returned to it on dying some fairly complex organic compounds of their own manufacture, the way is open for some larger occupants. These will, at first, be lichens and mosses and fungi, followed by higher plants—grasses, herbs, shrubs and trees. Among more highly organized animals, worms, mites and other small arthropods, insects and their larvae are perhaps the most important to the life of the soil. Vertebrate soil-dwellers, by comparison, are far less numerous, though more conspicuous to us through their visible soil-moving activities.

All, plants and animals alike, live, feed, excrete, reproduce and die, or are themselves eaten, so that organic matter is continually being built up, broken down and re-absorbed. There remains a reservoir of any momentarily unused organic matter in stock, intimately mixed with the mineral part of the soil by the daily activities of the living, which is known as 'humus'.

Humus is an exceedingly complex mixture of many substances, about the exact chemical nature of which very little is yet known, though its practical properties are familiar enough to gardeners, agriculturists and soil-scientists. It is an amorphous, dark brown, colloidal material, swelling enormously when wet, shrinking on drying, acting both as a cement between coarser mineral grains, binding them together, or to separate and render friable masses of stiff, otherwise unmanageable, clay. It is a reserve of available nutriment in the soil, both for plants and lower animals, containing nitrogen in a form which they can use to build up their own tissues. It contains acidic bodies which can combine with bases in the soil and it forms temporarily stable complexes with clay-minerals and soluble salts, thus preventing their too-rapid removal by percolating water.

A soil is thus an evolving complex of mineral and organic materials the latter living as well as dead. Beginning with a surface of scarcely weathered rock, inhabited only by micro-organisms and with hardly any reserve of humus (a youthful or immature soil) it may develop, after a sufficient lapse of time and under suitable conditions, into a deep, fertile mantle, covering the bedrock everywhere, supporting a rich flora and fauna in and on it—a mature soil.

Soils are of many types. The most potent factors in determining what type is formed in a given case are the nature of the parent rock and the complex of ambient atmospheric conditions which we sum up as 'climate'. The local effect of a major type of climate may be modified by topography and exposure; the species of plants and animals inhabiting the soil may influence it in turn and a sufficiency (a large measure) of time must be allowed for all the factors to result in the development of a mature soil.

A mature soil at any particular place, then, is the result of a number of environmental factors operating over a considerable time and is in virtual equilibrium with its environment. Such a soil is known as a 'climax-soil' for those conditions. Any change in any of the factors, as, for example, in climate, will initiate soil-changes in the direction of a new and different equilibrium or climax. On the climatic side, reasonably high temperatures with sufficient moisture during at least part of every year are needed for soil-development to any degree of maturity. Where these conditions are not fulfilled we find immature, but *permanently* immature, soils representing the climax of soil-development under those particular conditions.

When a weathering-soil is cut through vertically and is seen in section, it frequently shows more or less clear zoning in colour or consistency, the result of chemical and organic alteration, working down from the surface, on the bedrock materials. These zones, being approximately horizontal, are called 'horizons'. The whole section, from the surface to the unchanged parent rock, is termed the soil-'profile'.

Three main kinds of horizon may be recognized, distinguished by the letters A, B and C. A-horizons (subdivisible into A_1, A_2 and so on, if necessary) are those at or next to the surface, containing humus, and from which some, chiefly mineral, components may be in the process of being washed by percolation farther down the profile. B-horizons are those which are receiving and accumulating materials washed down from above. C-horizons are the chemically unaltered parent-rocks, at the most somewhat broken up by physical weathering and infiltrated by weathered material from above.

In this book, we can go no more deeply into the chemistry and classification of soils than we did into that of rocks, but just as it was necessary to have some systematic ideas about the different kinds of rocks available to man, so a broad description of the main types of soils must be undertaken if we are to understand their influence as part of man's natural environment.

Climates, as we saw in Chapter III, range from equatorial to arctic, with varying amounts and seasons of rain. The arctic and sub-arctic do not here greatly concern us, for the low temperatures, and even perennially frozen subsoils, prevent much chemical weathering, and agriculture, one of man's main direct interests in the soil, is in any case out of the question under such conditions. So, too, desert and sub-arid regions show no, or only slight, soil-development, because of the enduring lack of moisture and restricted soil-life. If such environments are inhabited at all, the people are hunters or nomadic pastoralists and the soil, if any, is therefore an insignificant factor in their environment. Our interest in soils, then, is confined to the cool-temperate to equatorial temperature-range and to regions enjoying at least a short annual rainy season.

Since soil-formation is so closely linked with climate, a soil-map of the world follows, in its broad outlines, those of the major climatic zones. Varying height above sea-level, by modifying the climatic factor, also affects the soil-type and introduces irregularities in the zoning corresponding to the distribution of high ground. Since the other main factor governing soil-formation is the nature of the parent-rock, under some circumstances the distribution of soil-types corresponds very faithfully with the outcrops of the chemically more distinctive rocks. This, however, is generally a small-scale effect which cannot be represented easily, or even at all, on a world map—though not for that reason unimportant.

Beginning with the cool-temperate zone, we find a fairly well-defined belt representing a major soil-type traversing the continents in the Northern Hemisphere from British Columbia to New England and from western Europe to eastern Siberia. In latitude, it lies on the whole between 40° and 60° N., extending farther north on the mild western continental margins and trending more southwards on the east. In the Southern Hemisphere it is represented only by small patches (relatively speaking) in Patagonia and the Falklands, in extreme south-eastern Australia, Tasmania and New Zealand. This is podsol-zone.

'Podsol' is a Russian word meaning ash-grey soil. Since pedology, or soil-science, began in the blackearth-lands of south Russia, several internationally recognized names of soil-types are of Slavonic origin. This type (Fig. 23a) takes its name from the well-marked pale grey, or almost white, horizon a little distance below the surface. Typically this kind of soil occurs on sands and rather coarse siliceous sediments of poor base-status. In the cool-moist conditions in which it is found, oxidation of plant-residues is slow and acid, or 'sour', peaty humus tends to accumulate in the A-horizon. It is the percolation from this, containing organic acids in solution, which washes iron-salts out of the upper parts of the profile. The iron is frequently redeposited as a cementing 'pan' in the B-horizon, some little way below. A well-developed iron-podsol, therefore, shows a dark, almost black, peaty A_1, a whitish or grey A_2, a yellowish- or reddish-black B-horizon and a lighter brown or yellow C, the boundaries between them being rather sharp and distinct. The parent-material is a more or less ferruginous yellow, brown or red siliceous gravel or sand, sandstone or quartzite.

Podsols are not everywhere typical throughout the podsol-zone, for wherever the parent-rock is at all fine-grained and clayey, and so does not permit rapid and voluminous per-colation, the typical podsol bleaching of the A_2-horizon cannot take place, because loss of bases and iron is not fast enough to produce the necessary degree of acidity. The same result ensues wherever the bedrock, even if of coarse grain,

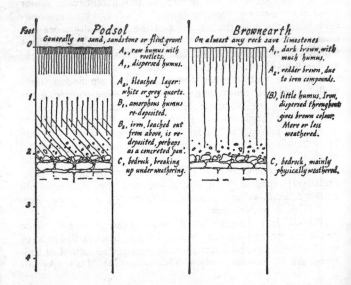

Feet	Podsol	
0	Generally on sand, sandstone or flint gravel	A_0, raw humus with rootlets.
		A_1, dispersed humus.
1		A_2, bleached layer: white or grey quartz.
		B_1, amorphous humus re-deposited.
2		B_2, iron leached out from above, is re-deposited, perhaps as a concreted 'pan'.
		C, bedrock, breaking up under weathering.

Brownearth	
On almost any rock save limestones	A_1, dark brown, with much humus.
	A_2, redder brown, due to iron compounds.
	(B), little humus. Iron, dispersed throughout, gives brown colour. More or less weathered.
	C, bedrock, mainly physically weathered.

contains some reserves of weatherable basic minerals, such as felspars. Thus, podsols do not typically occur, even on the more 'acid' igneous rocks such as granites, even less on those richer in variety of basic minerals, like basalts. In these circumstances, a brownearth soil develops, even if one distinctly acid.

South of the podsol zone, and at some distance inland from rainy western coasts, where climate is rather warmer and drier in summer, is the brownearth zone. Typical brownearths (Fig. 23b) do not show distinct colour-horizons, but are, as their name suggests, brown throughout the profile, the iron immobile and evenly distributed, the rather darker colour of the upper part being due to the presence of more humus above than below. The lack of clear zoning is in part due to the action of earthworms, which are numerous in such soils and continually work the profile over, mixing it thoroughly in the process.

Brownearths vary from rather dense, acid, almost podsolic types at the northern and western boundaries of their range, through the richer, deeper varieties, with a marked crumb-structure in the continental (C.2) climate zone with warmer, drier conditions, to paler, rather more highly coloured (yel-

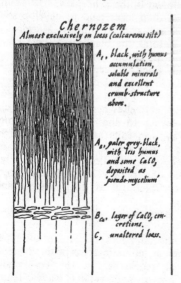

Chernozem
Almost exclusively on loess (calcareous silt)

A_1, *black, with humus accumulation, soluble minerals and excellent crumb-structure above.*

A_2, *paler grey-black, with less humus and some $CaCO_3$ deposited as 'pseudo-mycelium'*

B_{Ca}, *layer of $CaCO_3$ concretions.*
C, *unaltered loess.*

Fig. 23. Three characteristic soil-profiles: podsol, brownearth and chernozem.

lowish or reddish) soils, poor in humus because of the increasing summer drought, with approach to the Mediterranean (B.1) climate zone. They are also affected by the nature of the bedrock, richer and more fertile on the more calcareous or basic rocks, less so on the more acidic or siliceous. Many form rich agricultural soils.

In North America the brownearth zone is interrupted by the Rockies and their rain-shadow to the east. Indeed, because of the western Cordillera, soil-zones in both Americas tend to run north-south rather than east-west.

In the continental interiors large areas are covered by blackearths (Chernozem), frequently developed on loess, a wind-accumulated, porous, fine-grained silt of glacial origin, rich in weatherable minerals. Here there is pronounced continentality of climate (C.2) with insufficient rainfall in many areas to support forest. The same relative shortage of moisture ensures that no material, either mineral or organic, is lost to the ground-water by solution, so that both humus from the grassland vegetation and minerals, even soluble potash-salts, valuable as plant-food, tend to accumulate. The profile (Fig. 23c) shows a soil of magnificent crumb-structure and often of great depth, deep black above, greyer below, with a zone of calcium-carbonate enrichment in the B-horizon.

Even bedrocks less fertile than loess tend to develop soils of similar type under these sub-arid conditions. Marginally, where precipitation is less in total, the blackearths give place to chestnut-soils, red-brown in colour owing to their only slight humus reserves and much poorer vegetation. Westwards, into the more oceanic zone, blackearths grade into brownearths.

Round the Mediterranean and elsewhere under a B.1 climate soils become poor owing to the prolonged summer drought, highly coloured by iron salts and with only slight humus. Bright red or yellow loamy soils, called rotlehm and braunlehm, are the usual types, shallow, with indistinct horizons. They merge into the poorer brownearths where precipitation is a little more plentiful at their western and northern margins.

Next comes the world desert-belt, with poor, immature climax-soils, if any.

In the tropical and equatorial zones two main soil-types prevail. In the A.3, continental, climatic areas with savannah vegetation are the tropical redearths. In the continually moist equatorial regions brown and yellow clayey loams occur. Under rain-forest the latter are largely concealed by the deep, black humus accumulations from the luxuriant vegetation. The red colour of the savannah soils is due to sun-heating in the long dry season, whereby iron hydroxides are dehydrated to haematite. The brown and yellow loams are the result of intense chemical weathering under hot-moist conditions. In the long run even silica dissolves, so that little but iron- and clay-minerals remains. These are, in the presence of continual moisture, fully hydrated, the iron as limonite, whence the colour. In the case of these tropical soils, the nature of the bedrock is relatively unimportant. So few minerals can resist continual leaching with hot water that in any rock at all the end result is practically the same. Thus, the climatic factor here has overwhelming control.

Soils on limestone bedrocks, on the other hand, are strongly influenced by the peculiar character of the parent material, save under the above extreme tropical conditions. The characteristic type from the temperate zone is the rendsina —a generally shallow, grey-brown to black, crumbly, humic A-horizon lying directly on the calcareous C, with very little transition. Earthworms are plentiful and the crumb-structure is almost entirely due to their castings. Since the whole of the A-horizon is continually being worked over by them and because, in their deeper excursions, during frost or drought, into the fissures of the bedrock, they pick up much calcium carbonate and bring it to the surface in their castings, the humus is intimately mixed and chemically combined with it. Rendsinas vary from a rather pale brown, immature, dry-climate variety to the very black example described above, from an oceanic environment. Though shallow, they are fertile soils.

In warmer, more summer-dry conditions, not only is there some check through drought—always a hazard on limestones, which are notably porous—to the fullest development of the vegetation, but such humus as it does produce tends to be rapidly oxidized. All limestones contain at least a small percentage of sandy and clayey iron-stained insolubles and, with solution under weathering of the bedrock, this accumulates in the soil-profile. In a rendsina it is mixed with and masked by the dark colour of the plentiful humus, but if the humus development is checked, it forms a shallow dense loamy soil, yellow or reddish in colour, sticky under most winter conditions, iron-hard and cracked in summer. This is called *terra fusca* (Ital. dusky soil), and corresponds with a braun-lehm on a silicate bedrock.

In the sub-tropics, where it may undergo even severer summer baking, the iron- and clay-minerals of the terra fusca lose their chemically bound water and the colour turns to a bright brick-red while the consistency is altered to that of a dry, granular earth, not sticky even when wetted—a *terra rossa* (Ital. red soil). Owing to lack of humus and the initial small variety of minerals, both these are poor, hungry soils from the agricultural viewpoint.

Soils, in view of their varied origins in the natural rocks and supply of mineral plant nutrients, have a considerable direct influence on the vegetation which grows, or is able to grow, on them. Proceeding today by rail or road across a small country like England, of fairly uniform climate, comparatively low relief, but exceedingly varied geology, the observant traveller will be struck by the quite frequent and abrupt changes in vegetation and land-use, even within a distance of a few hundred miles.

Travelling from London to Holyhead (see geological map, p. 101) one crosses the geological 'grain' of the country and traverses a great number of different rock-outcrops. The older parts of London itself and its constituent villages were built on river-terrace gravels, the newer suburbs, perforce, on London Clay. The immediate riverside may have been swamp and fen in ancient times and the gravels and clays would have carried thick mixed oak forest on acid brownearths. Heading north-westward beyond the urban limits the traveller passes gravel-capped low hills on the summits of which oak-woods give place to thinner forest, with birch and pine, on lighter podsolic brownearths. Soon he is mounting the gradual rise of the Chalk dipslope of the London Basin, in the Chiltern Hills, where the soil is rendsina and the woods largely beech. As he reaches the crest, there lies at his feet a narrow strip of Gault Clay and Greensand, the latter a poor, siliceous bedrock, with a full podsol the typical soil, though here, close to calcareous wash from the Chalk, not so impoverished as in the wider corresponding belt in the Weald.

Beyond lies the Jurassic vale, with Oxford Clay, bearing oak-forest in earlier days, now rich plough and meadow land with tall elms lining the hedges. Past Edge Hill, in oolitic lime-stone, with woods of beech and ash, the traveller crosses a belt of Lias limestones, marls and cement-stones, leading to Birmingham. Here the soils are very red brownearths on

Triassic and Permian marls and sandstones, which, with minor changes to pale sandstones, dark shales and fireclays on inliers of the Coal-Measures, extend to Chester. Turning west here, he crosses more coalfields in Flintshire, then a strip of Lower Carboniferous Mountain Limestone in the Clwydian Hills, today open sheep-walks. Across older, dark Silurian shales which form moor and poor grassland, he passes the Snowdon range on his left. This range consists of igneous intrusions through Cambrian and Silurian rocks, and is mainly bleak moorland sheep-country. Soon he crosses the Menai Strait to Anglesey, which is lavishly striped across his route with Pre-Cambrian, Lower Palaeozoic and igneous rocks. In this journey we have ignored the superficial drifts, boulder-clays and alluvia of Pleistocene and Recent age, which will certainly have given yet more local variety to the soils and vegetation to be observed.

What we see today in the thickly populated cool-temperate zone are man-made landscapes—land which would naturally be largely covered with deciduous forest but which has been cleared, opened up, drained, fenced and cultivated or grazed, much of it for at least the last two thousand years, some of it, perhaps, for twice as long. During this time the soils have greatly influenced the patterns of settlement and land-use. Before man became an agriculturist and grazier in Neolithic times, the nature of the soil concerned him directly very little, but via the natural flora which it supported it nevertheless formed an important, if hidden, factor in his environment.

In the lower valleys of the great rivers of the Near and Middle East—the Nile, the Euphrates/Tigris and the Indus, for example—the soil is a pure river-sediment of great depth and fertility. Though the lands through which these rivers flow are for the most part in the desert or sub-arid climatic zones, their headwaters are in mountains or highlands, on which the seasonal rainfall is heavy and concentrated, so that regular annual floods, bearing large quantities of rock- and soil-material in suspension, overfill their channels and spread out like lakes over their wide flood-plains. Thus checked in its headlong career, the flood-torrent becomes an extensive, if shallow, almost stagnant, sheet of water. Much of it is absorbed by the soil, parched by the perennial drought save when flooded, and there is deposited on the surface a layer of fresh sediment which, being at least in part eroded soil-material, not only contains fresh minerals, but has a content of already humified organic matter. When the excess water has receded, been absorbed or has evaporated, the whole surface of the flooded area has its cover of new fertile silt, while the subsoil has gained a reserve of moisture which it can retain for months.

This, then, provides ideal conditions for settled agriculture. Crop after crop may be taken from the same patch as long as the deep water-reserve holds out. Next season's flood not only replenishes the moisture but restores depleted minerals and humus, so that no fallowing, manuring or crop-rotation is needed to maintain fertility. This natural irrigation was first exploited in Egypt by the Early Predynastic people in the first half of the 4th millennium B.C.

Similar conditions obtain in the Ganges/Brahmaputra, Hwang Ho and Yangtse Basins, and in the Mississippi valley, in subtropical and temperate climes. Great tropical rivers, like the Orinoco, Amazon, Niger and Congo, also supply vast volumes of silt in flood-waters, but the equatorial rain-forest covered all, so that until comparatively modern times no plant under human protection had any chance of competing.

Nowhere else has Nature been so accommodating in the matter of automatic renewal of soil every year. The earliest Near-Eastern cultivators (c. 600 B.C. at Jarmo), living in mountain foothills outside the great river-basins, must have learned in the school of hard experience that cleared land, even given an adequate water supply, would yield a crop only for a short time before becoming exhausted and that prolonged rest was required before it could be used again—if ever. Once the natural vegetation had been destroyed and the reserve of fertility used up, in many places the exposed soil would gully and wash away in the rainy season or blow away in the dry, so that there was only barren sub-soil left, incapable of supporting anything but scrub and cactus.

The Danubian Neolithic colonists of Europe about 4400 B.C. brought their destructive catch-cultivation practices from their eastern homelands. Their numbers were at first small and their agricultural equipment primitive—ground stone axes and hoes with more perishable implements of wood, bone or horn. The loess-lands of eastern Europe, along the ridges bordering the river valleys, offered deep, fertile, well-drained soils of blackearth or richer brownearth character, not heavily timbered and therefore easily cleared. The heavier, moister soils, in contrast, carried thick forest and swamp and were avoided. The coincidence of the early Neolithic settlement pattern and the distribution of loess is striking.

When their first fields ceased to produce a satisfactory crop they would move on to virgin land, slash off the natural vegetation-cover, burn it where it lay at the end of the dry season and, when the rains came, put in a crop. The ash from the burning was an useful fertilizer. As fresh tribes settled the land ahead, those older colonists forced to move on by the exhaustion of their fields would have to pass through the newly cleared territory in front of them until they came to suitable, unoccupied, virgin land, and so the onward migration pressed forward. The farther north and west the newcomers penetrated, the less fertile did they find the virgin soils in the brownearth and podsol belts and the more often would they be obliged to move on. This frequent shifting of ground made for speedy penetration by the Danubians, so that they reached even the Rhineland and Dutch Limburg by about 4000 B.C. There was, of course, no competition for land at this early stage in the growth of the new food-producing economy. In the deciduous forest zone even the lighter soils, under increasingly oceanic climates as they moved westwards, would recover fairly rapidly and within but a few decades regenerate secondary forest without catastrophic erosion. In the Mediterranean climatic region, however, the natural evergreen forest, once destroyed, did not recover in a short time, but gave place to eroded slopes and scrubland. The soils, often already over dry and humus-poor, became more impoverished yet, so that the longest-cultivated Mediterranean lands—Palestine, Anatolia, Greece, southern Italy and the islands, for example,—became agriculturally exhausted, a condition from which they are only today recovering under modern scientific soil-reclamation schemes and conservative management. To the perpetuation of the general deforestation and soil-devastation due to man, a large contribution has been due to uncontrolled browsing by his domestic animals.

In Britain, as we have seen, the Chalk lands offered to Neolithic immigrants *c.* 3000 B.C. a soil-environment similar, if less rich in varied minerals, to the Continental loess. Other light soils, such as those of podsol type on the Greensand of the Weald and the glacial-outwash sands of the Breckland in East Anglia, were already occupied by their Late

Mesolithic predecessors. The economic interests of these hunter-fishers and of the new agriculturists are unlikely to have clashed, for the sandy tracts were most unpropitious for primitive farming. The large areas of virgin mixed oak-forest on the clays and river flood-loams were of no use to either group. The contemporary warm-moist Atlantic climatic phase made higher, drier and more open sites preferable.

The succeeding Bronze Age coincided, in Britain, with a period of more continental climate (the Subboreal) with warmer, drier summers and colder winters. The exceedingly well-drained rendsina soils of the high Chalk must have been at least seasonally desiccated, so that one suspects that the Bronze Age peoples, who seem to have been more pastoral than agricultural, lived nearer to water, in the river-valleys, perhaps on gravel terraces, which would have been less thickly forested than the heavy loams. Though their cere-monial monuments, such as Avebury and Stonehenge Circles, and their burial-mounds, the round barrows, are most numerous on the Chalk, they are much more widespread and occur on a greater variety of soils than the Neolithic remains. Bronze Age dwellings, however, are scarcely known, and if they were not only impermanent huts, or even tents, it may well be that they were often sited by fords and river-confluences—exactly where, for reasons of water-supply, strategy or com-munications, most of the later inhabitants of these islands have elected to build, and so have since covered or obliterated the prehistoric traces.

The widespread and striking systems of 'Celtic fields' on the Chalk, largely attributable to the Early Iron Age, the enclosed steadings and prominent defensive earthworks on hill-tops show that this environment was still favoured by the immediately pre-Roman 'Ancient Britons'. The Subboreal drier phase had, in the last few centuries before Christ, given way to the wetter, more oceanic conditions (Subatlantic) which still prevail. Early Iron Age hand-tools and wooden ploughs were still inadequate to work the heavier soils, though the possession of iron implements—axes, bill-hooks and so on—enabled them to clear woodland and to construct buildings and defences with substantial timbers. Unlike the Neolithic people, they were thus much more adaptable to varied types of country, soil and livelihood, and the Romans found a numerous, sturdy and well organized, if technologically much less advanced, population to oppose their penetration and harass their flanks and rearguards.

Roman civilization brought the iron-shod plough and for the first time made practicable the cultivation of heavier soils, such as those on river floodplains and in the clay-lands of (for example) the London and Hampshire Basins and the Weald. Even in the Middle Ages soil-management was dependent on periodic fallowing to restore fertility. Crop-rotation and fertilizers, other than dung and lime, are modern developments.

All over the world, in earlier times, shifting agriculture was necessary outside the alluvial river-valleys. Exhausted soils might never have the opportunity to regenerate once their natural store of fertility had been used up. The results of single-cropping and inadequate restoration of humus have been seen in our own time in the Dust Bowls of the New World and in many parts of Asia. Man thus becomes a potent factor in influencing his own environment through the soil, to impoverish it by living on its capital or, by skilful management, to improve poor soil and make it yield many times what it would have done without human intervention. Only recently has science learned that the traditional destructive processes may be painfully reversed by contour-ploughing, mixed cropping, shelter-belts of trees to check wind-erosion, and adequate artificial additions to prevent exhaustion of plant foods. Much of the world is still cultivated in primitive and inefficient ways. Man will have to continue improving and conserving his soil-environment if his increasing populations are to avoid starvation, even in this scientific age.

Large areas of the world which are now desert or semi-desert were, in the past, fertile, well-watered lands. Desiccation by gradual climatic change we cannot prevent even today, but the fact that once these areas grew crops proves that if only the necessary water can by some means be provided, there is nothing lacking in the soil itself if erosion has not removed it altogether. This is being actively demonstrated, for example, in the drier parts of Israel, among other arid regions which are being intensively studied.* Irrigation, by damming rivers and by drawing on subterranean sources, is today successfully practised in many parts of the world where natural rainfall is inadequate. Modern irrigation mainly depends on huge civil-engineering undertakings—dam-building, tunnelling or deep drilling for water. The ancients had not these technical facilities, but irrigation in a smaller way—

* See for example: *A History of Land Use in Arid Regions,* ed. L. Dudley Stamp, 1961, UNESCO, Paris.

such as drawing off river-flow and the output of springs in oases and distributing the water by artificial channels to areas not naturally favoured—is an ancient device to increase cultivable acreage. 'Cursed is he that diverteth his neighbour's watercourse' seems to us, in the temperate climates, a great exaggeration of a not-too-antisocial action. In arid lands, diversion of water is not merely robbery—it may spell ruin and starvation to the owner of the parched field.

Fossil Soils

Since the type of climax-soil depends so far on climate and the nature of the parent rock, and since the parent rock still remains to be examined by us today, any ancient soil that by some circumstance, has been preserved as a fossil may give us information about the climate under which it was formed. Since, further, we know from geological and other evidence that climates have often been different in the past from what we find at the present day, evidence from fossil soils is one of the most valuable indications we have for studying climatic changes and the environments of ancient peoples.

Under a changing climate any soil exposed to the new influences will slowly begin to undergo changes in the direction of a fresh equilibrium with its environment. If the changes are large, and after they have been established for some thousands of years, the new climax-soil may show little resemblance to its former state. For a soil to become fossil, and to preserve its original character, it must, thus, be effectively removed from the influence of subsequent changes.

This most usually happens when it becomes sufficiently deeply buried, by the deposition over it of some naturally accumulated material—river-sediments, slope-wash, wind-borne dust or sand, or even a lava-flow. Soil material, though not a soil in its position of formation, may be preserved by being washed or blown into a cave or down a hillside, to be quickly buried beneath other deposits.

Whereas much of our knowledge of the course of events in the last million years depends on geological evidences from glacial features, such as moraines and climatic river terraces, these tell us only about the phases of cold climate. So also do the layers of loess which mantle a continental countryside, representing wind-borne dust accumulated in the unglaciated zones immediately adjacent to the ice-sheets.

It is the weathering-soils formed on such glacial and periglacial deposits which tell us most about the warmer interglacial periods, their durations and, by comparison with similar modern soils, the sorts of climate which then prevailed. The soils thus formed on the surface of, for instance, loess deposits, only to be gently buried by fresh loess with the onset of new glaciation, have greatly contributed to our knowledge of the number and nature of past climatic changes in continental Europe, so that a quite detailed sequence of climatic events is now known, with which we can associate what we know of contemporary human activities. The sites of such fossil soils, such as Göttweig, in Lower Austria, have even given their names to the particular phases of more temperate climate which they indicate.

Successive falls of volcanic ashes likewise lend themselves to the preservation of fossil soils. Central Mexico has, since Tertiary times, been the scene of repeated volcanic activity, interspersed with periods of quiescence, during which chemical alteration by weathering of the ejected materials could take place. The next outburst buried the weathered surface, preserving it with all its features intact, so that there, too, we can hope to obtain some valuable records of past natural events, within which to set in order the evidences of human occupation which may be found associated with them.

Petrologists, soil-scientists and climatologists will have to work closely together with the archaeologists on these problems.

Man, as well as natural agencies, is a great earth-mover. When ancient men heaped up cairns or mounds of earth over their dead, erected pyramids covering acres of land or dug defensive ditches and threw up banks and ramparts, they often covered parts, even if generally only relatively small areas, of the land-surface as it was in their time, so that all that has since happened has left the buried soil almost unaffected. By investigating these areas a growing volume of evidence is being accumulated about natural environments in times past which the archaeologists studying the cultures of ancient inhabitants of those lands cannot afford to ignore.

7
Plants

THE ESSENTIAL role of plant life in the formation and main-
tenance in fertility of the soil has already been mentioned.
The fundamental relation of the plant to all other forms of
life rests on its ability, by means of the green chlorophyll
which it contains, to synthesize, from the inorganic environment of earth, atmosphere and water, carbohydrates, pro-
teins and the multiplicity of other more or less complex
carbon compounds which all animals, directly or indirectly,
require for their nutrition. The statement: 'All flesh is grass',
written to be taken metaphorically, as showing the ephemeral
character of animal life, becomes almost literally true in
the light of modern knowledge.

Man, as an animal, with the rest of the animal kingdom,
lives by the green plant. The Eskimo, with his all-meat diet,
exists, if at several removes via unicellular animals, crus-
taceans, fishes and seals, as exclusively by virtue of the life
of green plants (in his case, the microscopic diatoms of the
arctic seas) as does the vegetarian Hindu, directly utilizing
rice and *dâl* and *ghî*.

The world's vegetation is roughly zoned according to climate, but soil also, through the parent rock, introduces
local differences of distribution of plant communities according to their chemical preferences, other things being equal.
History and palaeogeography have also played a part, for
in the north temperate zones at least the Pleistocene ice
ages played havoc with vegetation, and the variety of species
surviving from earlier ages in many parts has been severely
reduced. The long isolation of a land-mass like Australia,
for instance, has caused the development of a rich and
varied flora, very different from that of south-east Asia in
comparable latitudes.

Man himself, especially in the last few centuries, has

Ginkgo tree

changed the natural vegetation of vast areas, so that if we wish to visualize the world in ancient times we must put back on the map of today areas of natural forest, for example, which have vanished completely and will never be allowed to re-form as long as man needs the ground for crops, buildings and other works.

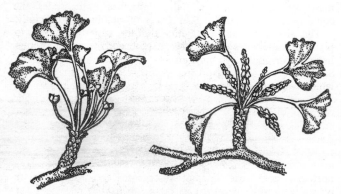

Ginkgo, female and male flowers

In Tertiary times, before the last (Alpine) phase of mountain-building, climate seems to have been far milder and more equable over large areas, far less varied, than it is today. A world-wide flora of great richness and variety then flourished, of which only relics in the warm-temperate forests of eastern continental margins (B.2 and B.2m climates) survive. In Asia especially, as in central and southern China, where the monsoon effect is strong, no catastrophic changes, even during the Pleistocene, intervened to extinguish this rich assemblage which, to some extent if not in the same variety, survives in the south-eastern United States also. *Ginkgo*, the maidenhair-tree, for one, known as a fossil in the Miocene of Greenland, survived until recently only as a garden ornament in China, the wild race being extinct. It has thence been brought back to European collections. The water-cypress, regarded by botanists as extinct, has recently been discovered living in Szechuan. This is the case with many other, less extremely marginal, survivors.

In Europe especially, the presence of the east-west barriers of the main Alpine mountains and the Mediterranean Sea left no retreat or refuge for many less hardy species of plants during the glaciations. Not only has there not since been time for those then succumbing to be replaced from farther afield, but it may well be that modern plant-competition is different from what it was in the Tertiary. Certainly it is not merely a question of present-day climate. The Asiatic magnolia, for example, formerly a widespread Tertiary inhabitant of northern Europe, still flourishes even under the conditions of northern Britain if it is re-established artificially.

The shape of the continents and the run of barriers to plant-migration seem to be largely responsible for such anomalies of distribution. In western Europe (see map, p. 94), the Scandinavian ice, advancing towards the Alpine massif, which was covered with its own ice-sheet, nearly pinched out a salient of the Eurasiatic plant-world. Barred from further retreat southwards by the Mediterranean, many temperate and warmth-loving species became extinct and have never since been able to recolonize the area. The desert and mountainous plateaux of central Asia had the same effect of an insurmountable barrier, but in eastern Asia, with increasing northern cold, the ancient temperate and warm-climate plants were able to retreat as far south as was necessary for survival and to readvance as conditions improved. Owing to the powerful monsoon influence, the continentality of climate in extreme eastern Asia was never so pronounced as it became in the west.

In North America, while the Rockies, their associated rain-shadow area and the Great Basin deserts formed obstacles to north-south plant migration, in the east no natural barriers intervened and, though the ice at its maximum extension almost reached a line from New York to St. Louis (see map, p. 95), the southern plants were able to survive to a large extent round the Gulf Coast. The end-results, in the glacial-stress zones of the two continents, have been strikingly different. While oceanic temperate Europe has its deciduous forests composed of but few species of trees, western North America, with a corresponding climate, is above all forested with conifers, some like the *Sequoias* (big tree, redwood) of Tertiary origin, known to survive nowhere else.

Vegetation zones follow those of climate closely (Fig. 24, compare climate-map, p. 81), owing to the dependence of plants on certain limiting conditions of temperature and moisture, which vary according to species.

In the Far North and on high mountains, temperature and the length of the growing season are the limiting factors. Bounding the regions of perpetual snow, more or less, to the

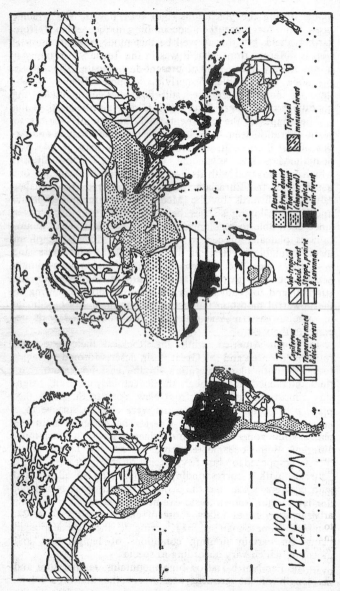

Tropical
monsoon-forest

Desert-scrub
& true desert
Thorn-forest
(chaparral)
Tropical
rain-forest

Sub-tropical
decid. forest
Steppe, prairie
& savannah

Tundra
Coniferous
forest
Temperate mixed
& decid. forest

WORLD
VEGETATION

north of the Arctic Circle, lies the tundra zone. The growing season of no more than two months enjoys continuous daylight, but is insufficiently long for upstanding trees. The vegetation consists of mosses, lichens and low, woody shrubs, such as crowberry and bilberry (*Vaccinium* spp.) with occasional dwarf birches or willows. Snow-cover in winter provides some protection from excessive frost and wind, so that even the trees have a prostrate habit. Permanently frozen subsoil, and the consequent waterlogging when the upper layers thaw in summer, check root growth, so that only shallow-rooted forms can live. Dormancy during the greater part of the year is enforced.

Towards the southern edge of the tundra scattered conifers begin, at first stunted and in small groups, then forming dense masses only a few feet high, consisting mainly of the dwarf Mountain Pine. Wind and frost tend to prune back any shoot overtopping the common level and on the close flat surface so formed snow lies clear of the ground, affording some protection in winter. This is the *taiga*, as it is called in northern Russia. It merges into high coniferous forest, which occupies a wide zone of 15 or more degrees of latitude, stretching across the northern continents almost unbroken. In Eurasia it lies, in the west, on the whole north of the 60th parallel, extending considerably farther south in central Asia and to the east. This was also formerly the case in North America, but clearance has been continuous since the first European colonization.

Pure coniferous forest next gives place, in the west of Europe, to mixed softwoods and deciduous trees, at first only

---

Fig. 24. The map represents an attempt to reconstruct the approximate distribution of natural vegetation, before it had been seriously altered by the activities of man. On such a small scale, any map must be very inaccurate in detail. Since vegetation is locally affected by all the factors of environment, only by ignoring much detail can any map be drawn at all. There are, of course, no hard lines in Nature—forest grades into parkland, into steppe, into desert, without exactly definable boundaries, and the vegetation-types which we choose to distinguish by symbols have quite arbitrary frontiers with their neighbours. The map serves, however, to demonstrate, in broad outlines, the dependence of vegetation mainly on place and on climate. The effect of relief is, on the whole, too small to be shown at this scale, though the influence of the larger and higher mountain masses cannot, even so, be overlooked. Rocks, soils, the biological factors and time are necessarily ignored completely.

birch, poplar (aspen) and willow, which are small-leaved and hardy. This assemblage is then replaced by the less resistant broad-leaved trees of the mixed oak forest, which, farther south, includes conifers only on the poorer soils and on higher ground. Most of the western part of the continent, between the Pyrenees and Scania, was so forested in ancient times. The summer-green trees, however, require plentiful moisture during the growing season and, eastwards, this zone wedges out between the more drought-resistant conifers pressing down from the north and the encroaching dry-steppe grassland. The high plateau of central Asia is, in any case, unsuitable for deciduous forest.

In North America the summer-green forest is missing in the west, where broad-leaved trees are replaced almost entirely by various conifers, which have better survived the glacial periods in the mountains. East of the Rockies the prairie-steppe marches with the coniferous-forest zone until, near the moister Gulf and Atlantic coasts, the warm-temperate forest with its more varied flora breaks in between them.

The Mediterranean evergreen forest, adapted to the long dry summer and mild winters, scarcely anywhere survives today in its natural state. Long ago cleared for timber, for fuel and for agriculture in Europe and western Asia where soils were suitable, the areas not closely occupied by man have reverted to a poor scrubland, known as *maquis*. The equivalent in California, with a similar climate, is called *chaparral*. Though the plant-species are different, the environment is very similar. Browsing animals have largely been responsible for maintaining this state of affairs. This zone, which includes all the north and east Mediterranean lands, and a narrow coastal strip of north Africa, has its counterpart not only in California but in other smaller areas (Chile, south Africa and south-western Australia) which share the very characteristic B.1 climate. Eastward in Eurasia, like the deciduous forest, it is pinched out by steppe to the north and the great desert belt.

The corresponding eastern-margin zone is the warm-temperate forest of south-eastern North America (where it survives) and of south-east Asia down to the Tropic of Capricorn, which we have already mentioned. Here, too, in crowded lands favourable for agriculture, the natural forest has been greatly reduced.

The steppe or prairie, called *veld* in south Africa, occupies large areas of the central parts of continents in middle latitudes, approximately between 40° and 50° N. In South America, steppe is represented in Patagonia and the *pampas* of Argentina. The limiting factor here is moisture, rainfall being insufficient to support trees, so that the natural flora consists largely of annual grasses and herbs with a rapid completion of growth and seeding between spring thaw or rains and the drought of high summer. The moister parts of the steppe zone, towards the forest borders, provide the world's best lands for straw-crops, the deep black soils being especially favourable. In their natural state these grasslands and the forest margins often support a rich fauna of grazing animals and are inhabited by hunting and pastoral peoples. The pampas are, today, cattle country *par excellence*.

Both the steppe and the Mediterranean-forest zones border the wide-sub-tropical desert belt, the transition being through semi-desert with thorn scrub, with other drought-resistant plants such as cacti. There is ample evidence that at least the margins of the area which now is desert have not always been so, but have been deteriorating since historic times largely as a result of human activities. Even though, during an European glaciation, large parts of arid north Africa, for instance, may have supported a relatively rich vegetation and fauna and have been suitable for human habitation, the desert zone has never entirely disappeared. It has at such times only been displaced southwards. If not actually reduced in area, the shift must have been at the expense of the tropical grassland zone.

Africa, among the other continents, most clearly shows regularity of tropical vegetation zones. Two belts, 10° to 15° of latitude in width, cross the continent to north and south of the western equatorial zone. On the drier eastern side the equatorial forest wedges out from between these two zones, which merge in the plateaux of Uganda, Kenya and Tanganyika. This is savannah, or tropical grassland, with scattered trees where sub-surface water is available. In nature, it here supports vast herds of game, grazers and browsers and their predators, the large carnivores such as lion and leopard. Here, too, are native cultures based on hunting, stock-raising and shifting cultivation. Up country, in Colombia, Venezuela and the Guianas, savannahs called *llanos* are wide-spread; on the Brazilian plateau to the south of the Equator they are called *campos* and occupy long strips of higher ground between the valleys of the great rivers. Height above sea-level and the comparatively dry climate maintain grassland here, where the moister valleys are thickly forested. In northern and eastern Australia, too, the summer-monsoon (A.3m) belt supports vast areas of grassland, used here, as elsewhere, for cattle-breeding and meat-production.

In the equatorial belt we find, in the lowlands and river-valleys, tropical rain-forest (A.1 climate), the *selva* of South America. With ample moisture at all seasons and high temperatures all the year round, vegetation runs riot and the variety of species is enormous, many being still undescribed. The canopy-layer is composed of tall timber-trees, often over 100 feet high, with a crown of foliage but unbranched trunks. Beneath grow smaller trees and tree-ferns, all being inter-laced and festooned with creepers and herbaceous plants (epiphytes) which grow on the branches and trunks of the others. On the forest floor the light is dim and there grow ferns and plants specially adapted to grow on the masses of decaying vegetation (saprophytes) in conditions of reduced illumination. Man has long made clearings and burned forests for cultivation and to extract timber, thereby disturbing the natural climax in many places and over considerable areas in our time. Secondary forest here replaces the high timber and would gradually revert to its original state if left to itself.

To north and south of the true equatorial forest, especially in coastal areas and in the Far Eastern monsoon belt, there is tropical forest with a marked dry season. This is luxuriant, but far less dense and with fewer different species. The jungles of India, Burma and the Far East are largely of this character. Fire is a serious hazard in the dry season. It appears, however, that modern sâl and teak forests are to some extent man-made, in that the natural propagation of these valuable trees at the expense of variety of species is favoured by occasional burning, accidental or otherwise, of the undergrowth, the larger trees being themselves somewhat fire-resistant.

Man's relation to his plant environment has always been a very close one. In the earliest times, perhaps in the Mio-cene, his forbears had separated from the apes. These, pursuing their own course of separate evolution down to the present day, have always been forest-dwellers in tropical conditions, living on the luxuriant produce of the rain-forest—fruits, buds, shoots and so on—available at all seasons for the taking. If it was the dwindling of the forest that made the first pre-Hominids descend from the trees, they doubtless continued at first to seek a vegetarian living where it could be found—roots, foliage, berries and seeds—until forced by necessity, when even this meagre supply failed, to feed on small animals. It seems that in the *Australopithecus* group proper, we have representatives of a carnivorous branch and in the *Paranthropus* fossils, remains of the surviving vegetarians, tied by their habits to the bush and waterside gallery-forest which alone could supply their wants. Their huge grinding teeth, often deeply worn, betoken specialization for a rough, fibrous diet. Freed from strict dependence on plant-products, the smaller *Australopithecus*-hominids could spread out into the seasonally dry savannah, learning to make and use tools and greatly widening their geographical range and adaptability to more stringent conditions.

True men, at the *Pithecanthropus* stage, were also sometimes tropical. The Javan representatives doubtless lived in a

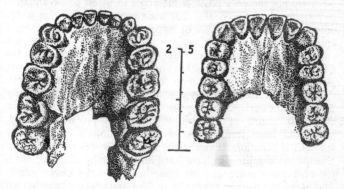

Vegetation teeth *(Paranthropus)* (left), and carnivorous teeth *(Australopithecus)*

forest environment such as would prevail there today, save for the vegetation changes caused by modern man. *Atlanthropus*, in Algeria, probably enjoyed a mild Mediterranean environment, with evergreen forest, but was certainly a tool-maker, as was the Chellean Man of Oldoway, and so probably largely carnivorous. The most northerly branch, at Peking, certainly lived on meat and endured hard winters, however pleasant and fruitful their summer temperate forest may have been. The man of Mauer, near Heidelberg, may have had rather similar, if less winter-cold, conditions. No direct evidence of vegetation is known from this district, but at so early a date (probably First Interglacial), it is unlikely that the European broad-leaved forest was as lacking in variety of tree-species as it is today, after three more severe glaciations have decimated them.

Of these, only the Peking men had fire, as far as we know. Since the Mauer jaw was found in a river-deposit, we have no means of knowing how the owner lived at home. For them, wood must have been a necessary fuel as well as a material for clubs and staves and tools. They and the rest may well have built huts or shelters of boughs and have thatched them with palm-leaf or grass against the wet or windy season. Fruits and nuts and roots, when available, would not have come amiss in a predominantly meat diet. We do not know whether they used fibres of bark for binding, but primitive peoples have always made good use of their plant-environment and if rawhide or gut makes a good lashing, these are not the only possible materials in forest or savannah surroundings. Nothing, alas, has been preserved, and one can only speculate about the use of gums and poisons, for instance, among vegetable products.

From Interglacial deposits we have the wooden spears of Clacton (Great Interglacial) and Lehringen (Last Interglacial) in Europe, both of them, curiously, of yew-wood.

A practical absence of vegetable products is also the case for the Mousterian and Upper Palaeolithic peoples of the west and centre of Europe. We have in profusion their stone and bone implements of gradually more varied and specialized functions. Even in the severe climates of glaciated Europe wood must also have been an important material, but the ubiquitous charcoal from their hearths is the only direct evidence of its use for any purpose. The flints must surely have been used for cutting and working wood, among other things.

Of Mesolithic peoples we have much more evidence. By means of pollen-analysis (p. 228), the Postglacial forest history of most of northern and western Europe is now well known. With the retreat of the Last Glaciation almost completed about 8000 B.C., the tundra and steppe which had covered even Atlantic Europe gave way to forest. Tree-species which had survived through glacial times only marginally, in sheltered valleys and along stream-courses in the south, now found more temperate, well-watered situations everywhere, while others, still less hardy, which had retreated to Spain, southern France, Italy and the Balkans, began to spread northwards and westwards again in their wake. Pine, birch, willow, aspen and mountain ash were the first-comers, with hazel and alder close behind. Then, as conditions continued to improve, and with time, the true climax-forest of broad-leaved trees, for example, oak, ash, hawthorn, elm, lime and finally beech and hornbeam—the mixed oak forest—returned. Varied as this was, in comparison with the birch-pine boreal forest, it nevertheless represented a bare remnant of the rich pre-glacial forest flora, from which the varied temperate conifers and such ornaments as the magnolia and Judas-tree were conspicuously missing. Even the sweet chestnut, widespread in southern Europe, has not found its way back to Britain in the far north-west. The tree flourishes when planted but sets viable seed (nuts) only in exceptionally warm and sunny summers. Large regions, according to soil, exposure, moisture and mere distance from the refuge-areas, from which some slower-spreading survivors had not yet had time to extend their range, were covered and still are today, by only one or two dominant species. These are represented by millions of individuals and make a pleasant picture in their summer green.

Increasing forest-cover changed fundamentally the ways of life of the human inhabitants of western Europe. Where, during glacial times, they had hunted the numberless herds of large grazing mammals of the open grassy plains, these migrated north and east with the steppe and taiga environments to which they were fitted and were replaced by the less easily located and pursued forest deer and wild pig. The forests were also haunted by adversaries dangerous to man, like bear and lynx and wolf as well as a great variety of smaller animals. More open country was only to be found by mountain and moor, fen and lake, on limestone- and sand-hills and on sea-beaches. The pervading virgin forest was often impenetrable as well as dangerous—very different from our generally well-kept woodlands of today. So it was that, living on forest verges, the Mesolithic peoples were trappers, fowlers, fishers, archers and boatmen.

Wood was one of their most important raw materials, and to fell and work it they developed the so-called *tranchet* (Fr., cleaver) axe, a flaked-down wedge-shaped tool, generally of flint, sharpened and resharpened by the skilful removal of a single transverse flake. Wood provided the hulls of dug-out canoes, paddles, tool-handles, harpoon-shafts, bows and arrows. Bark made them fishing-lines, nets and cordage. Birch-bark, in particular, furnished a large variety of boxes, pouches, trays and domestic vessels, as well as an adhesive in the tar or pitch which it exuded when it was heated. They made living-platforms and landing-stages by lake-sides with stakes, and brushwood behind them trodden into the mire, and on these they may have erected tents or shelters, thatched and walled with reed.

All this, as well as their stone equipment, we know from sites now buried in peat, which has preserved quantities of larger wooden objects and vegetable remains as well as the microscopic pollen, whereby the botanists can describe the contemporary forest and herb flora.

Tranchet axe

Hazel-nuts they ate in quantity, and no doubt gathered and stored them, for they are valuable food and plentiful, though their season is a short one. Other wild fruits and seeds they must have collected and used also when available—acorns, beechmast, raspberry, strawberry, crab-apple, blackberry, bullace, sloe, bilberry and others—palatable enough and indeed nourishing, but which, save by country children, are generally scorned and scarcely recognized today as potential food. In southern Europe, with a sunnier climate than the cool-oceanic north-west, the more delicate and nutritious chestnut and walnut would have been there for the picking up. Bulbs and corms, roots and fungi, foliage, stems and seeds of herbs as well as of trees must have served at times to furnish forth meals and stores.

All these natural products in their varying seasons call for intimate knowledge of the locality and appropriate time for their gathering and must have involved considerable travel for each family or tribal group exploiting them. It is likely that the sites, even such as Star Carr in Yorkshire or the numerous Danish stations, which have yielded the richest environmental information for the archaeologist, are only seasonal camps, occupied for the few days or weeks in every year during which they offered prospects of a particular harvest, vegetable or animal.

Where and how the Mesolithic peoples wintered we do not know for certain. Perhaps they travelled southwards and lived in earth houses during the colder and wetter months. The Abinger (Surrey) settlement rather suggests a more sedentary dwelling than most. Shallow pits dug in the sandy soil were covered with skins or thatch supported on poles. If the roofs were sound and a good fire was kept going within, these dwellings may have been quite dry and sheltered. Caves doubtless sometimes provided the necessary shelter, but are chiefly confined to areas with hard limestones as bedrock. Sheltered coves and coastal sandhills, with the sea's food always close at hand, would have recommended themselves. In Denmark the shell-mounds perhaps represent the sites of such winter settlements. Off rocky coasts, even seaweeds provide nourishment—the 'carrageen moss' and dulse, for example, still eaten locally in Britain.

The forest edges, especially where there were evergreens, such as holly, yew and conifers, would protect from gales and provide materials for shelter, cover and winter industries. A turf or wooden cabin roofed with a few poles and covered with skins or some sort of thatch would make reasonably snug winter quarters and, once abandoned, leave little enough trace for an archaeologist to find and recognize as an artificial structure.

One of the archaeological marks of the transition from a migratory gathering, hunting and fishing economy to the more sedentary life of a cultivator is the 'polished' stone axe, adze or hoe. This is, among other things, a sign of the serious necessity for an improved wood-working tool. The Mesolithic tranchet-axe, quickly made by flaking flint to a sharp-edged wedge, was but a clumsy tool, liable to jam in its own cut as often as not, and, owing to its inevitable asymmetry, incapable of work of any degree of precision. The ground axe, of some hard but fibrous and tough crystalline rock, represented a far higher degree of care, planning and patience in its preparation and, once made, was no doubt prized accordingly and kept in sharp condition. Smooth, at least as to its cutting edge, it would make a clean cut and could be easily recovered after each stroke in felling trees. Asymmetrically ground like a chisel and mounted at right angles to the plane of its haft, it made an adze, for hewing, shaping and smoothing timbers—necessary jobs for the quite intricate joinery in framing a more or less permanent building, to be fixed without nails of metal, or for erecting a post-and-rail fence for the corral. Similarly fixed on a longer shaft, it became a hoe for breaking the ground before sowing.

The plant world thus became at once of prime importance to the early cultivators. First the natural vegetation had to be cleared from the land, and felling, drying and burning the brushwood where it lay was the easiest way of achieving this. No doubt, in the process, the experienced man lopped and topped the longer and straighter trunks and poles, saving them for the innumerable construction jobs in which they would be needed about the house and steading—posts and tie-beams, ridges and rafters, gate- and fence-posts, perhaps a protective stockade.

Where timber, even for the frame of a house, is lacking, as with the Ma'dan of the Lower Tigris marshes, even long reeds tied in bundles may be made to serve. These are set in the ground in opposite pairs, bent inwards to overlap each other and so tied, forming a strong arch. A series of such arches, joined by longitudinal reed-bundles lashed on, makes the house-frame, which is then covered with reed matting. Exactly this type of house was used about 4000 B.C. by the early Sumerian settlers at Al'Ubaid not far away on the Lower Euphrates.

While the house was a-building, some of the Neolithic family or party would be hoeing a patch of burnt-off land and putting in the seed—wheat, barley, beans or whatever staple cereal they had, according to their country and traditions. Before the blades or first shoots showed they would have to fence and protect the coming crop from animal marauders—in Europe, wild cattle, pig and deer, only to mention rooks and pigeons among the even more numerous and voracious birds. The children would be out from dawn to dusk acting as bird-scarers until the crop was well and truly up and growing. So things would go on until harvest, apart from necessary weeding. The wild flora would still be required to provide firewood, timber, thatch, hurdles, basketry, fibres and the berries, fruits, nuts and herbs which all country folk collect for current use and storage when Nature provides them gratis.

With the maturing of their crops, police-work would have to be redoubled. Wild creatures know, even in advance of man, when the peas are green and juicy or the corn milky inside its coat of green, as every husbandman learns to his cost if protective steps have not already been taken. When ready for harvesting, all hands on the farm must turn out to cut, gather, bind, and carry the produce home.

This routine, or modifications of it according to crop and country, climate and culture, has imposed itself on agricultural mankind from the earliest Neolithic right up to our own day, in which a great part of the world's cultivators still grows only slightly improved crops by methods little more advanced than those of our forefathers of five or so millennia since. Farmers are tied to their land for a season or two at least, even under the most primitive conditions. With shifting cultivation, they need only move house and home when the walk to new fields becomes too long for the necessary supervision to be practicable. With any sort of workable system of fallowing, manuring and rotation of crops, the steading can become a permanency and the farmer and his family settled inhabitants.

With fixed settlements, the scope of the cultivator may be extended to kinds of produce which take longer than one or two seasons to yield their return from labour expended. If the fruits of the forest are welcome when others are lacking, the crab-apple or wild strawberry are poor things beside Cox's Orange Pippins or Royal Sovereigns in your own back garden. Even with modern methods and care it takes seven years or so to grow a bearing fruit-tree from a newly budded stock, and two even to bring a new strawberry bed into full production. If it is walnuts or mulberries, the planter's children are more likely to benefit than himself! Without astonishing good luck (and, preferably, some knowledge of modern genetics), half a lifetime can pass in breeding an improved strain of most vegetables. Continuity is everything in agriculture. Most of our modern food-plants are unrecognizably different from their wild parent-species and are the result of skill, selection and, latterly, of science, applied by generations of growers to their crops.

As to how it all began, we have only recently started to discover. Cultivation presumably started with gatherers of vegetable foodstuffs and probably in the tropics. The seeds of a plant of the cucumber or melon family, for instance— conspicuous, very numerous and, in comparison with the luscious flesh of the fruit, not obviously tasty or nutritious— may well have been shelled and eaten, as they are by some peoples today. Even if usually consumed as well as the flesh, some of the seeds would often have been dropped or discarded near the dwelling of the collectors. Given the right conditions of moisture and warmth, such seeds germinate within a day or two, producing a seedling plant large enough soon to be recognized, and this might yield ripe fruit within a few weeks. The advantage and convenience of a melon-bed at her very door, instead of a natural patch of the plant only fifteen minutes' walk away but under the hot sun, would soon appeal to the primitive housewife. If the plants should languish for lack of water, she would soon learn to supply the want. Encroaching weeds would obviously tend to smother the cherished crop and so would be uprooted. Once a crop had been successfully obtained from tended plants, deliberate resowing would not be a long step. In the same way, the beneficial effect of loosening hardened soil on germination and early growth of the seed, or of a first fortuitous dressing of dung would be observed. A family at first, then a whole tribe, would adopt the convenient habit of keeping cultivated melons, performing the necessary operations to ensure their welfare at the proper times. These might well soon develop into a semi-magical ritual of set form, unquestioningly followed by subsequent generations. Such a development would have survival-value.

It is, of course, not known what plant was first cultivated, when, by whom or in what part of the world. It is likely that the idea arose independently among different peoples at different times in different areas. Thus it is considered to be certain that the cultivation of maize, among other plants, probably in Central America, was a development on its own. The plant is indigenous there and it is thought that the ancestors of practically all American Indians reached the New World from Asia in a stage of culture which knew nothing of cultivation. Had the idea been introduced, it is most likely that the main food-plant of their homeland would have accompanied them.

Some stages in the early cultivation of maize have recently been described from dry caves in Mexico. Most attention has been devoted to discovering the development of cultivated cereals, but green vegetables, oil-seeds, fibre-plants, fruits, drugs, dyes—all must have their own histories.

Cultivated wheats: Einkorn, emmer, spelt

Wild grain was, no doubt, collected and stored long before the idea of cultivation arose. It is evident, therefore, that cultivation must have begun in an area where the parent-grasses of our cereal-plants existed in the wild state. In the case of the Old World cereals, wheat and barley, the possible parent-species are known today only in the Near East, from the area south of the Caucasus and in Abyssinia. The pre-Pottery Neolithic inhabitants of Jericho (Jordan) and Jarmo (north Iraq), the earliest known settled peoples (*c.* 6000 B.C.), used flint-armed bone sickles, but it is not known for certain whether they were cultivators, for these implements may have been used only to reap wild cereals or grasses for bedding, thatch, or fodder. Carbonized grain, certainly cultivated, is known from Egypt and Mesopotamia (4000 B.C.). It differs distinctly from any known wild species and may already have been in cultivation long enough for artificial selections, doubtless unconscious, on the part of the growers, to have produced the changes observed. Deliberate selection for desirable characteristics probably came much later. The mere actions of reaping and gathering, for example, would favour unconscious selection of ripe ears with a stronger rachis (axis). Those more brittle would break at a touch and scatter their grain irrecoverably, so that the harvest and the next year's seed would favour the produce of ears with a strong rachis. This feature, common to all cultivated cereals, would actually be disadvantageous to the survival of a wild grass, militating against the ready dispersal of its seeds.

Cultivation of cereals, especially wheat, first spread to eastern Europe with the immigrant Danubian Neolithic people and was being practised even in Britain by about 3000-2500 B.C. The evidence is not only in the shape of charred grain and parts of actual ears and spikelets, but in impressions of them in pottery, made by chance when the clay was still soft before firing. These impressions, made permanent by the firing, are still clear enough to be studied by botanists.

Oats and rye are thought to have originated in Europe in Early Iron Age times as weeds among more valuable cereals, their grain being threshed with the rest of the crop and re-sown in following years. This time (800-500 B.C.) in northern Europe was marked by a deterioration in climate (known as the Sub-atlantic phase) from its Postglacial optimum. Conditions became more oceanic, as they remain today—cooler and wetter—so that the introduced cereal crops, of Mediterranean or sub-tropical origin, sometimes failed because of cold summers or for lack of sun to ripen them. The related, but more hardy, graminaceous weeds in the field might nevertheless have set seed and have been gratefully gathered and eaten by farmers faced with starvation through crop-failure. Thus, in time they would of themselves have entirely replaced the original crop, or even have been knowingly adopted and improved for their own sake, in regions where wheat and barley were uncertain yielders.

What was disastrous to northern Europe may have proved a temporary blessing to north Africa. In Roman times, but a few centuries later than the onset of worst conditions in the north, north Africa had become the recognized granary of the Empire. Since then, however, throughout the Mediterranean and Near Eastern region, there seems to have been progressive desiccation up to our day. Although civilized man himself, by deliberate deforestation, injudicious single-cropping and by allowing uncontrolled grazing by animals, has affected the water-conserving power of the land and largely contributed to the spread of desert, there may be a climatic factor also.

We have learned today that it is at our peril that we interfere on any large scale with the natural vegetation in certain marginal areas. Strenuous efforts are being made by international organizations to make good some of the careless and ignorant damage of recent centuries and to restore where possible the productive conditions of the recognizable historic past. We have realized that world vegetation is a valuable asset which our growing populations cannot indefinitely squander without letting in the desert, to their own undoing. Oil and even atomic energy cannot yet directly create food as can the sunlit green plant, growing in suitable conditions of soil and moisture.

8

Animals

THE MOST primitive surviving cultures, such as those of the Australian aborigines, the Bushmen of south Africa or the Eskimo of the Far North, are based on hunting and collecting food in an unaltered natural environment. There can be no doubt that until man discovered or adopted from others the arts of cultivation and stock-breeding, so becoming a food-*producer*, all our European ancestors of the remoter pre-Neolithic past were mainly hunters. The purely vegetarian gatherer can find enough for his own and his family's year-round needs only in certain greatly favoured tropical environments.

Hunting, as we have seen, probably began when man's ancestor was 'cast out' of this sort of Eden by the gradual withdrawal from around him of the climatic conditions which made such a Garden naturally possible. His first animal food probably consisted of insects and their larvae, lizards, frogs, small rodents and any larger creature, immature or senile, which he and his band could surprise, capture and kill with their bare hands. Only later, when he had discovered how to use sticks and stones as extensions of his limbs, and had learned in the hard school of experience something of the habits and weaknesses of his intended prey, was he able to overcome animals much larger, swifter and stronger than, but not so intelligent as, himself—and become a fully qualified hunter.

As a hunter for meat man was entirely dependent on his natural environment—indeed, as an animal powerless to influence it permanently, still himself a *part* of the environment and in direct competition for his food with other wild species, notably the large carnivores, which were his chief natural enemies. How to eat without himself being eaten was his chief problem, in common with the rest.

Man started with one great advantage. He was physically unspecialized, save in respect of his large brain, and so able to adapt himself with the help of his intelligence to new and unforeseen circumstances. Had he been provided with the hoofs of an antelope or the claws and teeth of a lion—equipment which he doubtless had cause to envy at certain times!—he could never have been the agile climber or the grubber of roots with a sharpened stick which he certainly had to be on occasion in order to save his life.

Starting his hunting career, perhaps on the open African savannah, at the *Australopithecus*-stage, man, in his various forms, in time spread thence into all the environments we have by now considered, in each case finding a new animal assemblage—fresh and unknown enemies and competitors—and different conditions, to which his lately familiar hunting methods had to be adapted.

Dart has claimed that *Australopithecus* used the convenient bones, teeth and horns of the antelopes among which he lived for tools and weapons. The case in point is not generally regarded as satisfactorily proven, but *ex hypothesi,* among the first implements of a primitive hunter could not fail to be such things, lying to hand in plenty as waste from former meals and usable for a multitude of general purposes—as clubs, hammers, levers, punches, scrapers—without any, or only the slightest, adaptation. A straight antelope-horn would make an admirable dagger or, on a long shaft, spearpoint, without more ado.

No convincing bone implements, or evidence of bone-working has been adduced for any man, even at the *Pithe-canthropus*-stage. The European Neanderthalers may well have used bones unadapted—it would be surprising if they did not—but among all the numerous assemblages of Mousterian flaked stone implements which can confidently be regarded as their handiwork, even bones bearing general signs of bruising or wear are uncommon and hard to interpret as purposeful tools. None with a recognizable intentional shaping for a particular operation is known.

The animal bones and teeth found as fossils in association with the implements of Palaeolithic man in geological deposits are excellent indicators of environment, since even quite small fragments often enable the recognition of species, or at least of genera and families represented. If the fossils are reasonably plentiful, a quite long list of species may be compiled. However incomplete this is sure to be, what there is may be taken to represent the animal assemblage, the fauna, characteristic of the contemporary environment. It is a fair assumption that the habits and environmental preferences of the Pleistocene mammal species which are still living were much the same in the past as they are today. For those types which are extinct, the character of their ancient associates and the habits of their nearest living relatives will probably give some guidance. In the case of non-mammalian, and indeed invertebrate, animal remains, the assumption will be fully justified. Land- and freshwater-molluscs, for instance, had already reached their maximum diversity in the Tertiary and have evolved scarcely, if at all, during the last million or two years. The ecological preferences of the living species of snails and freshwater shellfish are sufficiently well known for their remains in geological and archaeological deposits to be useful indicators of environment. Here, it is not so much the individual species which may, or may not, be present—though there are some critical species which may be significant in isolation—but the total assemblage, and the relative proportions of the component species, that are important.

The history of animal assemblages in its outlines resembles that of the vegetation, having been affected by the same major natural changes during the Pleistocene—in particular, in more northern latitudes, by the alternation of glaciations and the intervening phases of more genial climate. In the absence of large land-areas in the higher latitudes of the Southern Hemisphere and the narrowing of the continents of America and Africa towards their southern extremities, the thermostatic effect of the oceans and the unhindered exchange of air- and water-masses between lower and higher latitudes prevented the development of ice and extreme cold, save in Antarctica, where it was too far from any other land to have much influence. Wetter periods, called 'pluvials', and intervening 'interpluvials' affected the tropical zones.

In the Pliocene there had been, as we have seen, mild, equable climates extending with great uniformity over vast areas. Just as the Late Tertiary floras were rich, varied and widespread, so were the mammalian faunas. They included many types of animals now extinct and some whose descendants still occupy, or in the recent past occupied, the much reduced areas of suitable climatic and floral environment which exist today. Among such areas are the great block of Africa south of the Sahara and parts of tropical, especially eastern, Asia south of the central high plateau and mountain ranges. Here, the Pliocene faunas, or their direct descendants modified by a million or so years' evolution, with some inevitable losses, still largely survive today—antelopes and other ruminants and the large flesh-eaters which prey on them.

In the earlier Middle Pleistocene, the African fauna of Oldoway, Bed II, for instance, has an extremely archaic-looking composition. Alongside more familiar forms were *Dinotherium*, an extinct relation of the elephants, with down-curving tusks in the lower jaw, which is found in Europe only in the Miocene; *Pelorovis*, a sheep with a horn-spread of 7 feet, known from nowhere else; and a pig the size of a rhinoceros! These were a little later than *Zinjanthropus*,

Oldoway Bed II. Warm savannah. Chellean man, *Dinotherium, Pelorovis, Samotherium, Notochoerus*

contemporaries of the Chellean hominid who, presumably, represents the local variety of *Pithecanthropus* Man.

Even as far north as Britain and the Rhineland the first of the four main glaciations (Günz of the Alps) did not effect any fundamental changes in the faunal situation. In the Interglacial that followed, and on through the first part of the next glaciation, during which flint-using men left their hand-axes in the valley of the River Somme, the associated fauna still had some Tertiary survivors—the great Southern Elephant, two species of two-horned rhinoceroses, hippopotamus, monkeys, a long list of deer, related to modern species but all now extinct, and a sabre-toothed large cat—among many others. This assemblage, with local variations, is found at a number of places from eastern England (the Cromer coast) through France (Abbeville), Holland (Tegelen, Limburg), Germany (Mauer, near Heidelberg; Süssenborn, near Weimar) and, at Mauer, was contemporary

Günz-Mindel Interglacial, Europe. Warm temperate forest. *Elephas meridionalis, Trogontherium, Machairodus latidens, Megaceros*

with the Heidelberg Man. These were the animals which he and the Abbevillian hand-axe makers probably hunted, though we have no direct evidence that they did so. The Chellean Man of Bed II at Oldoway, at the same cultural stage though not necessarily contemporary, seems to have been a successful hunter, by the evidence of broken bones found on his living-floors. The faunal assemblage in Europe is that of a warm-temperate forest or parkland environment, the bones and the implements being preserved in river deposits. In Africa it was savannah with a nearby lake.

The second phase of the next glaciation (Mindel II of

the Alps) was a very severe one and showed in many places the maximum known southward extension of land-ice. In Britain, for example, it covered all save the extreme south, from the Bristol Channel to the mouth of the Thames and even, in one place, invaded the Thames valley itself, at

Mindel II, Africa. Sub-tropical Mediterranean. *Atlanthropus, Hippopotamus gorgops*

Hornchurch in Essex. In north Africa *Atlanthropus* still enjoyed a warm, moist climate, as the bones of the animals found with his remains, including *Hippopotamus*, testify.

In the north the extreme cold caused the extinction of many of the archaic European mammalian species, so that when, in the Great Interglacial, temperate conditions once more returned, there were still, indeed, elephants, rhinoceroses and deer, but all of more modern types; only one monkey, no giant beavers or sabre-toothed cats. Instead we find, for instance, the modern beaver and fox, the cave-hyaena, bears, the great cave-lion (larger, but otherwise scarcely distinguishable from the modern lion and tiger), wild cattle, bison and horses. This was the time of the Swanscombe and Steinheim men, representatives of the widespread peoples who made skilfully flaked hand-axes in the Acheulean style. Several sites on the gravel terraces of the lower Thames are typical and the conditions which they indicate—forest and

Great Interglacial Europe. Warm forest and parkland. *E. antiquus,*
Macacus pliocaenica, Bison priscus, Dama clactonianus

a moist-temperate climate—are reflected over a large part
of western and southern Europe. The hand-axes and their
appropriate associated 'warm' faunas are found over most of
the tropical and temperate zones of the Old World, from
Britain to south Africa and from Spain to the Far East.

The Great Interglacial lasted for some 200 thousand years,
so that there was ample time for the establishment of a great
measure of uniformity in the distribution of species wherever
conditions were suitable. The extinct straight-tusked elephant
(*E. antiquus*), for example, with only minor variations, is
found from Britain and the Mediterranean to east Africa and
(called *E. namadicus*) in India and Java. The modern
Sumatran rhinoceros is the nearest surviving relation of the
Interglacial species of Europe, called Merck's rhinoceros
(*Dicerorhinus kirchbergensis*).

There followed another double glaciation, named Riss in
the Alps. Early in the second phase of Mindel there had
appeared in central Germany, at Süssenborn, with the last
elements of the temperate archaic fauna, some cold-climate

Riss glaciation, Europe. Cold snow steppe. *Elephas primigenius.
T. antiquitatis, Rangifer tarandus*

animal species. These included a steppe-dwelling species of elephant (*E. trongontherii*), a woolly rhinoceros (*Tichorhinus antiquitatis*), perhaps an immigrant from Siberia, and the present-day fully arctic reindeer and musk-ox, perhaps at that early time not so extreme in preferring a cold climate. With the advances of the Riss ice and renewed severe conditions, these and their descendants come into their own. *Elephas primigenius,* the woolly mammoth, even better-adapted to cold, replaced *E. trogontherii.* At Markkleeberg, near Leipzig, for example, there is, in the presence of flaked stone implements found in the gravels with the 'cold' fauna, evidence that man was already adapting himself to colder conditions also.

The Last Interglacial was, in comparison with the Great Interglacial, of only short duration—a mere seventy thousand years. By our standards, mindful of the mere ten thousand or so years which have passed since the last retreat of the ice, it was nevertheless a considerable period of time. The forests returned all over temperate Europe and the tundra-zone retreated once more eastwards and northwards, beyond the Arctic Circle, and with it, no doubt, the animals specially adapted to that sort of life. The temperate-zone fauna, how-

Last Interglacial, Europe. Warm forest. *Felis spelaea, Hyaena crocuta, Cervus elaphus, Megaceros euryceros, Dicerorhinus kirchbergensis*

ever, with few exceptions, now has a modern appearance. The outstanding species now extinct were *Elephas antiquus,* the straight-tusked elephant, *D. kirchbergensis,* the warmforest rhinoceros, *Hippopotamus* and *Hyaena*, all making their last appearances in temperate Europe. Some others, like the great cave-bear, the cave-lion and the giant Irish Deer (*Megaceros*), are also now extinct but held out into and, in the case of *Megaceros* in Ireland, even through the Last Glaciation, and all have near relations now living. For the rest, the list is much the same as that for Europe up to quite recent historical times: brown bear, wolf, fox, otter, wild horses, bison, wild cattle, pig, red deer, roe deer, fallowdeer and elk (moose) being among the most important. Ehringsdorf, near Weimar, for instance, has to show an early form of Neanderthal Man, living among, and hunting, these animals.

The three advances of the Last Glaciation (Alpine Würm) brought back, with additions and developments, the coldforest, tundra and steppe faunas, which had made their first appearance in Riss. Neanderthal Man in Europe was by now technically, and doubtless temperamentally and physiologically, equipped to withstand cold and to adapt his ways to the new conditions. Mammoth, woolly rhinoceros, bison, horses, reindeer, ibex, were his companions and his prey, which was doubtless at times disputed, as were his cave-dwellings, by animal competitors—bear, lion, wolf and lynx among the more powerful.

The Golden Age of the hunter came in with the First Interstadial of Würm, a period no longer than the Post-glacial to date and perhaps more continental in climate. The vegetation and fauna remained predominantly those of the steppes, but boreal mixed forest perhaps spread in moister and more sheltered places. *Homo sapiens* of modern type first appeared and absorbed or displaced—at any rate *re*placed—Neanderthal Man within a relatively short time.

These newcomers lived in the mouths of caves and under overhanging rocks, much as their predecessors had done—indeed, in the very same places, for their habitation-rubbish frequently overlies the layers formed in the time of the Neanderthalers, apparently without perceptible break. Some recession of the ice allowed for a considerable improvement of

Würm glaciation, Europe. Cold alpine forest and steppe. *Capra ibex, Ursus spelaeus, Homo neanderthalensis*

climate at this time, for evidence from buried soils in loess, especially in Austria and France, among the other more southern parts of the continent, suggest that it was, for part of the Interstadial at least, fully temperate in character. This is seen too in the composition of the fauna, which, if still comprising frankly steppe and taiga forms, like the horses, mammoth, wooly rhinoceros, elk and reindeer, included also some of forest and parkland, like the red deer, the roe, the pig and wild cattle.

Some of these species may have been seasonally migratory,

Würm I/II International, Europe. Temperate forest and steppe.
Homo sapiens, Equus przewalskii

so that at certain times of the year they passed in their thousands along well-defined routes. These would, of course, soon become known to the hunters, who would choose some narrow pass or valley in which to waylay them. Such are, among others, the Moravian Gate, a pass between the valleys of the Moravia and Oder Rivers, connecting the steppes of Hungary with the North European plain, and the limestone-walled valley of the Vézère in south-western France. Almost every yard of this latter was, at some time, occupied by successive cultures of Palaeolithic Man during the Last Glaciation. Among the hearths, with their flint implements and flaking-waste, which these occupation deposits contain, occur numberless bones and teeth of the animals on which they principally lived, from which the zoologist can list and study the species represented.

Würm II glaciation, Europe. Cold steppe. *Homo sapiens, Equus przewalskii Felisspelaea, Marmota marmota*

So rich and numerous is the fauna so described from these cave deposits, that it seems that the hunters had not far to go in pursuit of their quarry, the herds, at least seasonally, filing past for them to make their choice. With spear and dart and pitfall and trap the hunters took their toll, and, for a time, so easy was their living that, unlike most peoples of which we know at the hunting stage of culture, they had leisure from the mere business of getting a living to enjoy some speculation about their world and the animals which shared it. The walls of some of the deeper caves are covered with engravings cut with flint, and paintings in naturally occurring pigments like red and yellow ochre, black manganese dioxide and others. With few exceptions, these represent animals.

Since the people did not live in the depths of the caves, but in daylight, near their mouths, and because the animal-drawings are almost always in remote, dark recesses, it is evident that these often very skilled representations were not merely decorative—art for art's sake. Moreover, each clearly was, for the artist, a thing on its own—unconnected with any other which might already be there, for the cave-walls are often a veritable palimpsest of engraved lines and paint, whereby each figure partly covers, or is covered by, others. Nor, apparently, was there any attempt at erasure of existing pictures. It seems that the *act* of representation was the important thing, not the effect of the picture itself, once completed. When finished, it appears to have ceased to have any significance, for the next comer would ignore it entirely in laying out his own composition. It looks, then, as if the act of delineating must have had some important purpose, possibly a magical one, aimed at obtaining some power or influence over the creature or object depicted. Most, both engravings in line and paintings, as far as the tangle of superimposed lines can, in some cases, be interpreted at all, represent animals. There are extremely few figures of human beings—and those mostly impressions or caricatures, very different in style from the admirable naturalism of the animal drawings, at any rate in the hands of the more skilled artists. Belief in the magical influence of the act of representation would put a taboo on naturalistic drawings or portraits of human beings. Those which do exist are of personalities, perhaps deities or sorcerers, ritually presented by figures which are often evidently masked as they perform their ceremonies. Scenes involving any obvious groupings of figures are also uncommon. There are a few famous examples, but the meaning of most is often obscure, as is shown by the variety of interpretation offered by modern commentators. Some inanimate objects figure in the pictures, the most recognizable evidently being hunting weapons, others perhaps representing traps or cages.

With few exceptions, the general purpose of the drawings seems to have been to ensure success in hunting. Animals are often shown wounded by spears or darts. In the cave of Montespan in the Pyrenees there was a life-sized modelled clay figure of a bear, evidently intended to be fitted out with a real bear's head and perhaps the skin also. The body of the effigy was riddled with spear-thrusts, as if a bear-spearing ceremony, using the dummy, could guarantee the successful outcome of an engagement with the living animal, which, a cave-dweller also, doubtless was sometimes in competition with the men for winter quarters.

The south-west European cave-paintings continue into the next climatic and cultural phase—the second advance of the Last Glaciation, the time of the Magdalenian culture. Conditions now reverted to the near-arctic and the principal animals were the reindeer and other pronouncedly cold-climate forms —musk-ox, mammoth, woolly rhinoceros, steppe-horses, wolf, arctic fox, lemmings, marmots and so on. The bone, reindeer-antler and ivory implements—barbed harpoons and other weapon-points, dart-throwers—sometimes decorated with animal carvings and engravings, show the exclusive dependence of the culture on animal food and mainly animal materials. Eyed bone needles indirectly show the beginning of cut-and-sewn clothing of skins. A solitary human portrait of the period, the head-and-shoulders painting of a man in profile, on a limestone slab from Angles-sur-l' Anglin, Charente, suggests such fur garments.

The east Spanish cave-paintings, different in style from that of the Franco-Cantabrian of France and northern Spain, with its naturalism, may be later in date and clearly differ in content and purpose. They are mostly on rock-faces sheltered from weather but illuminated by daylight, and so meant to be seen by all. Stylistically, they have African affinities, resembling south African Bushman art. As well as animals, largely red deer and oxen, of more temperate climatic requirements than the Magdalenian animal assemblage of the more northern province, they depict numerous human figures schematically. These are often grouped into scenes of hunting or fighting, of dances or ceremonies. Among weapons, they show the use of bows and arrows, for which we have only indirect evidence in the Magdalenian. Their purpose was perhaps historical—recording events of note—rather than magical—seeking to bring them about. One scene represents a man gathering wild honey, surrounded by the infuriated bees—the earliest indication of man's use of this particular product, although until the introduction of cane sugar honey was the only concentrated sweetening available to anybody and correspondingly valued. Just as witchetty-grubs and ants are articles of diet for present-day Australian aborigines, and as desert-dwellers cook and eat locusts, insects themselves and their larvae must have formed a part, if generally only a small one, of the food of collecting peoples, mainly in the warmer parts of the world where sizeable insects are common.

Not only insects, but numerous other invertebrates, chiefly marine, have at all times contributed to man's menu. Snails invite the gourmet in restaurants today, but judging by the huge mounds of their empty shells found in parts of north Africa, they were at times in the past a principal source of animal food. These *escargotières* seem to belong to the same time, approximately, as the mounds of marine shells found on coasts and islands in western Europe—the period of the Mesolithic peoples who, deprived by climatic change and advancing forest of the herds of large grazers which had nourished the Upper Palaeolithic hunters of the steppes, had to turn to a more varied, and less easily obtained menu for animal protein.

We know that the Upper Paleolithic peoples took fish from rivers—there is the famous carved salmon of the Grotte du Poisson near Les Eyzies and various other engraved representations in cave-art—but it was not until early Postglacial times that fish, both marine and freshwater, became important sources of food. The numerous fish-hooks and gorges found at many Mesolithic sites and the deer-antler leister- (bident or trident fish-spear) prongs, which are the zone-fossils of the Maglemosian culture, show this.

The Azilians (early Mesolithic) of south-western France had a characteristic red-deer antler harpoon-head which must also have been a fishing implement; it had a basal hole for attachment of a line.

The taking of larger marine fish involves seaworthy boats, but the numerous species which frequent estuaries, the shallower brackish water and tidal reaches of rivers—sea-bass, flounders, whiting, pollack, among others—were more easily caught by baited line, net and spear, or trapped by weirs and creels. Among these, salmon and sea-trout, which run up rivers to spawn in the shallows of their headwaters, would be an important seasonal harvest for riverside dwellers.

The numerous lakes of recently glaciated areas (Finland today is an outstanding case) would hold stocks of freshwater fish, and these would be more easily captured from rafts or canoes than in either river or sea. Swan-mussels (*Unio* spp.) may be found in the shallows of stream and lake, by wading and feeling for them in the mud with the bare feet.

Besides fish, properly speaking, the sea is a lavish provider of invertebrate food. Between tidemarks the beachcomber on any rocky coast can easily provide himself with a meal of limpets, mussels, periwinkles and other molluscs. To one who knows the signs and is prepared to dig, sandy or muddy shores, between tides, yield razor-shells and other burrowing shellfish in plenty. Even today, cockles, whelks and winkles find an easy market. The more delicate mussels, scallops and oysters are nowadays more expensive, but not long ago oysters in Britain were a poor man's dish, plentiful and cheap. No Roman site in the country is without its oyster-shells among the rubbish. Shrimps, prawns, crabs and lobsters, among the Crustacea, are invertebrate delicacies much sought after today, over-fished round populous European coasts, but formerly much more common. Octopus is well thought of on Mediterranean coasts. All of these and many more would have been available to early man living by the sea and in it.

The species used as examples are the products of European waters, with which the writer is personally familiar. Clams, abalones, trepang and other well-known sea-foods are, to him, merely empty shells or names out of books. The reader must supply his own examples if these do not suffice as illustrations.

Prehistoric man was everywhere aware of what his environment could supply. One suspects, however, that shellfish, as a main article of food, were eaten for lack of something better rather than from choice—perhaps in bad seasons, in winter or when in unfamiliar surroundings, so that the better potentialities of the place had still to be learned. They undoubtedly afford a reserve supply of nourishment for which castaways of all times have been grateful—until they could do better for themselves.

A mark of the step to the Neolithic stage of culture which probably preceded the growing of crops and stemmed directly from the practice of hunting, as did agriculture from collecting, was the domestication of animals.

The dog seems to have been the first animal to become involved in this special relationship to man, and there is evidence from Denmark that domestication of a sort first took place there late in the Mesolithic period, at the time of the accumulation of the shell-mounds of the Ertebølle people. Authorities disagree as to the original wild species, but the wolf (*Canis lupus*) for Europe, and the jackal (*C. aureus*) for the Near East, are those most favoured.

Bands of wandering hunter-fishers would present a special opportunity to the pack of wild dog-ancestors, as providers, at and near their camp-sites, of numerous unconsidered edible trifles. At first the animals would merely be followers, scavenging around camps when the men had moved on, but given any encouragement, in the shape of direct offerings of food to the bolder scroungers, the relationship would soon become closer—a sort of symbiosis for mutual advantage: easier living for the dogs, in exchange for warning against the approach of strangers of either or any species.

It would not be long before the men, by one chance or another, acquired puppies as pets, and these, when they grew up, would be specially favoured as natural allies, their own instincts as guardians of territory, trackers and beaters of game and in giving warning of the approach of marauders being brought into man's service. While there may well have been some such alliance in Mesolithic times between dog and man, on more or less equal terms of mutual advantage, true domestication—entire subjection of the animal to man's requirements—would only ensue when man had first domesticated himself, by settling in one place and establishing territorial ownership.

The vegetarian ungulates, on the other hand, had little to gain by any relationship with man. With them, domestication probably began by man's capture of young animals alive, at first only with the object of keeping them as pets, later, when they grew up and became increasingly difficult to control, as convenient stocks of meat-on-the-hoof, to be killed when needed for consumption, but in the meantime to be protected against outside attack.

Wild sheep and goats occurred in the Near East and in Mediterranean lands. Their comparatively small size made them readily manageable, even as adults. If a number were kept together, they would breed readily in captivity and soon give rise to a flock which had never known freedom.

The same process would also apply to pigs, the wild

species being a temperate-forest animal of wide distribution in the Old World, though the adult boar, even in captivity, would remain a dangerous customer. Loosely herded in the forest margins, and not fenced, tame sows would often interbreed with wild males, and this would often, perhaps, obviate the necessity for keeping captive boars. The improvement of pigs to give the domestic varieties of today is a comparatively modern achievement. The prehistoric remains suggest beasts very like the wild race.

Cattle, too, in the form of the very large wild *Bos primigenius*, were to be found all over temperate Europe, and survived into the eighteenth century. The European bison, closely related to the North American 'buffalo', still lives at liberty in the Bialowieza Forest of Poland, where some specimens from zoological collections have been re-established. It was never domesticated, even in prehistoric times, when it was so plentiful a species.

In the Middle and Far East several other species (gaur, yak, banteng) of wild cattle may have contributed to domesticated races. The antecedents of the Asiatic domestic humped cattle (*Bos indicus*) are not certainly known, but it is possible that the kouprey (*Bos [Novibos] sauveli*), still to be found wild in remoter parts of Indo-China, is a parent. The Channel Island breeds of modern cattle, Jerseys and Guernseys, for instance, are thought, from blood-group evidence, to be descended from *Bos indicus*.

In Europe and the Near East, at least, it seems probable that most domestic cattle have a *primigenius* ancestry. It is significant that the remains of cattle, presumably domesticated, of Neolithic date are very large and closely resemble the wild species. Later, in the Bronze and Iron Ages, domestic cattle become notably small, and whether or not this is the result of deliberate selection by man for beasts more easily controllable when adult, is not yet clear. The fact, however, remains, and though the specific name *Bos longifrons* has been given to this type, a possible wild ancestor of comparable small size is not certainly known. It is generally thought to be only a race, or sub-species, of the domestic *Bos taurus*, in the main of *primigenius* lineage.

The horse and ass, until the invention of mechanical transport the chief beasts of burden in Europe and Asia, have a long history of domestication. The onager (*Equus hemionus*), a 'half-ass', was used to draw chariots in early Mesopotamia. The true horse, *E. caballus*, descendant of

steppe-dwelling species, was doubtless first tamed and domes-
ticated by nomad pastoralists in its own homeland. The
Hyksos 'shepherd-kings' of Egypt (seventeenth—sixteenth cen-
turies B.C.) owed their dominance to the horse and chariot.
The horse was brought to Europe as a domestic animal in the
Bronze Age.

Though apparently largely evolved in North America in
the Tertiary, the horse, having seemingly spread thence to
Eurasia, became extinct in America in the Pleistocene and
was re-introduced only in the sixteenth century A.D. by the
Spaniards. The 'wild' mustangs of the prairies were derived
from domestic escapees which had reverted to the wild.

The ass (*E. asinus*), native to savannah and scrub on
the desert margins, was also originally an Oriental acquisition. The several zebrine horses, surviving still in south and
east Africa, seem never to have been domesticated.

The cat (*Felis catus*) comes at several removes from the
sacred Egyptian cats, a tamed north African species (*F.
ocreata*). The Romans introduced it to Europe and to Britain, where it has doubtless since occasionally interbred with
the native wild-cat (*F. silvestris*). Other small carnivores,
the ferret, for instance, a descendant of some species of
polecat (*Mustela* sp.), have been tamed for special purposes
(in this case, combating rodents). The mongoose is partly
tamed in the East for the same reason. In Meso-America,
tame non-venomous snakes are used to keep down vermin.

Among birds, the domestic chicken derives from the
Indian jungle-fowl and also first appears in Britain with the
Romans. The farm-yard goose is a descendant of the easily
tamed wild European grey-lag goose (*Anser anser*); the duck
comes from the mallard (*Anas boschas*).

The list is far from exhaustive. In Lapland the reindeer,
in South America the llama, are used as beasts of burden.
The camel and Indian elephant are domesticated in the East.

Man's reliance on the animals for food, though important,
is not the whole story of his economic relationship with them.
It has been said of the modern pig that every part of it is
used, save the squeal! The animals which he hunted
or bred provided ancient man with a long list of valuable
materials—bone and antler, horn and ivory, hides and fur-
skins, gut, sinew and fat. He may, as did the Plains Indians
in North America, have used brains and urine for preparing
buckskin, and even dung is of value for fuel in an environment
without wood. The use of cow-dung as fuel in India is well

known and Gavin Maxwell (*A Reed Shaken by the Wind*, London, Longman's, 1957) has shown that the marshmen of the lower Tigris, the Ma'dan, keep and feed the water-buffalo, not for meat, but only for milk and—even more important—as a supplier of dung for fuel and as a cement for stopping leaks in their reed houses. Dung is nature's own fertilizer. At what point the early cultivators learned its value we do not know, but mixed farming was doubtless the economic basis of settled agriculture, obviating the recurring need to break new land.

Bone, antler and ivory were worked from Upper Palaeolithic times on to the present day and have only within our life-time been superseded by synthetic plastics as materials for combs, brush-handles and backs, knife-handles, billiard-balls and so on. Barbed harpoons and other weapon points, scrapers, smoothers, needles, fish-hooks and all kinds of ornaments from 'bâtons-de-commandement' to carved throwing-sticks, figurines, buttons, toggles and necklace-beads were made from them. Horn was doubtless so used as well, but has scarcely ever been preserved, because it so easily decays.

The strong hides of larger animals such as oxen nowadays serve as sole-leather and other durable leather-goods. In earlier days they made tents and house-coverings, groundsheets, protective clothing—even armour and shields—and, cut into strips, thongs for lashing and binding, laces, harpoonlines and any purpose for which, today, we use cordage. Rawhide, applied wet, shrinks on drying and makes the ideal lashing. Leather bottles and buckets only recently went out of use.

Thinner and more pliable skins and fur-pelts, perhaps treated with animal fat to make them soft and with urine or a lye of wood-ashes to de-hair them, then followed by much working, both wet and dry, with the hands and feet, served for garments, bed-coverings and rugs. Parchment was used in buildings to admit light, while excluding wind, until the invention of glass panes—and long after, for people unable to afford the luxury of transparent windows. The eyed bone needle for sewing was a Magdalenian invention, in part superseding the awl for finer work. Sewing thread was provided by teasing out the fibres of muscle-tendons and ligaments, or by twisted gut. Animal bladders, when inflated, made net- and harpoon-line floats; their stomachs, containers for food and fluids, bags and pouches—even contributing to the making of music, as in bagpipes and drums.

Fat was not only an essential energy-food in a cold climate, as it is for the Eskimo today, but a fuel for lighting and heating, a leather-dressing and waterproofing agent, a lubricant and an unguent, for personal use and beautification.

Animal food soon deteriorates under ordinary conditions, unless consumed soon after it is killed. Doubtless, in times of plenty, man, like his dog, gorged himself until he could eat no more; but hunger would return on the day after the morrow and famine the following week, unless there were a new kill. Our prehistoric ancestors, perhaps, were not as particular as we are about the freshness of food—they could hardly afford to be. Even if they did not dislike meat 'well hung' (i.e. in the early stages of decomposition), there comes a point for the human stomach when flesh-food becomes carrion and uneatable, if not actually dangerous to life.

There were three ways in which man could, at any rate for a time, postpone the spoilage of flesh and fish, and so have a store for times when food was scarce. In cold climates he must have observed how hard freezing would preserve meat. This would be useful mainly in lands with a frost-winter, for even temporary and intermittent thawing allows decay to proceed. Burying his frozen surplus in snow in a cave or under a cairn, to protect it from animal thieves and the sun's heat, or hanging it high in a tree or on a wooden frame beyond their reach, would serve while the frost lasted—but only so long. In hot, dry conditions, fish cleaned and filleted or meat cut into thin strips would soon become 'jerked' or dried in sun and air before serious spoilage set in. As long as it could be kept in that condition, it would last indefinitely. In climates where neither frost nor drought sufficed to preserve supplies adequately, it was found that a combination of steeping in brine, followed by prolonged smoking over a smouldering fire of green wood, chips or shavings would achieve the desired end. This is a much more complicated process, requiring not only the necessary knowledge and patience, but an industry for the production of dry salt, either from sea water or by mining, and a static settlement of houses equipped with a capacious chimney over the domestic hearth, or a special smokehouse. Thus, if it is an ancient practice, carried on even into our own day mainly for the characteristic flavours it imparts to the goods so treated, it can hardly be older than the Neolithic. Salt-mining in Europe (Upper Austria) is known to date from the Bronze Age and natural salt-pans under arid climates, as well as artificial ones made for the purpose in later times, provided the essential preservative. It may, of course, have been prepared by the expensive and laborious method of boiling down sea-water, if there was no other way, but this requires a capacious vessel, not readily available before the invention of pottery.

Animal enemies of man have at all times been even more numerous and varied than the allies and servants he has recruited from the animal kingdom to help him, and the species of use and value which he may exploit. They range from direct competitors for living-space and prey, like the larger carnivores, to microscopic but none the less deadly parasites, which cause diseases, and their larger, but usually still small, vector species, which transmit the infection. Only recently have most of the known disease-carriers, like the *Anopheles* mosquito, been recognized and appropriate steps to defeat them been taken. Others have doubtless still to be identified, but their number decreases year by year as the ever-improving armament of medical science is turned upon them.

Most of man's more obvious adversaries have long ago been exterminated, or defeated to the point where they are permitted to survive only where they can no longer do serious harm, at least in the more populous parts of the world. Even today, a man-eating tiger can terrorize several Indian villages at once. It is hard for us to imagine the predicament of a prehistoric family, armed only with primitive weapons, prevented from hunting for their subsistence because a cave-lion or bear has invaded their country and driven away the game. The alternatives were two only—either to kill the marauder or to move to other territory, beyond reach of the menace. We cannot help but see that, so ill equipped, they would often have to take the second alternative. Yet man has never willingly yielded first place to an animal. Some device must often have been imagined, and successfully carried through, to rid their world of the tyrant, short of a frontal attack, which could hardly hope to succeed without loss. As far as cave-bears were concerned, the carefully secreted skulls of several of them, found in the Drachenloch cave in Switzerland, show that Neanderthal Man knew how they might be overcome. Perhaps the possession of fire was the winning factor. So, too, it must have been, long after, for wolves also, not yet extinct in eastern Europe and Russia, but no longer the ever-present threat to man that we find constantly cropping up in the old nursery tales.

Less direct, and not so dangerous to man himself but to his crops, and so to his livelihood, were animals like elephants and pigs, among the mammals, which in a night can destroy far more than they consume. Creatures such as small birds in vast flocks, locusts or caterpillars, are just as destructive and more difficult to combat, because of their numbers.

Finally, there are the internal enemies of man himself— the intestinal parasites, the hookworm of tropical waters, the malaria and sleeping sickness organisms and their insect vectors, the legion of afflictions and diseases caused by lower animals to which man is subject. These are all parts of his biological environment, often closely tied to certain other parts such as a sufficiently high temperature, the presence of particular plants or other animals which act as intermediate hosts, and the necessary environmental factors to support them. Such enemies may sometimes prove crucial factors in the ability of a human culture to survive or progress in that environment. Endemic disease and the resultant chronic ill-health in many tropical areas is still the major obstacle to native enterprise and improved productivity which would raise standards of living among backward peoples. So it has always been in the past—a thing which, as archaeologists, we ought to recognize, even if the evidence for its incidence in particular cases is likely to elude us. So it will continue, as long as ignorance and superstition remain about matters which science today is capable of setting right, given the means.

Man in many places now controls his animal environment and has overcome the worst of his ancient enemies. Nothing now threatens him, with extinction at least, but his own species. Self control is the hardest of all disciplines, and remains for him to learn.

9

Time

ALL THE sciences relating to the Earth and its living inhabitants, vegetable and animal, are concerned with the time-dimension. Human calendars and written records, the materials of history, take us back only a few thousand years, to the early Dynasties of Egypt. Beyond that, for prehistory, and, even more, for the older revolutions of the Earth's crust, we rely on geological, palaeontological and other scientific evidence.

The geologists long ago worked out, from the super-position of strata, a detailed account of events in the Earth's past history, set in their correct order—a relative chronology. Lyell, in his *Principles of Geology* (1830-33), had contended that the vast changes to be observed in the rocks needed no worldwide cataclysmic explanation, but only the gradual operation of the geological agencies which we can to-day observe at work. These—heat and cold, wind and wave, shuddering earthquake—were quite adequate to effect the observed alterations of the Earth's face, *given sufficiently long periods of time*. The difficulty was: how to measure time-spans of the requisite magnitude.

Earlier attempts to do this, based on estimates of present annual rates of sediment-deposition in, for instance, the Mississippi delta, compared with the measurable thick-nesses of sedimentary geological formations, were far too low. Most were well below 100 million years for the time passed since the laying down of the basal beds of the Cambrian. One reason for this seems to be that today's rates of erosion and sedimentation are well above the average for geological time as a whole. Another approach was even less successful. This was based on the known salinity of the oceans, assumed originally to have been fresh but gradually having received salts leached out from the rocks composing the land masses, through geological time. The present-day accession of salt in rivers was estimated and thence an age for the oceans of some ninety million years was reached.

The stratigraphers, faced with a maximum vertical thickness of about 10 km. of observable geological deposits, among which they knew that there were many gaps, could not accept estimates of this low order but, themselves, could offer only guesses.

Little progress could thus be made until more reliable 'clocks' were procured, the use of which did not involve unverifiable assumptions about the constancy through time of rates of geological processes. The discovery of radium in 1898 and the subsequent developments, many of them only of recent years, in the fields of radio-chemistry and atomic physics have provided several new and powerful timekeeping instruments for the geologist, in the shape of radioactive forms both of relatively rare and of some common chemical elements. The fundamental advance lies in the fact that processes of radioactive decay are unalterable in rate by the application to the substance concerned of any form of energy—heat, pressure, magnetism, electricity, radiation, etc.—in intensities which we can envisage on the Earth. It is a fair assumption, therefore, that they have remained constant throughout the time-spans with which we have to deal.

Some elements, like the very heavy metals, uranium, actinium and thorium, are radioactive. Other, lighter elements have been shown to occur in several forms, called isotopes, chemically identical but some of which, generally occurring only in very small proportions in comparison with the common, inactive, form, are also unstable with time and give off radiations. By the emission of their radiations, all of these 'decay' at measurable rates, the product of the breakdown being, usually, a corresponding quantity of an inactive isotope of quite another element.

The rate of decay of a radioactive isotope is given by its 'half-life'. This is the time required for a given quantity of the active element to decay, so that only half of the original activity remains. Half-lives of particular isotopes vary between a few microseconds (10^{-6} secs.) and some thousands of millions of years (10^9 years). To be of use for geological or archaeological dating, radioactive isotopes with fairly long half-lives are required and the element concerned must commonly occur associated with the rocks or deposits to be dated, even if only in very small quantities. Of special value for dating the older geological formations are, among the heavy elements, uranium, actinium and thorium and, among the lighter, potassium forty.

The heavy elements occur in very small amounts in many rocks and minerals. Their processes of radioactive decay are complex, but ultimately result, by several stages, in residues of inactive isotopes of lead, each characteristic of the parent element. Thus, uranium-lead has an atomic weight 260, actinium-lead 207 and thorium-lead 208. Common lead, of average atomic weight 207.2, is a mixture of these and other isotopes not originating in any radioactive element (non-radiogenic lead). At each major stage of disintegration between (for example) uranium (atomic weight 238) and uranium-lead (atomic weight 206) an α-particle, which is an atom of helium gas (atomic weight 4), is given off, so that the whole process involves the loss from each atom of uranium of 8 atoms of helium (total atomic weight 32).

The half-life of uranium is estimated at 4,560 million years, more or less. From the moment that an uranium-containing igneous magma crystallizes into solid rock this process has been going on at an unchanging rate until our time, so that, assuming that the rock originally contained no lead, but only uranium, if today we measure the amount of unchanged uranium and the amount of lead produced by its decay, a simple calculation from the known half-life value will give the number of years which has elapsed since the rock was first formed. The helium-content may also be used to estimate the extent of radioactive decay, but since the element is a gas at ordinary temperatures and pressures, some is almost certain to have been lost by diffusion from the sample with the passage of time, so that helium-ages are only minimum values and so not as reliable as the lead-ages. Corrections for likely small proportions of actinium-lead, thorium-lead and non-radiogenic lead must also be applied.

In spite of some unavoidable assumptions and the necessity for such corrections, the method has, over recent years, given excellent results. It has been applied to igneous rocks of known relative ages from the Archaean to the Tertiary and the absolute ages obtained are not incompatible with the observed stratigraphical succession of the samples. We may be confident, therefore, that our dates are not impossibly far from the true values.

Thus, the oldest known rocks of the Earth's crust are dated to about 4.5 thousand million years ago. The earliest organic fossils are little more than 500 million years old. The mammals first became widespread only about 69 million years ago and the earliest undoubted fossil man dates from a mere half-million years since.

A radioactive isotope with a half-life of 1,350 million years is Potassium Forty (K^{40}), inactive potassium being K^{39}. In time, each atom of K^{40} loses an electron and, in this case without decrease in atomic weight, is converted to argon (A^{40}), one of the chemically inert gases of the helium-series. Potassium occurs in igneous rocks in the form of potash-felspars and potash-micas, so that any rock containing such minerals may be made to reveal its absolute age by estimation of the ratio between the unaltered rare isotope and its breakdown-product. *Zinjanthropus* (p. 51) has recently been dated by this means, though the value obtained, 1.75 million years, has been questioned because, among other criticisms, the underlying Lower Pleistocene basalt (which must be even older) has given a date of not more than 1.3 million years by potassium/argon, using a different technique. The K^{40}/A^{40} method is more recently developed than that based on uranium/lead, and we need many more check-determinations by different techniques before we can trust the accuracy of individual results. The order of magnitude given is, nevertheless, extremely interesting.

The difficulty about these particular timekeepers is their very long half-lives. For the later Tertiary and Pleistocene periods, back to less than twenty million years ago, in which the student of man is interested, the amount of radioactive decay which they have undergone is very small and hard to measure with sufficient accuracy. Another radioactive isotope, Carbon Fourteen (C^{14}), on the other hand, with a half-life of only 5,680 years, though admirably suited to measuring ages up to twenty or thirty thousand years ago, begins to fail for samples older than this. This is due to the extremely small residue of radioactivity to be measured. We really need some other radioactive substance, widespread in nature, preferably with a half-life of a few (under ten) million years.

C^{14} is formed in the upper atmosphere by collisions of energetic neutrons in cosmic radiation with normal nitrogen (N^{14}) atomic nuclei. The result of such a collision is the fusion of the N^{14} nucleus with the neutron and the immediate ejection of a proton (hydrogen nucleus) having a positive unit electric charge. By this event, the new nucleus still has the atomic weight 14 but is left with a net negative unit charge—a supernumerary electron. The possession of this electron gives it the chemical properties of Carbon, but with an atomic weight 14, instead of only 12, as in normal, inactive, carbon. On emission in due course of its electron, C^{14} reverts to N^{14}. While it survives, C^{14} enters, in a small proportion, into the carbon dioxide of the atmosphere, and thus into the carbon chemistry of all living matter.

Plants take up CO_2 from the atmosphere and synthesize from it sugars and all the other manifold vegetable carbon-compounds. These are taken over, when eaten by vegetarian animals, and are used to build their own tissues, which may then be consumed by carnivores. The substance of every living creature is therefore assumed to be in chemical equilibrium with the atmospheric concentration of C^{14}, itself due to a long-established balance between the rate of formation and that of decay of the isotope. (This assumption has recently been shown not to be strictly true, owing to certain systematic changes with time in the C^{14} concentration in the world's CO_2-reservoirs, especially the oceans.)

When a plant or animal dies its contained carbon is generally soon returned, by one route or another, to the common pool of atmosphere and living matter, but should any part of its substance chance to be isolated and preserved the radiocarbon in it decays at the rate of one half every 5,680 years and is no longer replaced, as it was in life, by exchange with the environment. If, therefore, the C^{14}-content of a piece of fossil wood, for instance, is determined, it is found to be less than that of similar living, or only newly dead, organic matter, in proportion to the time which has elapsed since it died. As organic materials of various kinds are used by man, and are sometimes preserved at his ancient dwelling-sites or in his tombs as well as in natural circumstances, we can use samples of them for C^{14}-estimation to date the death and burial of the material.

During the last ten years or so this method has given us numerous absolute dates for archaeological phases and natural events, occurring all over the world between about two thousand and thirty thousand years ago. Beyond this range the results tend to be unreliable. For a period of more than 5 half-lives of the isotope it involves measuring less than 1/32nd (2^{-5}) of the C^{14} originally present in the sample, which was itself a very small quantity. We have at least some well-established C^{14} dates for the later periods of European prehistory, back to the latest Upper Paleolithic, but those referring to the earlier Upper Palaeolithic stages are much less firm and open to considerable criticism.

When, under the heading of Climate (p. 91) we were considering the detailed glacial and interglacial subdivisions of the Pleistocene, their dating by Milankovitch's radiation-curves was mentioned. This remains the best time-scale available to us at present for the awkward gap existing between the usable range of C^{14}, on the one hand, and that of K^{40}/A^{40}, or the lead- and helium-dates for older geological periods, on the other. A large discrepancy at present exists between the extreme C^{14} dates and those of Milankovitch, in the area of overlap of their range in the Upper Pleistocene. Thus Milankovitch gives the date of Last Glaciation 1 as 115 thousand years before present (B.P.), while C^{14} would place it between 75 and 48 thousand B.P. The gap of 50 thousand years or so is not unimportant!

The Milankovitch radiation-dates for the glaciations, based on the computed summer minima of radiation received in Latitude 65^0 N., the zone of ice-accumulation, during the last 600 thousand years, are as follows:

		Thousands of years B.P.
Last Glaciation	3	25
	2	72
	1	115
Penultimate Gl.	2	187
	1	230
Antepenult. Gl.	2	435
	1	476
Early Glaciation	2	550
	1	590

These, of course, represent only the dates of the radiation-minima and give little idea of how long a glaciation took to build up to its maximum or for the ice to retreat and disperse when summers became warmer again. The time-lag between a radiation-minimum and the corresponding glacial maximum remains unknown. Allowing for these shortcomings, however, the events scaled by the radiation-dates obviously do, in the main, correspond remarkably well with the sequence and relative magnitudes of climatic phases in the

Pleistocene inferred from field-evidence by geologists and expressed by Penck, as early as 1909, as a curve, which is compared with that of Milankovitch in Fig. 9.

There did occur earlier glaciations in Europe than Alpine Günz, evidence for three of which have been noted by Eberl in the Iller-Lech area of the Danube basin. If Milankovitch's radiation-curve is calculated back to one million years B.P. (with less precision than to 600 thousand only), there appear on it four or more radiation-minima which may correspond with the three Donau (Danube) glaciations and some other early, probably glacial, gravels in the Alpine area, which precede Günz stratigraphically. Further confirmation of the latter half of the detailed Pleistocene chronology has been provided by the work of Emiliani on fossil Foraminifera (minute unicellular marine animals with a calcareous test) from deep-sea-bed cores. His results, expressed as a curve of water-temperature varying according to the proportions of different species of Foraminifera found, have been correlated by Zeuner with the radiation-curve as shown in Fig. 9 (p. 93).

The absolute chronology of the Pleistocene is thus seen to be very complicated, and, as yet, far from finally established in detail, though there is a large measure of agreement between various authorities on the main outlines, at least from 600 thousand years B.P. onwards. Earlier than that we have, as noted above, some European evidence for pre-Günz glacial phases. In Africa, however, it looks as if we are going to have to stretch even this long calendar to take in the apparently still older Bed I at Oldoway, for which an average of K^{40}/A determinations on several samples gave 1.75 million years B.P. There is as yet no firm definition of the date of the base of the long Villafranchian stage, formerly included in the Pliocene, but, since 1948, officially assigned to the Pleistocene. It seems possible, since Oldoway Bed I is regarded at the earliest only as Upper Villafranchian, if not Middle Pleistocene, that the base of this stage may prove to date from (say) three million years B.P., though this figure is at present no more than a guess. However, past experience in absolute dating in geology is that first estimates invariably prove to be too small. The whole Tertiary Era is nearly seventy million years long; the base of the Miocene is put at thirty million years B.P.; the Pliocene can hardly be less than ten million years long, so that a mere three million for the Pleistocene, including the Villafranchian, seems at least conceivable.

Another method of absolute dating, for Late Glacial times and the stages of retreat of the Scandinavian ice-sheet, was worked out by De Geer in Sweden. A retreating ice-sheet gives, during the summer thaw, large volumes of meltwater loaded with finer sediments, composed of rock-material ground small by the glacier. If such a meltwater-stream discharges into a lake, the coarser sand first settles out, but the grains of silt- and clay-size sink only slowly. With the onset of winter, melting ceases, the supply of new sediment is cut off and the lake may be frozen over, so that the water is perfectly still. Under these conditions, maintained for some months, even the finest clay is able to settle on top of the coarser sand and silt already on the lake-bottom. Every year's melting is thus represented in the sediment by a pair of layers, coarse, then fine, the latter being immediately succeeded by the next year's coarse sand. Such an annual pair is called a 'varve'. In numerous geological sections in south Sweden varves occur in banded sediments, often amounting to hundreds in number. All years (and so the corresponding varves) are not identical. A warm summer will give a thick band of sediment; a cool one a thinner. Particular sequences of years will give characteristic series of varves and this enables correlation between sections exposed at some distance apart, representing sediments from different stages of the ice-retreat, but overlapping at least as regards one recognizable sequence of bands. The years of retreat can thus be counted directly from the varve-plots, giving a chronology in years, but one which is not dated. To turn these figures into absolute dates requires that at least one year-event in the series be datable. This was achieved for the Swedish sediments by recognition of the widespread occurrence of a giant varve in the sediments of Lake Ragunda, accidentally drained in 1796. This giant varve according to De Geer, was the result of the release of water ponded up by the ice-sheet until the moment when it divided into two separate masses in the mountains of Sweden before disappearing entirely. Counting back from the last Ragunda-Lake varve (dated 1795) to the giant Bipartition-varve, a date for this event of about 6800 B.C. was obtained, and this was made the point of departure for the local Postglacial period. The varve of the Bipartition was recognized widely in the counted series relating also to preceding events, so that, for instance, the age of the

Central Swedish Moraine—the southern edge of the ice during a marked pause in the retreat of the Last Glaciation—is fixed by varve-counts at 7912 B.C. The preceding standstill, marked by the South Scanian Moraine, in the extreme south of Sweden, probably took place about 15,000 years ago.

A varve-chronology has also been set up by Antevs in the U.S.A. and is correlated by him with the European retreat-stages. If, as we suppose, the deglaciation was the result of extra-terrestrial causes, these must have been operative as much in North America as in Scandinavia, so that a general correspondence in time may be looked for. The details of the ice-retreat, however, will not necessarily correspond at all closely in continents with different topography lying some thousands of miles apart, so that correlation of particular features is likely to be hazardous. Here we need the support of some independent method of absolute dating, not relying solely on geological field-evidence.

Now, if varve-counts can be used to date events of the last glacial retreat, the varves themselves can have no direct stratigraphical relation to human settlements, for it is evident that contemporary men did not live at the bottom of ice-dammed lakes, or, probably, even near the ice-edge itself, though the latter is not impossible. At least one other independent relative chronology is required as the intermediary for transferring varve-dates to evidences of human occupation. In fact we have two—the successive systems of raised lake- and sea-beaches, associated with the glacial retreat, and the sequence of floral changes caused by improving Post-glacial climate. This sequence may be demonstrated by plant-remains preserved in the strata of peat-bogs and organic lake-sediments, especially by fossil pollen (see p. 228).

Relative sea-levels may change by local rising or sinking of the land, by a rise or fall in water-level or by unequal movements of both land and water. World sea-levels are lowered appreciably by the immobilization of water, ultimately from the oceans, as vast ice-sheets on the land, during glacial periods. They are raised again by the release of meltwater on deglaciation. This worldwide *eustatic* movement is complicated in and near the actually glaciated areas, by some local sinking of the land under the burden of its ice and its subsequent recovery when the load is once more removed (*isostatic* movement). The loading effect is obviously greater, and the recovery more marked, near the centre of glaciation. The net results of these two contrary effects, operating at different rates during different stages of glaciation and deglaciation, are complicated and, for the Baltic region, where they are of prime interest for their connections with the varved sediments, we have a known sequence of events during the last glacial retreat whereby the Baltic Sea was at one time flooded by the ocean and more or less salt and at another cut off from it as a freshwater lake at a somewhat higher level. These situations depended on the existing relative levels of land and ocean and the resulting opening or closing of shallow straits and sounds across southern Sweden and the site of the present-day Skagerrak.

A few fixed points are known at which the varve-dates may be applied both to the beaches of the different water-bodies, now well above sea-level owing to progressive isostatic land-recovery since their formation, and to sites of early Postglacial human occupation and industry.

Pollen analysis, however, provides the most far-reaching instrument for indirect Postglacial chronology, for it is applicable both to sites directly to be associated with raised beaches and the varve-dates and to those which are too far-removed to have any direct relationship with these phenomena.

Botanists have found that by a relatively simple, if laborious, technique fossil pollen-grains of higher plants and spores of cryptogams preserved in organic sediments, peat-beds or even buried soils may be extracted, recognized and counted, so that a whole plant-assemblage, with an accurate estimate of the relative frequency in it of different species, can be described for the time during which the sampling was forming. In this way a fairly detailed history has been compiled of the recolonization by vegetation of glaciated areas, after the retreat of the ice. This has been done for each main region of western Europe and has been widely adapted for many extra-European regions with totally different floras.

Especially in Scandinavia, where the method was first developed, local pollen-diagrams can be correlated with both geological and human evidences, so that at least approximate absolute dates assigned to different stages and events in plant-history may be transferred to prehistoric remains.

Excellent agreement has been obtained by the C[14] method as applied to Postglacial organic sediments and peats, which have also been examined for their pollen-contents and duly zoned in the succession. Thus, while the varve-dates for the Middle Swedish Moraines give about 8500 to 8000 B.C., this standstill of the ice-edge, at a time when the Baltic was dammed up as a freshwater ice-lake, is shown in the pollen-diagrams as a colder climatic oscillation with tundra flora in south Sweden, known as the Younger Dryas period. Between this and the Older Dryas period (both named from a typical tundra plant, *Dryas octopetala*) comes a warmer interval, the Alleröd Oscillation, called after the place in Denmark where the pollen-evidence for it was first observed. There was an earlier, somewhat temperate phase, called the Bölling stage, but Alleröd is the first well-marked and widespread temperate oscillation in the early Postglacial period, with pine- and birch-forest in north Europe, and has been recognized in many places over Europe and North America. In the latter it is known as the Two Creeks stage, between minor standstills of the Wisconsin glacial retreat. It is perhaps the best-dated climatic phase known, being set at 9500 to 8500 B.C. by the varves and between 10,000 and 9000 B.C. by a considerable number of C^{14} determinations which correspond very closely. This is, of course, the most accurate range for C^{14}-dating—about two half-lives of the isotope.

A Table of Postglacial events for southern Britain, unaffected by isostatic land-recovery, with geological, botanical and archaeological correlations, dated by these methods, is given on pp. 230-1. Since, during the gradual ice-retreat, the climatic and vegetational zones slowly shifted towards the areas which they occupy today, the dates in such a table are applicable only to one region or belt of latitude. By the time that the ice-edge had retreated to southern Sweden, for example, while Denmark and north Germany were still in the tundra-belt, central Germany must have been already covered with pine-forest and central France wooded with deciduous trees. Climatic improvement in Mediterranean Europe and southern North America must have preceded by thousands of years similar conditions in the higher latitudes of those continents.

It will be seen from the Table that after the Late Glacial Dryas stages, separated by the Bölling and Alleröd intervals, the climate became steadily warmer and less extreme seasonally up to the so-called Postglacial Optimum. This corresponds with the Altithermal of Antevs, or (not to commit the linguistic inelegancy of a Latino-Greek hybrid term) better called Hypsithermal. This was also a period of continuously rising eustatic sea-level, with the tempering effect on climate in Britain of shallow seas slowly spreading over

DATES (C.14)	GEOLOGICAL DIVISIONS		CLIMATIC STAGES (Denmark)	POLLEN ZONES (Jessen)	FOREST DEVELOPMENT
1000 A.D. B.C. 1000	POSTGLACIAL	Medithermal	**Subatlantic** Cooler, wetter, very oceanic, with mild winters	IX	Increase in birch maintained. Lime and elm very low. Beech and hornbeam increase. Continued slight decrease in alder and oak.
2000			**Subboreal** Drier, more continental	VIII	Slight decrease in lime, alder, even oak; increase in birch. Decreasing hazel.
3000 4000 5000		Altithermal (Hypsithermal)	**Atlantic** Oceanic, warm, moist Postglacial Optimum	VII	Mixed oak forest, with oak and alder dominant; elm & lime. Pine and birch are present but unimportant. Hazel plentiful.
6000		Anathermal	**Boreal** Continental, dry, with increasing warmth	VI	Pine decreasing, hazel max. Elm, oak appear and increase. Lime and alder appear at end.
7000				V	Pine dominant, birch decreasing, hazel appears.
8000			**Preboreal** Cold	IV	Birch dominant, pine increasing.
9000	LATE GLACIAL		**Younger Dryas** Arctic	III	Dryas (tundra) flora. Willow and pine, (perhaps drifted).
10,000			**Allerød Oscillation** Boreal	II	Birch maximum
11,000			**Older Dryas** Arctic c	I c	Dryas flora, willow, pine
			Bølling Oscillation Cold b	I b	Pine, birch, willow
12,000			**Oldest Dryas** Arctic a	I a	Dryas flora

FIG. 25. Postglacial events in southern Britain.

ARCHAEOLOGY (N.W. Europe)	SEA LEVEL CHANGES (S. Britain, eustatic)	BALTIC WATER-BODIES AND MORAINES (Isostatically affected).	DATES (C.14)
	(metres)		
Historic	± 0	Baltic Sea (as at present)	1000
	+2		A.D.
Early Iron Age			B.C.
Bronze Age	-5		1000
		3rd. maximum	
	+1		2000
Neolithic		Litorina Sea	3000
	-7		
	-7	2nd. maximum	4000
Mesolithic	-15	1st. maximum	5000
			6000
	-45	Ancylus Lake	7000
		Yoldia Sea	8000
Late Upper Palaeolithic	-60	Middle Swedish moraines	9000
		Baltic Ice-Lake	10,000.
			11,000
		Inland ice	12,000

the North Sea basin. There was a minor pause, or even set-back, in the improvement at about 2000 B.C., with a short interval of more continental conditions. The recovery from this has not reached, even in our day, the degree of climatic mildness which existed in (say) 3000 B.C.

Still another method of absolute dating, based on evidence of countable annual events, is tree-ring dating from tim-bers associated with archaeological structures. Dendrochro-nology, as it is called, was first developed in the early years of this century by Douglass, at Flagstaff, Arizona, a sub-arid region in which the growth of trees (conifers) is strictly con-trolled by the rainfall. In a wetter year than usual, a tree makes good growth, expressed in a wide annual ring in the cross-section of its trunk. Conversely, a dry year gives a nar-row ring, so that, when the tree is cut, its timber contains a more or less clear record of the variations in rainfall dur-ing the years of its growth. A large tree may be several centuries old. Its growth-rings may, in places, show character-istic sequences of good, normal and bad years, as, for in-stance, a ten-year group of three successive dry years, one normal and then another markedly dry, followed by four normal years and a final unusually wet one. Such a group, found near the centre of a log recently cut at a known date (i.e. formed when the tree was a sapling), may be recognizable in the latest wood near the periphery of an old stump, representing a tree already old when the first was still small. The rainfall-history given by the first tree may thus be extended back for some hundreds of years further into the past. Another characteristic growth-ring sequence from the youthful period of the old stump might be found repeated in the later growth of a beam from a still inhabited Indian house, and an earlier series from this, in turn, might correspond with a pattern to be recognized in a timber from a ruin of unknown age. Provided that the cross-identifica-tions of ring-sequences between one trunk and an older, all along the line, can be made with some confidence, the date of cutting of the oldest timber in the series may be dis-covered by a simple summation of the number of annual rings intervening in the different logs between the upward and downward correlation-points.

In practice, this was achieved only by the examination of hundreds of timber cross-sections and painstaking plotting of their particular seasonal variations in ring-thickness.

Clearly, there must sometimes be anomalies in individual cases, due to peculiarities in the actual sites of growth, making difficult the recognition of well-known sequences of variations. By the study of many examples, however, a standard plot may gradually be compiled with which the variations in any individual specimen of unknown date may be compared. If correspondences are found, its age may be determined with some accuracy.

This method has been applied, among other things, to the dating of Pueblo and Basket-Maker Indian buildings and ruins in the south-western United States, back to the fourth century A.D.

Attempts have been made to correlate tree-ring counts between widely separated areas, in some of which tree-growth is not as critically controlled by available moisture as it is in the Arizona homeland of the method. In Europe, for example, a correspondence has been claimed between records from southern Swedish prehistoric timbers and from California *Sequoia* ring-series. Since the climatic conditions are so different in the two places, such long-range correlations are regarded as too speculative for much credence. There is, nevertheless, evidence of a worldwide effect on tree-growth, connected in some way which is not at present fully understood with the well-known 10/11-year cycle of varying solar radiation to be seen in the sunspot-record. If such cycles of worldwide incidence can be discerned, despite the probably more marked growth-variations due to purely local factors, the likelihood of long-range correlations between tree-ring plots giving useful dates will be greatly increased. The established American tree-ring dates have afforded useful checks on the C^{14} method, when applied to samples of wood from dendrochronologically-dated zones of timbers.

Archaeological dating proper was, until the recent advent of scientific methods giving absolute age-values for archaeological and geological materials, the only available means of answering the recurring question: 'How old is it?' Archaeological dating is based, ultimately, on written historical sources. If our scientific methods are still often lamentably imprecise, the archaeological method is liable to be still more ambiguous, for the earlier periods, at least. Ancient literature and classical references to, or quotations from, now lost works of earlier authors have given us a very few fairly fixed points.

Perhaps the earliest literary date is that for the accession of Sargon I of Akkad, in lower Mesopotamia. This is given at 2750 B.C. (in terms of our calendar!) by Nabonidus of Babylon, whose own Empire fell to the Persians in 539 B.C. This was the result of his own historical researches, and a creditable one, considering that it spanned a period longer than our Christian Era to date. Modern opinion puts Sargon at about 2340 B.C.

Both for Mesopotamia and Egypt there are surviving lists of kings and dynasties, with the years of the reigns, mostly compiled long after the times to which they relate. The main catalogue for Egypt, for instance, is due to Manetho, an Egyptian priest of the early Ptolemaic period (280 B.C.), whose *History of Egypt*, in Greek, compiled from the native sources, though itself lost, is extensively quoted by classical and early Christian authors.

The Egyptian calendar was based on the annual simultaneous appearance of the star we know as Sirius (Sothis) with the Sun (heliacal rising), after a period of invisibility. This event coincided closely with the yearly beginning of the Nile flood, on which the whole Egyptian economy depended. Owing to their omission of a Leap-Year day, which we insert once in four years to prevent just that, the opening of their calendar-year moved round the seasons with a period of $365 \times 4 = 1,460$ solar years (Sothic Cycle).

We have, from a Latin source, the information that one such cycle began in A.D. 139, so that the dates of the beginning of earlier cycles must have fallen in 1321, 2781, 4241 and 5701 B.C., in one of which years (it is supposed) the Calendar was probably instituted. The Calendar is known, from the Pyramid Texts, to have been operative in the Vth and VIth Dynasties of the Old Kingdom, so that there is a choice of dates possible for this period of Egyptian history. Modern opinion, supported by C^{14} estimations, selects the 2781 B.C. date.

The Fayum Neolithic, according to C^{14}, appears to cover the fifth to the fourth millennium B.C., so that the date of Menes, the traditional first ruler of an united Upper and Lower Egypt, can hardly be much earlier than 3000 B.C. He is dated today at 3200 B.C., in round figures.

The chronology of the Near East and the eastern Mediterranean, formerly based almost entirely on the Egyptian, linked by 'synchronisms' of datable objects exchanged between Egypt and other civilizations and the peripheral barbarous cultures, is now supported by the independent evidence of C^{14}-dates.

The Neolithic with pottery had been established at Jericho, in Jordan, for some one thousand years before the first European cultivators pushed up the Danube about 4400 B.C., reaching the Rhineland and eastern Netherlands (Limburg) by 4000 B.C., according to C^{14} dates. It was nearly five hundred years more (3500 B.C.) before agriculture and stock-breeding reached the more southern parts of western Europe, and perhaps some centuries yet before the Neolithic way of life was brought over to Britain, possibly from the Low Countries or western France, somewhere about 3000 B.C.

Dating by synchronism of exchanged objects is often precarious because several removes may often be involved. The argument might run:

> Culture A is synchronous with B,
> Culture B is synchronous with C,
> Culture C is synchronous with D,
> Therefore Culture A is synchronous with D.

On paper, the logic is inescapable, but in so arguing we forget that cultures have a dimension in time. *Part* of culture A may well be contemporary with *part* of culture B (and so on), but the correctness of our final conclusion is in serious doubt unless we can assure identity with the parts of culture B (for instance), linking it with A on the one hand and C on the other. By the time we reach D, certainty has vanished—the cultures are only *diachronous* (overlapping in time).

One-way exchange (an object of culture A found at a site or in association with objects of B) is only slender evidence of contemporaneity. There may have been a long time-lag between the manufacture of the object and its eventual arrival, perhaps via several intermediaries, at the place where it was found. Valuable or decorative imported objects may have become heirlooms, handed down through several generations before being lost, discarded or buried. All that can be said with certainty is that associated objects are contemporary with *or later than* the import: *how much* later does not appear.

Double exchange, in which objects of culture B are also found in the homeland of A, is proof positive of contemporaneity—and comparatively rare!

Numerous examples could be given of synchronic datings, but only a single, more or less related, group from north-west Europe will be mentioned.

In some Early Bronze Age round barrows of southern Britain (Wessex Culture) there has been found a fair number of segmented faience beads, almost certainly of XVIIIth Dynasty (*c.* 1550 B.C.) Egyptian manufacture. We do not know for certain how they reached these islands, but seeing that geographically intermediate finds extended from the western Mediterranean across the south of France to Brittany via the Garonne, it seems most likely that they were traded mainly by sea. They may, therefore, have reached their destinations without serious time-lag, whereas, had they passed from hand to hand across Near Eastern and European land routes, it is probable that their journey would have taken many years.

The shaft-graves of Mycenae, in Greece, themselves dated by Near Eastern synchronisms to about 1600 B.C., contained beads and spacers of amber of north-European origin. Their date may, therefore, be transferred back to the Danish producers and their intermediaries in the amber trade, who must have been active at least a little earlier than this. (See map, p. 108.)

The same Wessex barrow-builders who acquired Egyptian faience beads also wore amber disc-ornaments in gold mounts, perhaps sun-symbols, of which the nearest known parallels are from Mycenae, while the amber probably came, as did that of Mycenae, from Denmark; the gold, perhaps, from Ireland. A whole complex of long-distance trade-relations is thus revealed, dating, with very little doubt, to about the middle of the second millennium B.C.

Most cultural influences are less well established than these. At Stonehenge, also in Wessex, carvings of a dagger and bronze flanged axes were recently found on the standing stones. The former was similar to a well-known type of bronze weapon made at Mycenae; the axes were of local Wessex type. May one justifiably transfer, without modification, the date of the foreign object in its home centre to Salisbury Plain? If, as seems likely, the Mycenaean influence at Stonehenge was a fairly direct one, the dating is probably nevertheless valid, especially in view of the above independent evidence of links with Mycenae. The carving may have been due to some small party—or even individual—hailing from the centre of Mediterranean civilization, cast away or wandering far from home in the barbarous confines of Europe.

Iron Age chronology in Europe also goes back for its basis to the Mediterranean and Classical sources. The use of iron probably reached Greece from Asia Minor and entered central Europe via the Adriatic, at first only as imported objects. European working of iron began in the Alpine/Illyrian area and was based on Austrian ore-deposits by 1200-1000 B.C. The Bronze Age peoples of Upper Austria, we remember (p. 155), had been notable copper-miners and metallurgists. The dating of the different stages of the central European Iron Age depends on synchronisms with the north Italian iron-using cultures, which are not very accurately dated themselves.

The Hallstatt sword

The spread of iron-using peoples was to the west and south, activated basically by pressure from eastern steppe-dwellers, perhaps economically affected by the onset of climatic deterioration in the early part of the last millennium B.C. (Sub-atlantic phase). A series of invasive waves emanating, as far as concerned western Europe, from the north Alpine area and the Danube basin, crossed the upper Rhine and Rhone valleys and fanned out into France by the natural river-valley and coastal-plain routes. Contained to the north of the Lower Rhine by a similar folk-pressure from the north German plain, bearers of different stages of culture, called Hallstatt and La Tène (after sites in Austria and Switzerland respectively), invaded and pervaded western and southern France, pressing their predecessors inexorably before them. These ethnic movements and cultural influences, much diluted, were felt even across the Pyrenees and the English Channel in the latter half of the first millennium B.C. The pressures were only intermittently effective and resulting movements took place over a number of centuries, a tribe displacing one in front of it, or leapfrogging beyond, when itself urged on by a mounting territorial pressure behind. The Dorian invasions of Greece were part of this process.

Many of these peoples had trade relations, exchanged goods with and acquired notions from the more advanced civilizations of the Aegean and Mediterranean. The foundation of Greek colonies in the western Mediterranean, such as that of Massilia (modern Marseilles) in 600 B.C., made for even more direct relations. In particular, Greek wine was appreciated by the barbarian Keltic chieftains of central Europe and the vessels of bronze, mainly of north-Italian manufacture, and painted Attic pottery, used in its serving and consumption, afford important evidences for such exchanges and the dates at which they took place. They are found throughout Languedoc, in central and northern France, Switzerland and in the middle Rhine and Moselle valleys, many perhaps distributed via Massilia, but others arriving probably more indirectly over the Alpine passes. (See map. p. 108.)

Some of these peoples emerge into the light of history through Greek and Latin sources, though their identity and the correct correlation of their classical names with the archaeological remains, revealed by excavation and chance finds, are often matters of dispute among scholars.

As Roman empire-building, with its written records, pushed

ever farther west and north, both the curtain of anonymity hiding prehistoric peoples and personalities and the uncertainty about their chronological position are slowly lifted. Though there exists a framework of historical dates for Britain from the invasion of Julius Caesar in 55 B.C. on, many events unrecorded in Roman and Anglo-Saxon writings are susceptible of clarification and dating only by the archaeological method.

10

Conclusion

THE FIELD of archaeology and, with it, the study of environment, extends right up to the Industrial Revolution. From mediaeval times on environmental studies may be called 'human geography' or 'economic geography', but they remain, in essence, the same, whatever university Faculty undertakes research in them.

With town-dwelling, division of labour and specialization of society human ecology merges with economics, and even with politics. Economic history relies mainly for its facts on written records, but cannot fail to be interested also in economic data to be obtained, for example, from the excavation of deserted mediaeval villages. Though in Britain today we may draw our supplies of iron-ore from Sweden or Lake Superior, our wool from Australia, and innumerable products unknown even to our near ancestors from every corner of the globe, even as recently as the eighteenth century England was largely self-sufficient. The daily necessities of town life were mainly produced in the surrounding countryside, or at no great distance, so that local environment still played a very considerable part in the lives of the people.

Environmental studies are basic for understanding the way of life of man the savage. For the barbarian agriculturist or stock-breeder they remain of the first importance. By the time man becomes a townsman or citizen, politically conscious, even literate, his dependence on geography and the natural world around him seems less clear, and certainly is generally thought to be of secondary importance. It would nevertheless, be instructive for the student of Roman or Anglo-Saxon Britain, for instance, to consider how the towns and villages of his period were maintained—on what area did they draw for their supplies; what products were locally obtainable; which did they have to procure from elsewhere; whence, how and in what quantities did they obtain them?

In the absence of written documents, the only way in which this sort of information can be gained is from the archaeological and natural materials laid bare by excavation.

Pollen-analysis, as we have here seen, has greatly added to our knowledge of the environment of Mesolithic, and even of Neolithic, Man, especially in its dating function. Seldom has it been applied to samples of the Roman and later periods, yet in an agricultural area a suitable sample might preserve evidence of the sort of crops grown and of changes due to human occupation in the natural flora.

We section hundreds of Neolithic stone axes and trace them to the spots where the rock was quarried. Has any petrologist ever been asked to examine (say) tesserae from a Roman mosaic pavement and to tell what rocks are represented and where the materials originated?

Numerous analyses have been carried out on Bronze Age metal weapons and ornaments in an effort to identify the ore-bodies exploited in their manufacture. To the writer's knowledge, this has never been attempted for Roman or later iron-work, yet the metallurgist's findings here ought to be just as interesting as in the former case.

There were no glaciations in the Middle Ages, but we have documentary evidence of a minor period of unusually hard winters in western Europe in the thirteenth century A.D. Tree-ring studies might well give us a more detailed account of the climatic events of this time, if the historians were sufficiently interested to enlist the help of a dendrochronologist. The material doubtless exists, and, indeed, some work in this direction has been done, but there has been small encouragement from those who would stand to gain most from the results.

Examples could be indefinitely multiplied. The fact is that we have used the methods to hand to investigate the environments of some prehistoric peoples, because we had no other way of understanding how they lived. Where historical records are silent, a similar approach could be helpful for later times also.

Even for prehistoric studies, available scientific methods have not always been used to the full, or to the best advantage. Although the archaeologist must continue to concern himself primarily with the ancient objects themselves, he must be prepared to look beyond his flints, potsherds, bronzes or town-plans for the natural economic motives behind what he is studying. These include the availability of materials, the suitability of climate and soil for particular crops and animals, the effects of the changing seasons on the habits of his people, their relations, as to trade or exchange, with neighbouring groups, depending on geography and economic needs.

The archaeologist cannot be expected to make himself an expert in all the manifold aspects of the natural environment of his site and period, but he must, nowadays, be prepared to consider them and to call for assistance in any branch of natural science where he cannot himself form a reliable opinion. Secondly, he cannot any longer afford to ignore matters having so close a bearing on his own conclusions. If he is bound to call for specialist guidance he must know enough of what a specialist can, and can *not*, do to help him, in order to frame his inquiry in such a way that the answer may be relevant to his own problem.

Ideally, the archaeological excavator should be a scientist also. Unfortunately this is seldom the case, because the history of the subject has rooted its approach, for all periods except the earlier Stone Ages, in the humanities. Our present system of education (in Britain at least) denies to the committed humanist much serious participation in scientific work from the time that he joins the Faculty of Arts at his University. Similarly, the scientist has probably ceased to have any formal contact with any Arts subject since he left school, so that if he knows anything of the detailed content of Archaeology it is due to his personal interest and reading 'out of school', not to any part of his University curriculum.

The two (or more) participants in any environmental study of ancient communities thus tend to have different technical languages, but the gulf is readily bridgeable if there is community of purpose. The bridge is best constructed by each taking the other into his full confidence and by facing the problem side by side, if possible in the field and at the scene of the excavation in progress. Both are then in possession of the relevant facts, each considering them from his own viewpoint and trying to communicate his mental arguments and to share those of the other. Discussion on the spot, with the evidence in front of them, will enable an agreed plan of action to be concerted, aimed at extracting particular, defined information from the facts. It will, at the same time, become clear to both parties which possible lines of approach are unlikely to be profitable in a given instance. This will save much wasted time and disappointment at a later stage.

Without this meeting in the field and sharing of information, not only may important evidence be overlooked by the excavator, for lack of the scientific eye, but the consulting scientist may face the materials submitted for examination without any clear idea of what the archaeologist hopes to learn from him. His report is then in danger of being archaeologically valueless, for lack of orientation towards an agreed objective.

A result of this is the apparently still-lingering belief of some excavators in Magic as a branch of science! From reading the publications of the more enlightened of the fraternity they know that it is, nowadays, the proper thing to have, as Appendices to the excavation-report, a string of specialist studies on any natural materials discovered in the course of the 'dig'—rocks, minerals, soils, timbers, charcoals, plant-remains, pollen, foraminifera, snails and other Mollusca, bones of fish, fowl, mammals and of man himself. Seemingly without really understanding why or how such additional investigations may be helpful, an archaeologist may collect samples of one or more materials in the list and send them to specialists with a request for 'analysis'. Supporting archaeological information is often lacking, or any indication as to what light the results of an analysis may be expected to contribute to archaeological problems. If interrogated, he may often, indeed, have a problem connected with the material submitted, but since this is obvious to himself he has not thought it necessary to explain more fully to the consultant. Such an undeserved reputation for clairvoyance may be flattering to the scientist, but does not help him to understand what sort of information to be obtained from the sample might be of interest to the inquirer.

If, in fact, the specialist undertakes any analysis without sufficient supporting information it is certain that his report will only by the merest chance be relevant to the excavator's problem. From total belief in the powers of science, the resulting disappointment is likely to swing the inquirer to extreme scepticism of its usefulness. Both attitudes are equally mistaken. Science can sometimes do wonders, but it has its limitations and only some understanding of what is likely to be possible will make for useful co-operation between archaeology and science.

These are extreme cases. Often when the specialist cannot visit the site archaeologists can, and do, take the necessary samples themselves and, when sending them for examination, supply sketch-plans, drawn sections, a statement of their own thoughts about the field of inquiry. In this way satisfactory results are often obtained, even though a conference on the site, which might have elicited even more, has not been possible.

Many environmental inquiries involve the work of two or more specialists. Once more, it is extremely helpful to everybody if the field-evidence can be seen by all and discussed on the spot. Without this there may well be differences of opinion about the facts. Whatever conflicting interpretations may later be offered, the observable *facts* can always be agreed upon. When, as is often the case, a field-conference is not possible, the archaeologist should at least inform one consultant that others are also concerned. Results of one man's work may have a bearing on another's, so that they should be in touch with each other as well as with the excavator. Failing this, they may reach opposite conclusions and submit conflicting reports, each in ignorance of the existence of a contrary opinion, founded on equally valid evidence and argument. Such lack of co-ordination is to be deplored, as showing imperfect planning and understanding of the problems. There may, in any case, be divergences of opinion and in conclusions between workers in adjacent fields of study, but they should be expressed, if unavoidable, in the full knowledge of the other's dissent. Even if evidence from independent sources appears to be contradictory, the very fact, if known in time, may lead to reconsideration and new conclusions of value, or at least to a balance or compromise acceptable to the protagonists. When archaeological matters are at issue it is clearly the responsibility of the archaeologist, and in his own best interests, to see that his scientific colleagues are kept properly informed of the progress of events.

Finally, the archaeologist in reaching his own conclusions must give full consideration to those of his collaborators. It is not unusual to read excavation reports accompanied by several specialist studies as Appendices, in the main text of which the latter are accorded no comment, or even recognition, by the author, beyond a polite mention under the head of 'Acknowledgements'. As the co-ordinator of all the work connected with his site it is the duty of the main author to sum up the results in full, embodying those of the subsidiary studies in his conclusions. Without so much, the full implications of the specialists' work may easily pass unrecognized by readers who may not trouble, or be technically incompetent, to derive them from the Appendices directly. The author of an Appendix, furthermore, is probably not in possession of the final archaeological results at the time of writing his report; he can only state the conclusions which his particular material justifies on its own. The main author may be able to arrive at further, or more exact, conclusions, after taking all the available evidence into account. Even if he cannot, he should show, by saying so, that he has considered the possibility and has not merely printed the individual reports without reading them!

But enough! We are, all together—historians, prehistorians and scientists—students of one or another aspect of the development through time of the altogether astonishing species *Homo sapiens,* to which we ourselves belong. The better we understand each other and bend our several disciplines to the common task, the better shall we come to understand how man has attained the unique position in his world which he occupies today.

An important part of that task is to reach a fuller understanding of his relation to the varied natural environments which he has occupied in the past.

Suggestions for Further Reading

ASHBEE, P. *The Bronze Age Round Barrow in Britain.* London, Phoenix House, 1960.

ATKINSON, R. J. C. *Stonehenge.* London, Hamish Hamilton, 1956. New York, Macmillan, 1956.

BROOKS, C. E. P. *Climate Through the Ages.* 2nd ed. London, Benn, 1949. New York, McGraw-Hill, 1949.

CHILDE, V. G. *The Bronze Age.* Cambridge University Press, 1930. *New Light on the Most Ancient East.* 2nd ed. London, Kegan Paul, 1952. 4th ed. New York, Praeger, 1953.

CLARK, J. Desmond. *The Prehistory of Southern Africa.* Harmondsworth, Penguin Books, 1959. Baltimore, Penguin Books.

CLARK, J. G. D. *Prehistoric Europe. The Economic Basis.* London, Methuen, 1952. New York, Philosophical Library, 1952. *World Prehistory: An Outline.* Cambridge University Press, 1961.

COLE, S. *The Prehistory of East Africa.* Harmondsworth, Penguin Books, 1954.

CORNWALL, I. W. *Soils for the Archaeologist.* London, Phoenix House, 1958.

DURY, G. H. *The Face of the Earth.* Harmondsworth, Penguin Books, 1959.

FOX, Cyril. *The Personality of Britain.* Cardiff, National Museum of Wales, 1932.

GODWIN, Harry. *The History of the British Flora.* Cambridge University Press, 1956.

HEIZER, R. F., and COOK, S. F. (eds.). *The Application of Quantitative Methods in Archaeology.* New York, Viking Fund Publication in Anthropology, No. 28, 1960.

HESSE, R., ALLEE, N. C., and SCHMIDT, K. P. *Ecological Animal Geography.* 2nd ed. New York, John Wiley, 1951.

HOWELLS, William White. *Mankind in the Making: The Story of Human Evolution.* London, Secker & Warburg, 1960. Garden City, Doubleday, 1959.

LEAKEY, L. S. B. *Adam's Ancestors.* 3rd ed. New York, Longmans, Green, 1935. 4th ed. London, Methuen, 1953.

LORENZO, J. L. *La Revolución neolítica en Mesoamérica.* Mexico City, Instituto Nacional de Anthropología y Historia, 1961.

MONKHOUSE, F. J. *Principles of Physical Geography*. 4th ed. London, University of London Press, 1960.

NEWBIGIN, M. I. *Plant and Animal Geography*. London, Methuen, 1936.

PIGGOTT, S. *The Neolithic Cultures of the British Isles*. Cambridge University Press, 1954.

PYDDOKE, E. *Stratification for the Archaeologist*. London, Phoenix House, 1961.

STAMP, L. Dudley (ed.). *A History of Land-use in Arid Regions*. UNESCO, Paris, 1961.

TANSLEY, A. G. *The British Islands and Their Vegetation*. Cambridge University Press, 1939. Reprinted with corrections, 1949.

THOMAS, W. L., Jr. (ed.). *Man's Role in Changing the Face of the Earth*. Chicago, Wenner Gren Foundation for Anthropological Research Symposium, 1955.

WOOLDRIDGE, S. W., and GOLDRING, F. *The Weald*. London, Collins, 1953.

ZEUNER, F. E. *The Pleistocene Period*. 2nd ed. London, Hutchinson, 1959.

Dating the Past. 4th ed. New York, Longmans, Green, 1958. London, Methuen, 1961.

A History of Domesticated Animals. London, Hutchinson, 1963.

Index

Abrasives, 142, 147

Acheulean (Lower Palaeolithic) industries, 140, 201

Adobe (mud brick), 152

Adze, of stone, 189

Agriculture, 36, 41, 89, 169
cultivation of cereals, 193
influence on flora, soils &c., 169 ff.
Neolithic, shifting, 170, 190
on floodplains, 169
use of dung as fertilizer in, 215

Alaska, land-bridge Asia/America, 60, 68

Amber, beads and ornaments of, 148
trade-routes, 108

America, colonization of, by man, 60, 68

'Ancient Britons' (*see also* Early Iron Age), 18, 172

Animals (Fauna), archaic species of, in early Interglacials, 200
as agricultural predators and pests, 191, 218
as factor of environment, 26, 40, 196 ff.
as food of primitive man, 196

as soil micro-fauna, 161
as source of industrial materials, 214
carnivorous, as competitors of man, 196, 217
domestic, influence of flora, 171
drawings and paintings of, in caves, 208
invertebrate, as environmental indicators, 198
migrations of, 57, 206-7
of steppe and forest, contrasted, 187

Ape/man transition, 46-8

Archaeology, 21

Atlanthropus (fossil man), 55, 185, 201

Art of prehistoric man, 208

Australia, colonization of, 69, 119
land-bridge to, 121
rock-shelters in, 116

Australian aborigines, 69, 82, 87, 119, 210

Australopithecines (African subfamily of ape-men), 49, 185

Austria, copper-mining in, 154-5

249

SIGNET SCIENCE Books
on Related Topics

THE WELLSPRINGS OF LIFE *by Isaac Asimov*
The chemistry of the living cell, and its relation to evolution, heredity, growth and development.
(#P2066—60¢)

THE NATURE OF THE UNIVERSE *by Fred Hoyle*
A noted astronomer explains the latest facts and theories about the universe with clarity and liveliness. Illustrated. (#P2331—60¢)

A BRIEF HISTORY OF SCIENCE *by A. R. and M. B. Hall*
The course of science from ancient times to the present, an account of this century's advances, and a forecast of the future. (#T2542—75¢)

THE DAWN OF LIFE *by J. H. Rush*
A lucid, absorbing explanation of the most recent and authoritative scientific thinking about the origin of life. (#T2192—75¢)

MODERN THEORIES OF THE UNIVERSE *by James A. Coleman*
A concise, impartial explanation of the two leading contemporary theories concerning the origin of the universe. (#P2270—60¢)

THE NATURE OF LIVING THINGS *by C. Brooke Worth and Robert K. Enders*
A fascinating exploration of the plant and animal kingdoms—the origin and structure, the life habits and relationships of living organisms. (#P2420—60¢)

THE WEB OF LIFE *by John H. Storer*
An easy-to-understand introduction to the science of ecology showing how all living things—bacteria, insects, plants, birds, and mammals—are related to each other and to their environment, and how man can help maintain the delicate balance of nature. Illustrated.
(#P2265—60¢)